Government in Metropolitan Areas

Edited by Luther Gulick

THE FEDERAL GOVERNMENT
AND METROPOLITAN AREAS

Publications of the
Governmental Affairs Institute of Washington, D.C.
under the
Government in Metropolitan Areas Project of the
Edgar Stern Family Fund

THE FEDERAL GOVERNMENT

and

METROPOLITAN AREAS

ROBERT H. CONNERY

RICHARD H. LEACH

Harvard University Press, Cambridge

1960

FOREWORD

THE Government in Metropolitan Areas Project was designed as a nation-wide exploration of the governmental problems thrust to the fore by the revolutionary expansion of urban populations in the United States and the resulting new patterns of metropolitan settlement.

The Project was underwritten by the Edgar Stern Family Fund in August 1955. The general plan of action was developed, over a period of many months, in conference with Dr. Will Alexander, representing the Stern Family Fund.

In line with Dr. Alexander's suggestions, a special project development committee was appointed by the American Political Science Association on vote of its Executive Committee in March 1955. This committee, whose membership was continued as the advisory committee on the Project, met, exchanged comments through correspondence, and developed the final plan as adopted by the Council of the Association and the Board of the Fund.

The project has involved four distinct parts: first, a series of technical studies designed for publication, of which the present study is one; second, six regional studies of selected issues and the structure of political leadership, summarized in a series of informal papers on community decision making; third, the holding of a number of workshops and conferences to discuss techniques and problems involved in the course of the Project; and, finally, a considerable number of appearances, speeches, and papers designed to present facts and ideas growing from the Project.

This entire effort was made possible by the grants of the Edgar Stern Family Fund. Certain parts of the work were also financed by the Ford Foundation and the Social Science Research Council, through grants for specific conferences. The Institute of Public Administration made its contribution through the assignment of personnel and the assumption of certain administrative costs.

Robert H. Connery and Richard H. Leach are joint authors of this volume. Both are political scientists and members of the faculty of Duke University.

Professor Connery was graduated from the University of Minnesota in 1929 with the B.A. degree and received the Ph.D. from Columbia University in 1935. He taught successively at Columbia, Catholic University, Stanford, University of Illinois, and Duke.

Over the past twenty-five years he has served as consultant to numerous federal, state, and local governments and officials, including among others the National Resources Planning Board, the President's Committee on Administrative Management, the New York State Legislative Committee on Interstate Cooperation, the Secretary of the Navy, the Secretary of Defense, the Hoover Commission, and the City Administrator of New York. He has been a Fellow as well as a senior staff member of the Brookings Institution.

During the Second World War he served for five years in the Navy as a commissioned officer. In that capacity he was assigned to Secretary Forrestal's office to write an administrative history which later was published as *The Navy and the Industrial Mobilization in World War II* (1950). He is also author of *Governmental Problems in Wild Life Conservation* (1936), *Administration of an NRA Code* (1939), and other government reports and articles.

Professor Leach is joint author of *The Administration of Interstate Compacts* (1959), of *In Quest of Freedom: American Political Thought and Practice* (1959), and of numerous articles. He was graduated from Colorado College in 1944 and received the Ph.D. from Princeton in 1951. He taught at Georgia Institute of Technology before joining the Duke faculty in 1955. He has had considerable practical experience in government as a member of the staff of the Southern Regional Education Board from 1953 to 1956, and of the Army Security Agency.

The views expressed in this study are those of the authors. Under the circumstances neither the Edgar Stern Family Fund, nor the Governmental Affairs Institute, nor any other contributors to the Project, including the eminent social scientists associated as advisers, are in any sense responsible for the Project publications. The Project is, however, under deep obligation to Professors Connery and Leach for their notable and original contribution to this inquiry.

LUTHER GULICK

New York
February 1960

CONTENTS

LIST OF FIGURES

Government in Metropolitan Areas Project

Director

Luther Halsey Gulick
Institute of Public Administration
New York, New York

Associate Directors

Robert H. Connery
Duke University

Norton E. Long
Northwestern University

Advisory Committee

Harold Alderfer
Governor's Office
Commonwealth of Pennsylvania

Victor Jones
University of California
Berkeley

Louis Brownlow
Washington, D.C.

John Harrison Rohrer
Georgetown University

A. M. Hillhouse
Cornell University

Coleman Woodbury
University of Wisconsin

Staff Associates

Edward C. Banfield
University of Chicago

George M. Belknap
University of California

Arthur W. Bromage
University of Michigan

Charles R. Cherington
Harvard University

Charlton F. Chute
Institute of Public Administration

Frederick N. Cleaveland
University of North Carolina

Lyle C. Fitch
First Deputy City Administrator
City of New York

L. Vaughan Howard
Tulane University

Maurice Klain
Western Reserve University

Richard H. Leach
Duke University

Alvin K. Peterjohn
Institute of Public Administration

Dorothy R. Swift, Editor
Institute of Public Administration

1

FEDERAL PROGRAMS
IN METROPOLITAN AREAS   ·

THE average American probably feels that the country pictured in Katharine Lee Bates' poem and hymn "America
the Beautiful" is still his America, a country

> . . . beautiful for spacious skies,
> For amber waves of grain,
> For purple mountain majesties
> Above the fruited plain.

And it has not been so long since that stereotype was accurate,
and we were in fact a rural and agricultural country. Fredrika
Bremer, who visited the United States in 1853, was most impressed by the farms and fields, the open country crossed by
rivers "bright as a mirror" and dotted by "golden woods . . .
in the bosom of the hills." [1] Virtually every other visitor to the
United States in the nineteenth century echoed her sentiments.[2]
Indeed, such a vision of the nation became part of our national
myth, and it is still embedded deeply in our national consciousness. As late as 1935, when Ernie Pyle wrote nostalgically
about his homeland, he thought first and foremost of the nation as one of "the summer wind," "the infinite flow of Old Man
River," and the "dusty plains" of the prairie country.[3]

But if the vision was appropriate in Miss Bremer's day, it
was a false one by 1935. Even as early as 1910, Henry van

Dyke noted how the early "transformation of the Indian's hunting trail into the highroad" and the later transformation "of the highroad into the railway" had resulted in the "growth of enormous cities . . . in places that three generations ago were a habitation for wild geese and foxes." [4] By 1935, the increase in urbanization had become the outstanding characteristic of American life. Even as Miss Bates herself had predicted in the fourth and little-remembered stanza of her poem, the "alabaster cities" seen originally only in patriots' dreams had by then become a reality. Indeed, urbanization had already begun to give way to metropolitanization, and the latter has accelerated to the point where today the metropolis is the "irresistible magnet" which draws "big business, big money, big reputations, big decisions, big league baseball, big theatre, big industry" ever more closely to it.[5] So rapid has been the change that the facts of metropolitanization—of the metropolitan explosion, as some writers like to put it [6]—are so stupendous they almost seem to defy acceptance.

The Rise of the Metropolis

In 1790, the first decennial census showed only 24 urban places [7] in the United States, and their population totaled a bare 5 per cent of the nation's population. By the seventeenth census, in 1950, there were more than 4,700 urban places in the nation, and they contained some 64 per cent of the total population. Even more striking than the growth of the urban portion of the population, however, was the increasing congregation of urban dwellers in a relatively few metropolitan areas after 1900. Although the concentration of people in cities was evident throughout the nineteenth century,[8] it was not until after the turn of the century that the tendency of urban residents to spill over the boundaries of cities into the country surrounding them became noticeable. Suburb after suburb developed as cities grew, and together they formed that peculiar product of modern times, the metropolitan area. Metropolitan areas owe their development largely to the automobile and to the rapid movement between home and work that the automobile made possible; but new materials, new ideas about out-of-door living, new gadgets, more machines, and more leisure time all contributed their share to the desire for suburban living.

By 1910, the Census Bureau had begun to note the existence of "metropolitan districts," and by 1950, the Bureau had

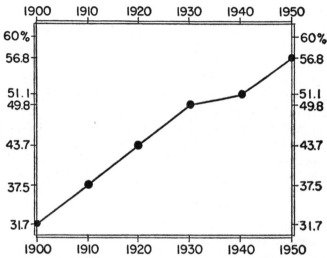

Fig. 1. Percentage of United States total population in standard metropolitan areas, by decades, 1900–1950.

adopted the term "standard metropolitan area." [9] Between 1900 and 1950, the over-all population of the country increased very nearly 100 per cent; in the same period, the population in areas defined in the 1950 Census as standard metropolitan areas grew 177.8 per cent, or nearly twice as fast as that of the nation as a whole. "At each census since 1900, a greater share of the total population has been found to be living either in or in the immediate vicinity of metropolitan centers than lived there a decade earlier." [10] Figure 1 shows the percentage of the total United States population living in what were defined as standard metropolitan areas by decades from 1900 to 1950.

Since 1950, most of the nation's continued increase in population has taken place in metropolitan areas, and the trend does not seem to be abating. Indeed, it is entirely logical to anticipate that by 1975 over two-thirds of the total population of the nation will live in metropolitan areas. The day of the metropolis is upon us.

Government Parallels Urban Growth

Just as astounding as the growth of the nation's population since 1790 and the development of metropolitan areas has been the radical change which has occurred in the size and role of government in the same period. In 1790, and for several decades thereafter, government corresponded to the predominantly rural pattern of the times. The federal government was concerned primarily with foreign affairs and national defense, and even here, contacts with foreign nations were limited. The defense problem consisted chiefly in protection against Indians on the frontier. The principal sources of federal funds were the tariff and excise taxes. So small was the entire federal establishment when the capital was moved from New York to Washington during Adams' administration that only about 150 government employees were involved. During the same period, even the state governments performed few functions. They were chiefly concerned with such matters as the maintenance of law and order, the establishment of courts for the settlement of disputes, and the registration of land titles. By and large, the few services of government were performed by cities and towns. Cities built docks, constructed elementary water works —more often than not the town pump—built crude sewage systems, constructed rudimentary streets, and began municipal lighting systems, if only by requiring every seventh householder to hang out a lantern on moonless nights.[11] On every level, government was a very simple and uncomplicated process, admirably adapted to the circumstances of the day.

But the whole nature of the American scene changed when the Industrial Revolution came, bringing with it as it did a rapid increase in the number of factories and cities. Before long, urban communities clustered around industrial locations began to dot the eastern seaboard. The building of the railroads, the great influx of immigrants, and the movement of the frontier westward carried urbanization across the continent.[12] The movement that was well under way by 1880 gathered further momentum during the first half of the twentieth century, and government on every level vastly increased the scope of its activities to accommodate itself to the developing urban pattern. Nowhere was the change more evident than in the relations of the federal government with local communities. In the beginning, local government was considered to be solely a matter for the states. Cities were chartered by state legislatures, and their later development was pretty well guided by what the legislatures would allow. In spite of the tremendous growth of municipal home rule, state governments never relinquished their hold over cities. The federal government was thought to have no part in local government; it was simply a bystander.

The inadequacies of this concept were first revealed during World War I, but it took the Great Depression to bring about wide recognition of the fact. The depression forced the federal government to initiate urban welfare and public works programs on a gigantic scale, and almost immediately a totally new relationship between the federal government and the nation's cities was brought about. Once established, this relationship persisted, and World War II and its aftermath of continued crisis served to extend the new relationship into still other areas of activity. Where once it had no connection at all with urban development, today the federal government finds itself, through its fiscal policies, grants-in-aid, subsidies, regulations, research activities, and development programs, heavily involved in a great many programs affecting the growth of metropolitan areas.

Indeed, a list prepared by the Bureau of the Budget in 1957 showed twenty-one programs of the federal government which were operating in metropolitan areas: [13]

1. Highway construction
2. Flood control and prevention
3. Improvement of rivers, harbors, and waterways
4. Water pollution control
5. Control of communicable diseases, including tuberculosis and venereal diseases
6. Services to crippled children
7. Health centers and clinics
8. Disaster relief
9. Civil defense
10. Housing, slum clearance, and urban redevelopment
11. School lunch program
12. Special problems of federally impacted areas
13. Airports and air terminals
14. Old-age and survivors' insurance for local government employees
15. Hospital planning and construction
16. Suppression of crime
17. General welfare assistance
18. Social security
19. Vocational education
20. Vocational rehabilitation
21. Employment security

Most of these programs are concerned with services to people; thus, the school lunch program is of benefit to children wherever they may live. General welfare assistance, old-age and survivors' insurance, suppression of crime, and control of communicable diseases concern every American whether he lives in the city or in the country. The same thing is true of vocational education and rehabilitation, disaster relief, and employment security. Nevertheless, all these programs result in the expenditure of money in metropolitan areas and so have an effect on their economy. Indeed, the federal government today spends a very large proportion of its annual budget in metropolitan areas.

Federal Expenditures in New York: An Example

At the request of the authors of this study, the Budget Bureau collected some figures on federal expenditures in the New York metropolitan area.[14] The Urban Renewal Administration, it found, had granted $120 million to underwrite 52 slum clearance and urban renewal projects in the area, this amount constituting two-thirds of the cost of acquiring the land in slum areas for redevelopment. The Public Housing Administration was supporting the construction of 90,000 low-rent public housing units by pledging contributions of $30 million a year for forty years. By the end of 1957, about 54,000 units had been completed, and the rest were in either the planning or the construction stage. In the ten-year period 1947–57, grants of almost $10 million in federal funds aided construction of 10 airports in the area, and an additional $6 million has been approved for further work. The Bureau of Public Roads had allocated grants of $129 million since 1953 for the federal government's share of the $270 million highway and bridge program in the New York region, and these figures did not include expenditures under the new 1956 highway building program. The Federal Housing Administration insured in the calendar year 1955 alone 16,000 home mortgages in the area, amounting to $170 million, and 85,000 home improvement loans, totaling $70 million. The volume of loans guaranteed by the Veterans Administration during the same period was estimated to be considerably larger than that from the FHA. Veterans Administration hospital construction in the New York area exceeded $54 million in fiscal 1957; the Public Health Service made additional grants for the same purpose of approximately $10 million, and the Defense Department added another $3 million for a hospital at Fort Monmouth. The Army Corps of Engineers had some 30 projects, involving expenditures of well over $100 million, under way for port improvement in the New York area. Once these port improvements have been constructed, they are maintained by the Corps of Engineers at the expense of the federal government.

What is true of New York is true on a lesser scale of every other metropolitan area in the nation. Obviously federal expenditures of this magnitude are significant to the economy of an area. Moreover, such programs have a great impact on government in the area. For these reasons a clinical examination of the federal government's major programs in metropolitan areas—housing and urban renewal, water resource and pollution control activities, airport construction, military installations and defense industries, civil defense, and highways—is important. Such an examination will show how the federal government became involved in these activities, what the several programs were intended to accomplish, and, above all, what impact they have had on government in metropolitan areas. An analysis of each of them will also point out the problems which must be solved if these programs are to make the most effective contribution to government in metropolitan areas in the future.

Moreover, a critical study of the programs will demonstrate that federal involvement in metropolitan areas is no longer a matter of conjecture. Further commitment is the direction in which the federal government inevitably will move in the future. For however much its policy may shift from administration to administration in the years ahead, the course is already clearly marked. As the history of these programs demonstrates, metropolitan problems cannot be solved without federal leadership. Inevitably, the needs of two-thirds of the American people will make the case for federal action even stronger in the future.

Housing

The federal government became an active participant in housing development for the first time during World War I, when some 16,000 units were built for shipyard workers. After the war, they were sold to private owners. It was not until the depression in the early 1930's that the government's interest in housing was again awakened. Then the immediate problems were met by a series of emergency relief measures which gradually emerged as a federal housing program of broad proportions. The story of the evolution of this program can be divided into three parts: pre-World War II, the war period, and the postwar period.

The depression years brought threats of widespread mortgage foreclosures on homes, unemployment in the construction industries, the drying-up of mortgage funds for new construction, and the spread of slums in the cities as available housing grew older and was not replaced. At first, these were regarded as financial problems to be met by providing more capital for home construction. The Federal Home Loan Bank Act of 1932 [15] was the first step in the direction of providing credit for home financing. The Home Owners Loan Corporation, established in 1933,[16] was intended to refinance mortgages and thus to relieve both distressed home owners and lenders. In 1934, federal insurance up to $5,000 was provided for deposits in building and loan associations.

The National Housing Act of 1934 [17] went a step farther. It insured small unsecured loans for home modernization and repair as well as for new homes and moderate-rental housing projects. Furthermore, under various emergency relief acts, a number of public housing projects were built by the federal government on an experimental basis. Although most of this housing was intended to improve living standards of rural families, almost as many housing units were built in urban as in rural areas. Finally, in 1937, the United States Housing Authority was created by the Housing Act [18] of that year to administer a long-range low-rent public housing program. This new program provided federal financial aid to local public agencies established under state law for the construction and operation of low-rent public housing projects. This was a departure from earlier programs, in that the projects were built, owned, and maintained by local agencies. The federal government simply supplied the funds.

As war approached and defense activities expanded, Congress appropriated funds for housing for defense workers and military personnel. Before the war ended, sums totaling over $2 billion were provided for these purposes. In addition, war housing was built under the Housing Act of 1937 which was intended to become low-rent public projects after the war was over. But some of the housing, unfortunately, was constructed in areas where postwar housing was not needed, so that much of it was torn down after the war.

Postwar Expansion of Housing Programs

Recognition of the special needs of the returning veterans led to the Servicemen's Readjustment Act of 1944,[19] which provided, among other things, for guaranty by the Veterans Administration of credit extended to veterans for purchase, construction, and improvement of homes. This was the so-called "G. I. Loan Program." Various acts followed, liberalizing and extending the veterans' housing legislation.

But the need for new housing after the war extended far beyond the veterans. Population growth, shortage of materials, and a long period of less than normal home construction left most communities with insufficient housing to meet their needs. A study made shortly after the war found that the nation would require 1.5 million additional non-farm housing units each year for a period of at least ten years, assuming that one-half of the substandard housing would be replaced during this period. It recommended that the federal government encourage private home construction through expansion of credit and provide financial assistance for public housing to replace slum dwellings, as well as conduct research to reduce production costs.[20]

The National Housing Agency had been created as a temporary war agency in 1942, bringing under one roof the Public Housing Administration, the Home Loan Bank Board, and the Federal Housing Administration. At the end of the war it was decided to continue this arrangement, and in July 1947 the Housing and Home Finance Agency was established under

Reorganization Plan 3.[21] In a series of housing acts beginning in 1949, and continuing each year during the next decade, Congress provided funds for loans, refinancing and insurance of home mortgages, public housing, urban renewal, and slum clearance. Not only were large sums of money committed for public housing, but billions of dollars' worth of loans for private housing were guaranteed by federal agencies.

As a result of all these programs, the whole pattern of urban land use has been affected in the past twenty-five years. Through loans, grants, mortgage insurance, mortgage guarantees, and urban renewal, the federal government has greatly influenced the development and character of land use in virtually every American city.[22] Moreover, as a result of the broad scope of these activities, an extraordinary number of different federal agencies became involved in some aspect or other of housing. By 1958, not only was the Housing and Home Finance Agency with its several subdivisions in the field, but also the Departments of Defense, Commerce, Health, Education and Welfare, and Agriculture. In addition, the Department of Labor, TVA, the Veterans Administration, and the Atomic Energy Commission were all concerned with parts of the housing program. Although the presence of all these agencies in the field creates problems of co-ordination, most metropolitan communities continue to deal principally with the Housing and Home Finance Agency.

During the past ten years, there has been not only an increase in the amount of federal activity, but also a development of an underlying housing philosophy. The former Housing Administrator, Albert M. Cole, speaking before the National Housing Conference in Washington, D. C., on June 17, 1957, summed it up in these words:

Twenty years ago we thought in terms of individuals, of houses to shelter them, of special aids administered through special and separate governmental units. Then we recognized that this was too limited, too piecemeal. We began to think in terms of local areas and neighborhoods and we tried to bring some unity into government aids through a loose coordination in a single overall agency.

In the Housing Act of 1954 we moved another long step forward. We dealt with the community as a whole and with housing in relation to other aspects of the community. In the urban renewal program, we established an approach that was based on overall planned action for the whole community and on closely integrated administration of government aids.

But as we top one hill and look ahead, we find an even wider horizon ahead of us—another hill to climb if we are to continue to progress. In these few years I have discovered that even the community is not the final entity that we must consider—that it is part of a growing and expanding urban economy which moves with giant stiides not only into the suburbs but into the interurban stretches that no longer define the country and the town. Today it is in these broader terms that we must think and plan—the community as part of the region, the neighborhood as part of the community, the individual home as part of the neighborhood. This is a far cry from the hope of twenty years ago that we could solve our city's problems of slums and bad housing simply by providing good homes for low-income families and tearing down the city's slums one by one, as we went along.[23]

Planning Assistance Provided

The Housing Act of 1954 [24] was especially significant for metropolitan areas, in that it provided grants-in-aid for planning on a metropolitan basis. Based on studies of the President's Advisory Committee on Government Housing Policies and Programs, the Act provided federal grants not to exceed 50 per cent of the estimated cost to provide planning assistance to small cities and to official state, metropolitan, or regional agencies for planning in metropolitan or regional areas. Whereas the 1949 Act directed the Housing Administrator to encourage metropolitan planning, the 1954 Act specifically provided grants for this purpose. Congress has so far appropriated slightly more than $9 million for the entire program, of which $3,606,707 has been allocated for metropolitan area planning. As of June 30, 1959, 93 metropolitan areas, urban regions, and special areas in 33 states had had their planning projects approved for federal aid.[25] Amendments to the original act have extended the program and made it more flexible. Even areas not urban are authorized to receive grants for planning if they are threatened with rapid urbanization as a result of the establishment or rapid expansion of a federal installation. This change took place after King County and two adjoining counties in California applied for an urban planning grant and were refused. All these counties were essentially rural, but they maintained that a new Air Force installation would make them urban. The original application was rejected as coming from an area neither urban nor a region. Appeal to Congress, however, soon led to an amendment in the Housing Act of 1957 to permit this type of grant.

The first agencies to take advantage of the new program were those already in business under authority of state laws, since they had resources to match the federal grants-in-aid, as in the case of the Detroit Metropolitan Area Planning Commission, which received $35,000. Many of the early applications, however, were received from planning agencies which had no funds or which could not meet other legal requirements. Unfortunately, official planning agencies operating on a metropolitan basis were all too rare.

Both in 1958 and in 1959, the Congress put housing legislation high on its priority list. But in both years the omnibus bill which finally emerged from conference did not have the approval of the President. The 1958 omnibus bill died in the House, and President Eisenhower vetoed the bill passed in 1959 (S. 57) as "a bill so excessive in the spending it proposes, and so defective in other respects, that it would do far more damage than good." [26] S. 57 reflected the conviction of both houses of Congress that considerable expansion in the housing and urban renewal activities of the federal government was warranted; it authorized commitments over a forty-year period of $2.2 billion, as opposed to a two-year authorization of $810 million proposed by the President. In particular, the bill sharply increased authorization for urban renewal and public housing units, while at the same time it authorized a new program of housing for elderly people, expanded the college housing loan program, provided subsidy prices for mortgage purchasers, and proposed a new device for bolstering the private mortgage market. In his veto message, the President scored all these measures as inflationary.

Whatever the final disposition of S. 57, it is clear that even President Eisenhower is committed to a federal housing program for the indefinite future. The question now to be resolved is how to accomplish the objective in a manner fiscally satisfactory to the Administration and philosophically compatible with the broad purposes of the Housing Act of 1949 and the sentiments of the more liberal members of Congress. Testimony before congressional committees was replete with evidence that the nation is losing ground in the fight against slums, in providing adequate housing for the low- and middle-income groups and for minority groups, and in achieving urban renewal. Congress can be counted on to reconsider the whole matter; urban citizens' organizations, the metropolitan press, the National Housing Conference, and scores of other influences are being brought to bear on Congress for action. Unfortunately, the whole housing question has become a political football, and it may well be, as Senator Joseph Clark has suggested, that no significant action can be secured until after the presidential election in 1960.[27]

Impact on Metropolitan Areas

Viewing the federal housing program as a whole, one can hardly help but conclude that it is in fact a hodgepodge. To begin with, one should note that much of the original support for government aid for housing was primarily for the purpose of stimulating the national economy. Even much of the testimony in support of the 1958 and 1959 Housing Acts emphasized the need for reducing unemployment. And, as one might expect, the housing program has had a number of unforeseen results that have had a tremendous effect on metropolitan areas. It has been partly responsible, at least, for the rapid construction of "cracker-box suburbs," since the G. I. and FHA programs encouraged construction of single-family homes rather than of multifamily and rental units. The financial requirements of the federal housing programs work to the special disadvantage of the builder of multifamily rental properties. In the case of a single-family dwelling, the buyer's down payment and the proceeds of his mortgage—as high as 100 per cent in some G. I. loans—reimburse the builder for all his costs and give him his profit in cash immediately. His profit is not restricted to any specific percentage of his costs, but the amount of the FHA mortgage is based on an appraisal of the value of the completed house. If the builder is especially efficient, he can make a larger profit.

The apartment-house builder, however, is faced with many restrictions. He must file a cost certificate, and if he builds especially efficiently and below original estimates, he is penalized by having the amount of his mortgage loan reduced, regardless of the value of the property. Moreover, his profit rate is restricted, his rents are regulated, and he must manage the building over a period of years to get out his profit. All these factors make building multifamily rental housing much less attractive to developers, and explain, in part at least, why so much new housing since the war has been in single-family units. Since land for single-family dwellings inside the central cities generally is limited, developers go to the suburbs and erect small houses. For example, it is interesting to compare location and type of housing in the Chicago metropolitan area in 1927 with that in 1954. In 1927, before the advent of federal-aid housing, builders' permits for 55,000 housing units were issued in the metropolitan area, as compared with 47,000 in 1954. But in 1927, 74 per cent of the new construction was inside the city of Chicago and 26 per cent in other parts of the metropolitan area. In 1954, on the other hand, 28 per cent was inside the city of Chicago and 72 per cent in other parts of the metropolitan area.[28] Of the 41,000 new housing units authorized in the city of Chicago in 1927, 86 per cent were multiple dwellings and only 14 per cent were single-family. In 1954, total new housing units were slightly over 13,000, and 37 per cent of these were multiple-family, while 63 per cent were single-family dwellings. The same story could be repeated with similar statistics for other metropolitan areas.[29]

In 1955, more than 90 per cent of all new housing was in single-family units. The FHA insured about one in five units, the Veterans Administration guaranteed about one in three, and the rest were financed through conventional loans. Moreover, federal insuring of multifamily rental housing was greater in the period 1946 to 1950 than it was from 1950 to 1955. Multifamily units in the whole ten-year period were never more than 17 per cent of the total housing started in any given year, but the proportion of this new housing insured by the federal government steadily declined between 1950 and 1955. In the latter year only 3 per cent of the mortgages insured by FHA were for new rental units.[30] Not until 1958–59 was the trend reversed and the number of multiple-family housing units increased.

The whole question of the movement of population into and within metropolitan areas, as influenced by the various federal housing programs, needs further exploration and careful study. The movement to the suburbs, to be sure, probably had many causes, of which the federal housing program was only one. And many people would agree that it should be encouraged. But it has also created a demand for municipal services in suburbs, increased waste disposal problems, and placed a tremendous strain upon available water resources, educational facilities, and recreational areas. These are all by-products of the federal-sponsored housing programs, and all in turn are interwoven in the complex pattern of metropolitan living and are bound to affect government in metropolitan areas.

Moreover, there has been considerable criticism of the design of public housing. "Cities are freezing on a design for living ideally calculated to keep everybody in suburbia. . . . These vast, barracks-like superblocks are not designed for people who like cities, but for people who have no other choice." [31]

It is argued further that the new housing developments are cut off from city life. They are, to use a term frequently applied to them by their builders, "self-contained." There is no place for the development of community life in the big new housing projects. It is not surprising, as one witty commentator points out, that "a host of little enterprises has sprung up on the bad side of the street as witness to the vacuum of the design. Visually, the effect is enough to drive an architect crazy; grocery stores with fruit out in the street, discount houses covered with garish signs, pastry shops, delicatessens, a Happy Time Bar and Grill, and a host of perversities to clutter up design. People are just no damn good." [32]

Though the federal government of course is not solely to blame for the design of the new housing, neither has it done anything to improve the situation. Since it provided such a large share of the funds, it must be held at least partly responsible for the results. On the other hand, it should not be overlooked that FHA and VA regulations have often been more important than local ordinances in protecting the purchaser and the community, particularly in regard to soundness of construction. Frequently, too, federal zoning and subdivision standards have been much higher than those of local communities.

Moreover, the Housing Act of 1949 required that the urban renewal plan under Title I conform to the general city plan. This was the first federal law requiring a measure of city planning before a grant-in-aid could be made. The Act of 1954 went further in requiring each city to submit a "workable program" outlining among other things the progress it was making in city planning and indicating how the new housing would aid in carrying out the plan. This, of course, was an important step toward encouraging the development of sound city plans.

As one might expect in so large a field, administrative headaches have been numerous, and some of them, at least, have had an effect on metropolitan areas. Although some steps have been taken to bring about better understanding between federal and local housing officials—the National Association of Housing and Redevelopment Officials, for example, has sponsored a Federal-Local Relations Committee to discuss mutual problems and to simplify administrative regulations—hearings before congressional committees are full of complaints by local officials about delays caused by federal statutory requirements and administrative red tape. The Baltimore Urban Renewal Study Board, reporting to the mayor in September 1956, complained that "many of the delays and problems encountered . . . by local government agencies are due to limitations imposed both by law and administrators at the Federal level. A comprehensive renewal program . . . is being hampered through unnecessary controls." [33] The House Subcommittee on Intergovernmental Relations found that "Federal supervision of the public housing and urban renewal program was strongly and almost universally criticized for hampering local effort. . . . cities attributed their dissatisfaction to several factors: (1) detailed and cumbersome Federal procedures and requirements for obtaining project approval, (2) tight centralization of administrative authority in Washington, and (3) inadequate staffing of field offices." [34]

The very complexity of federal housing laws is another problem. Amendment has been piled upon amendment over the years until considerable "expertise" is needed to prepare an application for a grant, and delays are frequent. As the mayor of Philadelphia recently testified, the public housing law "is so full of 'provided thats' and 'notwithstandings' that it is a nightmare to try to track down just what is provided for." [35]

Even more important from the point of view of this study is the fact that cities are seldom prepared to absorb the impact of several major federal programs simultaneously. Their financial resources are almost always limited, and virtually every program requires considerable expenditure. Moreover, each city is faced with the problem of synchronization. Charles E. Slusser, Commissioner of Public Housing, explaining delays in the public housing program, commented that "cities are absorbed in their urban renewal programs. Their timing schedules are a little different. . . . the highway and freeway programs are having their impact. The cities must pace and time themselves as to their most urgent need." [36] Furthermore, when a city accepts a federal grant, it undertakes the obligation of relocating people who must be moved from the site. Sometimes the same family has to move several times as housing becomes more and more difficult to obtain. Urban renewal programs will eventually increase the amount of good housing, but in the meantime, they often cause temporary housing shortages. Slums must be torn down before new housing can be built, and too many projects undertaken in a single metropolitan area can create a real housing crisis. If cities wish to take advantage of federal grants, they must become involved in what in many cases constitutes a major population-moving function, in which they have no experience and which therefore they often handle very badly.[37] Relocation of dispossessed families is properly a matter for local action, but federal programs fail to appreciate the magnitude of the problem.

The whole problem of synchronization is made even more difficult for cities because not only do the various aspects of the housing program have to be meshed together, but housing has also to be geared to other federal aid programs. No provision is made in the new federal highway program, for example, for the relocation of the families who will inevitably have to be moved to make way for superhighways built in urban areas.

As Mayor Richardson Dilworth of Philadelphia pointed out, "If people are given no help in relocating from the path of highways this obviously augments the housing problems which the renewal program is trying to solve. And renewal activities must be closely related to the programming of highways if we are to avoid, on the one hand, the creation of new blight along new highways and, on the other hand, the chewing up of a newly renewed area to make way for a new highway." [38]

The result of these programs certainly entails one of the

largest mass movements of urban population in American history, yet very little is definitely known about it. Some people, perhaps a third, move to other parts of the central city, another third to the suburbs, and the remaining third simply disappear so far as existing records are concerned.[39] Indeed, only recently have records begun to be kept, and even today in New York City, where relocation is handled by the developer, records are incomplete.

Looking over the whole program, it is obvious that the federal government has given very little thought to the possible effect of its housing and urban renewal activities on the larger problem of government in whole metropolitan communities. Though no one can doubt that federal aid has gone a long way toward removing some of the worst instances of physical blight in individual cities, at the same time it may well be that these programs have unwittingly helped to create social problems of large magnitude in the encompassing metropolitan areas.

Water Resources

The federal government has long had an interest in the development and use of water resources. The roots of present activity go back to 1824, when Congress authorized the first river improvements. For almost a century thereafter, federal interest and activity in this field was limited largely to improvement of navigation in rivers and harbors.[40] Later, as forests were cut down and farms and cities covered the valleys, flood control came to demand more attention. Then, as settlers moved into the Far West, irrigation and water resources development became increasingly important. In modern times, all the earlier interests have remained, and prevention of pollution created by dumping of untreated sewage and industrial wastes and the maintenance of adequate water for human and industrial needs have been added.

Over the years, the federal government's relation to water

resources has become perplexingly complex.[41] Today, the government is active in irrigation, navigation, power development, soil erosion control, drought relief, flood control, fisheries development, recreation, and prevention of water pollution. Since World War II alone, more than $15 billion has been spent on these programs.

A great many federal agencies now carry on water resources activities. The Bureau of Reclamation handles irrigation matters; the Corps of Engineers, flood control and river and harbor development; the Soil Conservation Service and the Forest Service, watershed protection and development; and the Division of Sanitary Engineering in the Department of Health, Education and Welfare, water pollution control. TVA, the Federal Power Commission, the Bureau of Mines, and a dozen other agencies carry on additional programs.

Some of these programs may seem to have little direct impact on metropolitan areas, but all of them influence living and working in such areas. Irrigation, for example, might at first glance seem rather remote from urban concerns, but irrigation is a consumptive use of water. Once water is used for irrigating, it is lost for use by downstream areas. Thus use of water for irrigation depletes the total amount available for metropolitan needs. The whole water supply picture of metropolitan Los Angeles, for example, is closely related to irrigation projects which draw water from the Colorado River. The same competition takes place in many other areas.

Too much water can be as disastrous as too little, and the federal government's activities have been equally important here. For example, in 1957 the TVA dams prevented the flooding of the Chattanooga metropolitan area.[42] Since limits of space make selection necessary, no attempt will be made here to describe the impact of irrigation and flood control programs on metropolitan areas, however real it may be in some instances. Somewhat more evident in their impact are the long-established federal harbor development activities, since location of port facilities may change the flow of business enterprise. In the discussion that follows, however, attention will be centered chiefly upon water resources and water pollution, the major problems in the field.

"The greatest single weakness in the Federal Government's activities in the field of water resources development," said a recent Cabinet committee studying the problem, "is lack of cooperation and coordination of Federal agencies with each other and with the States and local interests." [43] This Cabinet committee was only the last of a series of groups to examine federal water policy since the end of World War II. Both Hoover Commissions had task forces working in the area,[44] President Truman appointed a President's Water Resources Policy Commission,[45] a survey was made by Temple University,[46] the Missouri Basin Survey Commission made its report in 1953,[47] and finally in 1955 President Eisenhower's Presidential Advisory Committee on Water Resources Policy, which was composed of three Cabinet members, reported its findings.[48]

Lack of Co-ordination

All the survey groups pointed to the number of programs and to the lack of co-ordination between them. Thus they were all forced to give some attention to two major administrative problems. They all considered what sort of administrative organization should be created in the executive branch of the federal government to administer and co-ordinate federal water resource programs. Some groups proposed a new Department of Natural Resources, and others suggested centralization in the Department of the Interior. Most proposed a board of review in the Executive Office of the President, although there was considerable difference about how the board should be constituted and how it would function. Even with these differences, however, there was agreement that federal water resource programs ought to be reviewed at the presidential staff level.

Better field co-ordination was likewise recommended. All the groups agreed that some sort of drainage or river basin committee was required, as the first Hoover Commission said, "to facilitate 'grass roots' decision, interservice cooperation, and local participation in planning." [49] There was less unanimity of opinion on how this basin committee should be constituted and how it should operate. Some thought that it should be simply a survey and planning group on which each federal agency interested in water would be represented, each with a veto over the plans of the others. Some recommended that appropriations be made to the basin committee, which would supervise their expenditures. Eisenhower's Presidential Advisory Committee would have added a representative of each affected state to the basin committee. None of the proposals would have included any metropolitan or other local representatives on the committee.

Conflicting policies established by Congress have been one of the principal obstacles to obtaining a unified and intelligent water use policy. To some extent, this conflict results from the fact that water resources programs, like many another program affecting metropolitan areas, are divided among a great many committees of Congress, preventing any one committee from getting the whole picture. President Truman's Water Resources Policy Commission pinpointed this conflict of policy and recommended that "a set of clearly defined material objectives established by Congress" be used by all federal agencies to judge new river basin programs. [50] The Commission, however, was not very definite in regard to what these objectives should be. It did assert that they ought to achieve maximum sustained use of water resources for all purposes, and that federal agencies ought to co-operate among themselves and with state agencies in co-ordinating their planning efforts. The Commission, in a pious exhortation, urged Congress to consider future water development programs only if they were multipurpose and for a whole basin.

Failure to Consider Urban Needs

Five years later, the second Hoover Commission's Task Force on Water Resources reported that there was still "no Federal legislation which recognizes municipal and industrial water supply as being of national concern on a quantitative basis." [51] It found, however, that

various bits of legislation recognize the right of municipalities and industry to participate in the benefits of Federal water resource development. Rapidly increasing urban population indicates the need for careful evaluation of the effect of Federal multipurpose projects on municipal water supply. There may be both advantages and disadvantages in these projects with the advantages more likely if municipal needs are included in the planning. The rate of water flow permitted by flood control dams has a direct effect on the clearing of pollution, the growth of aquatic plants and the amount of taste and odor in waters drawn off dam streams.

The operation of hydroelectric power facilities which call for a great range of discharges may result in many operational problems for downstream water intake installations. . . . In the event that a municipality is located on a reservoir the reduction in velocity and the development of counter currents may permit waste from that or a downstream community to travel upstream to the water intake. This phenomenon has been known to occur at Cincinnati, Ohio, on the Ohio River.[52]

These factors may be taken into account and a policy including the needs of metropolitan areas developed when the newly created Senate Select Committee on National Water Resources makes its report. This committee, established by the Senate during the Eighty-sixth Congress, was charged with studying the development and co-ordination of water resources and making recommendations for "an adequate and comprehensive legislative program." [53] Such a program can hardly avoid encompassing metropolitan water supply.

Although metropolitan water needs are small as compared with those of irrigation and industry, they are crucial for community existence, and they have been largely neglected in federal programs.[54] According to U. S. Geological Survey estimates, withdrawals for irrigation amount to 95 billion gallons a day.[55] Industrial use is estimated at 70 billion gallons a day, which includes great amounts used for cooling, but which does not represent actual consumption, since the water is returned to rivers and lakes little reduced in quantity. These figures are to be compared with an estimated 12 billion gallons daily for all municipal uses, including drinking, sanitation, sewage, street cleaning, and air conditioning.

Irrigation projects not only increase the amount of mineral matter in water by leaching it from the soil, but also increase the cost of developing municipal water supplies through preempting low-cost water sources. All these factors make an evaluation of federal water programs in terms of urban needs necessary, and the competing needs of municipalities within each metropolitan area make an approach to water supply on the metropolitan area or region basis even more vital.

Metropolitan difficulties arise from a number of different causes. Sometimes the central city in an area needs more water, but for the most part large cities have so far been able to obtain sufficient supplies. It is principally the rapidly growing suburbs that lack adequate water reserves. When deep wells are unproductive and the suburbs are individually too small to build their own water systems, the only answer is some approach on the basis of the whole metropolitan area.

President Truman's Water Resources Policy Commission urged the creation of metropolitan water districts to cope with the problem, and it cited the Massachusetts Metropolitan Water District in particular as representing "a conspicuously successful means of meeting the water-supply needs of a densely populated metropolitan area overriding the municipal boundaries, and establishing authority to develop and sell water at wholesale." [56] Differences in state constitutions and state water law have led other areas to approach the matter somewhat differently, but the New Jersey District Water Supply Commission and the Metropolitan Water District of Southern California indicate how cities can associate with one another for the purpose of procuring water from a multiple-purpose federal river basin project. The federal government ought to do all it can, the Commission said, to encourage the formation of metropolitan water districts as the most economical way to meet metropolitan needs. The Commission also noted the "pressing need for improved cooperation in the planning of river and drainage basin studies which necessarily involve municipal water supplies." [57]

An interesting variation of the usual metropolitan pattern is found in Pinellas County, Florida, part of the St. Petersburg–Tampa metropolitan area. There a county water district has been created to serve just its suburban communities. This device might provide another answer to the difficulties of suburban communities whose rapid growth has made local water resources inadequate, and which thus are faced with the need for spending sums of money far beyond their individual means to bring water from a distance.

There is a limit to what the federal government can do to bring about the creation of metropolitan water districts. It is largely a matter for the states. Fortunately, in most of the nation except the West, where water law is pretty well developed on the basis of appropriation, water law is still in the developmental stage. As it is converted from its old basis of riparian rights to a doctrine based on use, urban citizens can be active in behalf of their interests. If they do not take an interest in the development of water law, however, metropolitan needs may be largely overlooked.

All in all, it is evident that despite expenditures of great magnitude in a variety of water programs, the federal government has not developed either a consistent and all-inclusive water use policy or a co-ordinated program. Nor has it recognized the implications of the suburban explosion on water supply. For the most part, flood control, irrigation, and navigation have held the attention of Congress to the exclusion of the requirements of the city dwellers. Metropolitan needs, however, are becoming increasingly demanding, and the federal government cannot long ignore them.

Water Pollution Control

Just as important as water supply is the problem of controlling pollution. As the Senate Committee on Public Works declared more than ten years ago, "Water pollution has become a matter of grave concern in many areas, and its damaging effects on public health and national resources are a matter of definite Federal concern as a menace to national welfare." [58]

The federal government's first major attempt in this field was the passage of the Water Pollution Control Act of 1948.[59] That act was principally a research and planning measure. The research program of the Public Health Service was expanded, a Sanitary Engineering Center was established in Cincinnati, and a Water Pollution Control Advisory Board was created. Simultaneously, a model state water pollution law was worked out, and pollution control plans were developed jointly with states for a number of river basins. The basic philosophy of the 1948 Act was that pollution was primarily a state responsibility, but that the federal government had an interest in seeing that water resources were conserved. The principal objective of the legislation was to make sure that every state had an effective pollution program.

Though the passage of this act represented the fruit of many years of effort to provide comprehensive stream pollution control legislation based on local, state, and federal co-operation, it proved to be inadequate in abating pollution. The Hoover Commission Task Force on Water Resources reported in 1955 that "expanding industry and urban populations are creating pollution at a rate greater than it is being abated." [60] In 1956, Roswell B. Perkins, Assistant Secretary of the Department of Health, Education and Welfare, commenting on the progress states were making in controlling stream pollution, said:

I think we would have to, in all candor, say it has been inadequate. . . . We think that the State pollution control authorities themselves are doing an excellent job with the relatively inadequate support that we think they are getting. . . . Some of them have annual appropriations of less than $30,000 a year. In fact 23 states do. And more have less than $50,000 a year. So we would say this is a relatively meager support for a very important function.[61]

In 1956, Congress amended the 1948 Act by the passage of Public Law 660, which authorized $500 million to be spent in the next five years as matching grants to help states build sewage treatment plants, the federal government to provide 30 per cent of the eligible cost of the plant or $250,000, whichever was less, and $3 million to assist states and interstate pollution control agencies in expanding their efforts. In fiscal 1957, fiscal 1958, and fiscal 1959, Congress appropriated $45 million a year as allotments to the states. In 1957, the first full year of grants under Public Law 660, $351 million was spent for municipal water pollution abatement plants, as compared with an average of $222 million between 1952 and 1956; and in 1958, tentative figures show that the amount municipalities spent for treatment plants jumped to about $390 million. By October 1, 1958, about 200 plants had been completed with this federal aid.[62] Although the grants are small, and thus are of most assistance to small communities, a few plants of substantial size have been built under the program in major metropolitan cities. Even so, Secretary Perkins felt that the preference given under the law to small municipalities was unnecessarily great. He argued that "the principal objective of incentive grants should be to stimulate the construction that is most urgently needed to abate pollution. From this standpoint, stimulating the construction of treatment works by larger municipalities is—generally speaking—of relatively greater importance." [63]

Moreover, as Daniel Bergson, State Health Commissioner for New Jersey, pointed out, the bill did not provide aid for the construction of sewage collection systems. Yet, in many metropolitan areas, new treatment plants were not needed nearly so much as collection systems to take care of the new suburbs.[64] Just as with water supply, the problem of water pollution is most acute in new suburban areas. For the same reasons, big cities need federal aid far less than older small cities that have reached their bonded debt limits. Some of these latter cities have never had sewage treatment plants and have simply dumped their wastes untreated into a near-by stream. Others have increased in population and now find their old plants inadequate. Still other cities have developed new suburbs. In any case, water pollution is part of the problem of the efficient use of water resources as a whole. Again the danger of the partial approach is quite apparent.

Bills were introduced in the Eighty-fifth Congress and in the first session of the Eighty-sixth to amend the 1948 Act further by increasing the maximum from $250,000 to $500,000 for any single construction project, permitting municipalities to join together in building joint treatment plants with no effect on the amount of each grant, authorizing an appropriation of $100 million in any fiscal year for grants, and establishing an Office of Water Pollution Control in the Department of Health, Education and Welfare. By the end of the session, one such bill (H. R. 3610) had been passed in slightly different form by both houses of Congress, and there was considerable pressure building up for its final passage. Whether the President would sign such a bill in the face of the recommendation of his Joint Federal-State Action Committee that federal aid for sewage treatment plants be dropped is problematical.[65]

Whatever the outcome, the federal government is committed to aid in attacking water pollution, at least on a small scale, and chiefly in smaller communities, until 1961. It probably cannot avoid further involvement in the future. The rising population, the rapidly increasing per capita water use, and growing industrial water needs make current levels of expenditures for pollution abatement facilities grossly inadequate. The worst part of the whole pollution picture is in connection with the water supply of metropolitan areas, and the years ahead can hardly help but see increased federal aid to remedy this problem.

Airports

Although the federal government spent a considerable amount of money before 1942 to aid civilian aviation, there was no national program specifically for the construction of civilian airports. Before 1942, as a means of assisting unemployed persons, approximately $100 million was spent on some 1,000 airport projects through the Works Progress Administration, the Federal Emergency Relief Administration, and the Civil Works Administration.[66] Some of this went for new airfields, but most of it was spent to extend runways and to build access roads. During the war further federal money was allotted to airport construction, but this was essentially an emergency military program. Under this program, about 550 airfields were constructed, most of which were occupied by the military. At the end of the war, these airports were declared surplus and turned over to cities, counties, or states for civilian airport use.[67] In addition, the federal government has borne the cost of radio and light beacons, teletype communications, and intermediate landing fields from the time the aviation industry first developed. Local communities, however, were estimated to have spent $350 million to $400 million up to January 1, 1938, and much more by the end of the war, to build airports.[68]

At the end of the war, the nation was faced with an acute problem in the field of air transportation. Airports had been located on what appears to have been a hit-or-miss basis across the country, depending upon local initiative or military need. Frequently, funds were lacking to maintain them after they had been constructed. In the face of a probable tremendous expansion of the air transportation industry, a whole series of questions had to be resolved. The major one, however, was, Who should have the responsibility for planning, constructing, and operating airports—the federal government, the states, or local communities?

So far as the states were concerned, it was argued that "large cities . . . had spent . . . more than $100 million in airport construction and the state governments had spent relatively little. . . . Aviation has been and is peculiarly and largely a matter of local and federal concern. . . . there is nothing about aviation that is of state-wide significance. Some states do not have aviation agencies. It would be unfair to expect cities to impose taxes and issue bonds in connection with airport projects for the purpose of turning over the proceeds to state agencies which would act as intermediaries in matching federal appropriations." [69]

The Federal Airport Act of 1946 reflected these objections and provided for a federal-local pattern of grants. Under the act, states might apply for federal aid for specific projects, but grants were not limited to states. Any "public agency"—a city, a county, a town, a parish, a port authority, for example—might be a sponsor, but the majority of the sponsors were municipalities. Thus the state governments could be by-passed by their political subdivisions unless this was prohibited by state law. [70] The federal portion of the grant was limited to 25 per cent of the cost of acquiring land for the airport and 50 per cent of the other costs.

In fixing standards for aid, the Civil Aeronautics Administration decided to include "only existing and proposed public airports serving communities which have a substantial requirement, and which will require airport development within the period covered by the [National Airport] plan." [71] Any one of fourteen different grounds could qualify a community as having "a substantial requirement." It might be permanently certified for scheduled service by the Civil Aeronautics Board, or it might have ten or more airworthy aircraft based in the community, or if none of the fourteen justifications applied, the airport might be needed because of some special circumstance essential to the public welfare. Indeed, it would seem hard to find a community which could not qualify for some federal aid under this policy. Eventually, the size of commercial airports was determined by a formula based on the number of passengers enplaned and the length of their trips. All other airports for general use were put in a category which limited their size. Thus, although small communities were encouraged to build airports, the amount of federal assistance was determined by a formula based on actual and potential use.

The 1946 Act provided that appropriations be made annually, thus requiring operation of the federal-aid airport program on a year-to-year basis. Some 1,100 airports were built or improved during the period 1946–55 with grants-in-aid from the federal government. In an endeavor to permit longer-range planning and to give local sponsors greater flexibility in arranging their financing, the 1946 Act was amended in 1955 [72] to authorize a four-year program of annual grants of $63 million. At the end of the first year, it was reported that the new program included 334 projects located in every state except Wisconsin and Wyoming, "which [were] expected to submit programs in the near future," and that a total of more than $52 million had been allotted for the continental United States and nearly $3 million for the territories.[73] Metropolitan area airports fared quite well. For example, out of a total of $2.69 million for the whole state of Michigan, the Detroit-Wayne Major Airport received $1.25 million. The portion which great metropolitan centers received was much the same from state to state. In New York State, out of a total of $4 million, some $2.5 million went to the New York Port Authority for La Guardia and Idlewild airports. In California, Los Angeles and Oakland each received $1.25 million and San Francisco $765,000 of a total of $4.7 million for the state. Among the sponsors were cities, counties, airport districts, port authorities, towns, states, universities, and sometimes a combination of two or more of these.

But if federal money was made available, the CAA was not prepared to see that it was used properly. Indeed, the Planning Division of the Office of Airports was for all practical purposes abolished in 1953 and was not re-established until July 1958. The last official CAA guide to airport planning was published in 1952! Thus during the period of the most rapid growth in the history of civil aviation, the federal government had no unit specifically directed toward airport planning. During the whole period, as a consequence, airport construction was allowed to drift and to be based on local and often transitory considerations, which in very few cases took adequate account of long-term, area-wide needs. There may have been a great deal of construction made possible by federal money inside the airport fence, but no consideration was given to the relation of the airport to the community outside the fence. Since 1958, the planning function has been resumed by the Federal Aviation Agency, but it will be a long time before the effect of planning will be felt across the country.

In the 1959 session of Congress, the first bill introduced in the Senate once again provided increased federal assistance for airport development. It again authorized the appropriation of $63 million a year for the next two fiscal years in the form of grants-in-aid to states and local communities. Passed by Congress, this bill was signed by the President on June 29, 1959. Thus federal aid to airports is guaranteed through 1961.

The National Airport Plan for 1959 indicates that a total of $1,285,394,000 worth of airport development is needed for the period ending June 30, 1962. "Of the total cost [of this projected construction], about $590 million is available from local and state sources." [74] The balance will probably have to be met by federal funds, for it has become an accepted fact that it is clearly "in the national interest to continue a strong and effective Federal aid to airports program." [75]

If the federal government is making substantial contributions for the construction of airports, it has done little to encourage the establishment of an approach to the problem on a metropolitan basis. To be sure, some local areas have gone ahead on their own. St. Paul and Minneapolis, Minnesota, have established a joint Metropolitan Airport Commission, and the federal government has dealt with such airport authorities where they exist just as it has with individual cities or counties. As a matter of fact, it has stated that metropolitan areas are eligible for more than one grant-supported airport, contrary to its general rule. On the other hand, the federal government has done little or nothing to press for metropolitan planning of airports where special authorities do not exist. Its policy has been to work with whatever tools are at hand, rather than to exercise leadership in bringing about planning for air transportation for whole metropolitan areas.

Other intergovernmental problems have arisen in the airport program.[76] There have been conflicts between the civilian and military programs, and they have had their amusing sides. As one Air Force major said, "Hell hath no fury like a sleepless taxpayer," and military jet planes have kept many a taxpayer awake nights. Military men argue the necessity for dispersion of aircraft in the interest of national security. In many areas, both civilian and military traffic is increasing at all airports located near big cities, and accident rates continue to climb. Both civilian and military users claim that they need airports close to centers of population, and the fact is that the military frequently have the best sites because they got there first. Sometimes this leads to friction. The rapidly growing city of San Diego, for example, was told by the Civil Aeronautics Administration that its municipal airport, Lindbergh Field, was obsolete and that a new airport should be constructed. Good sites were difficult to find. The city, after a long search, found a site that the CAA approved, but the Navy objected on the ground that the new field would interfere with operations at the near-by Naval Air Station. This conflict aroused a great deal of interest among city officials everywhere. American Municipal Association representatives appeared before the Air Coordinating Committee to protest, arguing that "the basic principles involved in this dispute may well affect every other city in America having any branch of the armed services in its general area." [77]

The American Municipal Association summed up the military-urban conflict at its 1956 congress: "The combined pressures of civil and military airport requirements have over-taxed terminal facilities and are creating serious airspace problems in many localities. . . . Until steps are taken to resolve conflicting use interests between civil and military aircraft, the purposes of the federal aid program cannot be attained and military authorities can continue to prevent cities from seeking to cooperate in planning, providing and operating adequate civil airport facilities essential to the normal growth and development of national civil aviation requirements." [78]

There are a number of other airport problems involving federal-city relations. Most of them can be solved only by a broad approach for entire metropolitan areas. Jet planes promise more noise and demand longer and better-constructed runways.[79] Zoning around airports to keep out high buildings and dwellings has already been used to some extent, but it may need to be greatly expanded in the future. Large-scale approach clearances may involve considerable population movement, intensify housing shortages, and complicate highway patterns. To date, there has been little consciousness on the part of the federal government that all these problems interrelate. It is to be hoped that that trend will be reversed and that the airport problem will be tackled, as it must be, on a metropolitan basis.

Military Installations and Defense Industries

There are few metropolitan areas in the country today that do not have some major defense activity within their borders. Whether it be in areas like Norfolk, San Diego, San Antonio, or Corpus Christi, where the armed forces play an important role in the community's total life, or in areas like Detroit, where war industry plants are erected with financial help from the Department of Defense, the military functions of the federal government have had a major impact on the nation's great urban centers.

The most direct and obvious impact has been through the

establishment of navy yards, air bases, and army posts which involve control of real property. As of June 30, 1957, the military departments controlled somewhat more than 27 million acres of real property in the continental United States, the original cost of which was $19.5 billion.[80] Some 7.6 million acres were fee-owned and the remainder was held under lease or easement or was part of the public domain assigned for military use. These figures are so large that they have meaning only when related to other data. The total land area of the United States is approximately 2 billion acres. The federal government owns 408 million acres, or 21 per cent, and the Department of Defense alone controls 27 million acres, or 1.4 per cent. Thus it can be argued that the area set aside for military use is very small as compared with the total held by the federal government. This argument is only partially valid, however, because a good deal of military property is in well-settled urban areas.

Each year new military programs involve additional land in urban areas. In fiscal 1959, for example, the Army spent some $147 million for the surface-to-air missile program for defense of key military bases and metropolitan industrial centers; the Navy constructed a dry dock at the Charleston, South Carolina, Navy Yard, as well as new facilities at San Francisco, New London, and the District of Columbia; and the Air Force acquired 4,500 acres of land to enlarge airports and extend runways and to extend its operational and support program generally. In the same year, moreover, 679,000 officers and upper-grade enlisted men required family housing. To meet this need, over 450,000 units already were in being, but approximately 58,000 more were needed immediately.[81]

Even housing on a military reservation can have an impact on the surrounding community. In the summer of 1958, the chairman of the Fairfax County Planning Commission in metropolitan Washington, D. C., charged that the $10 million military housing project at Fort Belvoir would violate county land use plans in the historic Mount Vernon–Woodlawn Plantation area.[82] The chairman was particularly critical of the fact that the county "was not told that the project was in the offing." The area involved was characterized by high-priced single-family dwellings surrounded by wooded vistas. The Army's project included 309 duplex homes "dropped between Woodlawn and its view of Mount Vernon several miles away." Army spokesmen replied that the project would be hidden behind a barrier of trees and that access would be through Fort Belvoir and not directly from the main highway passing Woodlawn. The Army apparently could not understand why the County Planning Commission should be consulted in these circumstances. The Commission argued, however, that it was interested in the development of the whole area, and this involved what was built on the Fort as well as off.

On the other hand, the Department of Defense also disposed of some 1.75 million acres of real estate in the three-year period 1953–56. Nevertheless, military holdings continue to be very large, especially in certain metropolitan areas. It can be readily admitted that much of this land was obtained years ago and that urban settlement grew up around the military part, but this is precisely one way the military holding of land influences the development of a whole area. Army installations mean more housing; some of it may be supplied on the base, but supplementary housing is always needed outside. Even what might seem to be the purely military matter of permitting servicemen to leave the base in civilian clothes rather than in uniform may make necessary proportionally large increases in police forces in neighboring communities.[83] Men in uniform are disciplined by military police, but military personnel in civilian clothes are under municipal control until their identity is established.

Determining Location of Military Installations

The Pentagon reports that strong pressure is brought to bear on the military services by congressmen and local chambers of commerce to locate new military installations in their communities. Far from forcing new military projects on reluctant communities, the military usually finds itself in an excellent bargaining position and able to demand assurances that adequate water, sewage, and roads are available or will be made available before it comes into an area. There are exceptions, to be sure, but they are few and far between. Usually cities are anxious to have military bases located in or near them. The reason, of course, is the expectation that military payrolls will bring money into the community, and, conversely, that if an installation is moved the community will lose business. Even New York City was concerned about the moving of an army quartermaster center to Philadelphia. Whether these local expenditures are as large as they are generally thought to be is an open question. Certainly expenditures in post exchanges and pay allotments sent home reduce the amount. Business groups, however, have campaigned against military commissary stores, post movies, and military housing on the base with considerable success.

Whatever the facts of the situation, local businessmen are certain that a defense establishment spells prosperity. Rarely is the cost to the community in terms of increased public services, the growth of slums, and the need for street and traffic aids considered. In the negotiations to obtain a military installation, usually a representative of the chamber of commerce and the local congressman sit on one side of the table and the military authorities on the other. The city planning director is seldom included. This is not a deliberate evasion on the part of the military authorities, since the local people determine the composition of the negotiating group. Moreover, some cities do not have planning staffs, and there are very few metropolitan planning bodies. In the Norfolk–Hampton Roads area most of the military establishments had been built before any community planning agencies were created. Norfolk itself did not have a city planning director until after World War II.[84]

In recent years, the Army has established informal community councils in areas near military posts, made up of leading citizens, civic officials, and military leaders. Though these are intended primarily to assist in solving day-to-day problems by better understanding and co-operation, they have also been useful in adapting military base planning to community needs. The eagerness of local business groups to obtain bigger and bigger military posts, however, as well as the fact that much of the damage has already been done, continues to handicap efforts of metropolitan planners.

The indirect impacts caused by the location of war industry in a metropolitan area may be even greater than these. When war came in 1917 and again in 1941, defense industries had to be greatly expanded to meet the requirements of the armed services. To be sure, many factories could be converted from the manufacture of civilian goods to military items, but, in addition, many new plants had to be erected. This plant expansion was financed in several different ways. Sometimes the federal government built the plant and leased it to the manufacturer; sometimes it simply certified the new construction as necessary for the war effort, and the owner was able to take advantage of the rapid amortization provision of the income tax laws.[85] There were variations of these plans, but the result in every case was a tremendous expansion of industry largely financed by the federal government. In the early days of World War II, the determination of plant location was left pretty much to the manufacturer. Later, labor shortages and pressure from Congress led the armed services and the War Production Board to exercise a veto on site selection. In the main, however, this veto power was used to keep new plants out of congested communities. The federal government did everything it could to help obtain public utilities for the new plants, and during the war, a request from the military carried great weight. New plants also meant new highways and access roads constructed by the state with federal aid. Utilities and transportation facilities attracted non-war industry, housing, and recreational establishments. As a result, metropolitan growth in the areas where there were war plants was profoundly affected.[86]

Willow Run: A Case Study

The story of Willow Run makes an excellent case study to illustrate the point. When Henry Ford II and the Defense Plant Corporation agreed in April 1941 to build the world's largest bomber plant, Willow Run was a rural crossroads in Ypsilanti Township, Washtenaw County, Michigan.[87] The first step after the construction of the 60,000-employee plant was to build highways giving ready access to Detroit, with the expectation that workmen in the new plant would not move their residence and that it would not be necessary to create housing and community services. Contrary to these anticipations, however, people began to drift into the region directly adjoining the bomber plant. Shack towns sprang up with their attendant menace to health. No single political division found itself in a position to assume full responsibility for this industrial colossus. The general area included several cities, parts of counties, a score of townships, and numerous school districts, but there were only a handful of part-time town officials in the immediate vicinity of the plant. Gradually state laws gave state administrative agencies more responsibility over health and authorized county authorities to regulate sanitation in cabin camps, location of septic tanks, and water supply for private dwellings. The federal government advanced funds to state and county highway units for highways and also made grants-in-aid for hospital expansion. But county zoning and the prohibition of wildcat subdividing were slow to come, and there was little planned development. On January 31, 1942, the *Detroit News* stated: "To date, there has been absolutely no coordinated planning by federal, state, metropolitan defense area, county, township, municipal and bomber plant officials. So far as inter-communication is concerned, each might be dwelling on separate planets."[88] So far as the federal government was concerned, the secretary of the Ypsilanti Chamber of Commerce said: "I have managed to record the names of only fifteen representatives of federal agencies of all those calling here since last summer.

They pop in and pop out and are never seen again. They tell us how big our problem is going to be and ask what we are going to do about it. We say: 'You tell us what you want us to do. If you don't know, who does?' But they go away and each one asks the same questions of the persons around here and that's the last we hear of it." [89]

Eventually many of these problems solved themselves, but the early confusion long left its mark on the area. Moreover, the location of war industries at Willow Run encouraged a strong westward movement of metropolitan Detroit, thus altering the normally expected growth pattern. It is a well-known principle that urban areas attract each other and that normal growth patterns will ordinarily lead to settlement between urban clusters. War industries constructed at the expense of the federal government altered this pattern. Willow Run was a problem in intergovernmental relations made more complex by the stress and strain of a war, but the federal government, through its decision to erect a huge war plant at Willow Run, was the catalytic agent that created the problem. It is an excellent answer to those who argue that government of metropolitan areas is solely a local problem in which the federal government properly has no concern.

Civil Defense

The civil defense activities of the federal government potentially could have the largest impact on government in metropolitan areas of any federal program. Indeed, they could remake the face of America. Forty per cent of the population and over half of all persons employed in manufacturing live in forty metropolitan areas, according to the 1950 Census.[90] It is pretty well agreed that scattering urban population and industry would decrease the nation's vulnerability to atomic bomb attack. Though this would not mean abolishing big cities, it would mean shifting a large percentage of the nation's strength to scattered small cities and to the suburbs of the larger cities.

Any serious program of this character obviously would have a tremendous effect on metropolitan areas and on government within them. Even an adequate bomb shelter program estimated to cost from $10 billion to $20 billion,[91] for example, would involve a vast amount of construction work in metropolitan areas. No such ambitious civil defense programs have been undertaken, however, and it is unlikely that they will be. To date, indeed, Congress has shown great reluctance to vote large amounts of money for civil defense. It has appropriated some funds each year for the administrative expenses of the Federal Civil Defense Administration, and limited amounts have been granted to cities and states for equipment. Thus, although the potential effects of a national civil defense program are tremendous, civil defense has not had a major effect on government in metropolitan areas up to the present time.

The Federal Civil Defense Administration was first created as part of the Office for Emergency Management by executive order on December 1, 1950, during the Korean crisis, and it was subsequently made an independent agency by the Civil Defense Act of 1950.[92] By that act, the FCDA was charged with developing, co-ordinating, and guiding a national program to protect life and property on the home front in the event of war. The act declared that the states and their territorial subdivisions had the primary responsibility for civil defense on the state and local level, but it did not make clear what the federal responsibility was, or where it stopped and local responsibility began. This later proved to be a major problem.

Three types of work were assigned to the federal agency: research on the effect of modern warfare on civilian populations and the best means of meeting it; the development of a nation-wide warning and communication system; and the procurement and storage of civil defense equipment. The FCDA was to advise states and local governments, conduct training programs, and prescribe insignia. It could make no grants-in-aid to states for administrative expenses, but it could provide 50 per cent of the cost of materials and facilities to be used for civil defense. With federal advice, states were to develop survival plans and to negotiate interstate compacts for civil defense. State plans were to be in conformity with national civil defense plans, and thus by implication the federal agency was to develop national plans.

Civil Defense: Federal or State Responsibility?

In operation, the program ran into considerable difficulty, principally on the ground that it was inadequate to meet the needs of the situation. Extensive hearings to investigate the charges were held in 1956 before the Subcommittee on Military Operations of the House Committee on Government Operations.[93] In six months of hearings, the Subcommittee took over 3,000 pages of testimony. Its conclusion was that "Federal civil defense legislation should be redrafted to rest the basic responsibilities for civil defense on the Federal Government, with the state and local units of government having an important supporting role."[94] Further recommendations included the establishment of a Department of Civil Defense, the inauguration of a shelter construction program with federal funds, the preparation of a national master civil defense plan, a better definition of the role of the military in civil defense activities, and the strengthening of state and local civil defense organizations through federal grants-in-aid.

These recommendations were embodied in H. R. 2125, introduced by Representative Chet Holifield of California in January 1957. Hearings were held during the spring months of 1957, at which time numerous civic organizations, including the American Municipal Association and the United States Conference of Mayors, endorsed the bill.[95] The Bureau of the Budget, however, representing the Eisenhower Administration, was unwilling to approve the allocation to the federal government of primary responsibility for civil defense, and instead argued for joint federal-state responsibility. Eleven Republican members of the thirty-man House Committee on Government Operations also objected to increasing federal responsibility in the area of civil defense. This group issued a minority report condemning the proposal for a new department. H. R. 2125 was unable to overcome this opposition and failed to pass.

Subsequently, the Budget Bureau, realizing that civil defense would be a continuing problem, began a new study which resulted in the President's sending to Congress on April 24, 1958, a reorganization plan that combined the Office of Defense Mobilization and the Federal Civil Defense Administration into a new agency to be known as the Office of Civil and Defense Mobilization.[96] One of the arguments advanced for the merger of the two mobilization agencies was that it would remove duplication in developing and testing emergency plans and would provide better co-ordination of the civil defense activities of other federal agencies.[97] Hearings held by the Subcommittee on the new plan revealed some unhappiness in Congress that an executive department could not be obtained, but there was a willingness to accept the new agency.[98] Even if it was only half a loaf, it was better than none.

The complaint of the Subcommittee that national defense plans were inadequate was met, in part at least, by the testimony of FCDA Administrator Leo Hoegh, a former governor of Iowa, that a new national plan for civil defense was already in draft form which covered all the points of H. R. 2125. Hoegh said: "We have worked diligently with governors, mayors, city and state directors, with all Federal agencies, to the end that we could come up with a co-ordinated, simple, practical, effective national civil defense plan." [99] In addition, Hoegh pledged his efforts to further research and public education on the possible effects of nuclear weapons, to sample existing structures to determine their capabilities for providing shelter against fallout, and to construct a limited number of prototype bomb shelters. He recognized that there could not be a "massive federally financed shelter construction program," but he promised that the federal government would provide leadership in planning and by example.[100]

The whole matter of responsibility for civil defense still had to be settled. H. R. 2125, it will be recalled, had made civil defense the primary responsibility of the federal government. The Budget Bureau, as spokesman for the Administration, had disagreed and supported a middle-of-the-road concept of joint responsibility. This concept was embodied in H. R. 7576, which was introduced by Representative Carl Durham of North Carolina, passed by Congress, and signed by the President in August 1958.

There can be no doubt that congressional discontent was largely responsible for these changes. It brought about a merger of ODM and FCDA and a re-examination of the concept of responsibility for civil defense. Although those who wanted civil defense made primarily a federal responsibility were not successful, they did succeed in emphasizing the need for federal leadership and for a larger federal role in the program. Though a massive shelter construction program was not authorized, a national civil defense plan has been prepared, and research and public education programs have been expanded. These have been substantial changes, to be sure, but a massive bomb shelter program and the dispersal of industry which would be necessary in a defense emergency would have immensely greater impact on government in metropolitan areas. To date, however, except for a national plan at the top, civil defense is largely a myth. Congress, which controls the funds, is indifferent, and so is the public.

No Adequate Program for Metropolitan Areas

There is another aspect of the civil defense program that also ought to be examined, and that is the extent to which the Federal Civil Defense Administration in its day-to-day activities influenced government in metropolitan areas. In general, it was FCDA policy to work through state civil defense directors, who then dealt with the local governments. But there were many exceptions to this rule. Early in his career as administrator, Val Peterson told state directors that he would not hesitate to deal directly with local people if access to them was unduly obstructed by the state offices. Actually, there were many direct contacts between national headquarters and major local governments. This increased the importance of direct federal-municipal relations.

The FCDA, however, made grants-in-aid only to states. The old difficulty of metropolitan areas' having no corporate existence made them unable to receive funds. On the other hand, an occasional grant was made to a state with the understanding that it would be used to finance studies or plans for metropolitan areas and even for those stretching across state lines. Everyone recognized that this was not a satisfactory solution. For metropolitan areas wholly within a single state, FCDA recommended that each state by legislation provide for a single corporate civil defense planning and operating agency. Ohio acted upon this recommendation, and Dayton established a metropolitan civil defense agency. Miami has attained the same end through the new Dade County Charter. FCDA was much less positive what to do about interstate metropolitan areas. It hesitated to recommend a single pattern, because of the possible political repercussions. It did recommend a coordinator for each metropolitan area in its national plan, and the use of a Metropolitan Area Target Authority. Generally the metropolitan target area would coincide with the standard metropolitan area as defined by the Census Bureau, except where one target area might include two or more standard metropolitan areas.

In 1955, Congress provided $10 million for grants for survival studies to aid in the development of an operative civil defense plan, and most of these grants went to finance studies in metropolitan areas. Unfortunately, few cities were equipped to make such studies themselves, and most therefore had to contract with public or private research organizations to do the work. Some of the early contracts were over expensive and were not very well drawn as to the nature of the studies to be undertaken. This difficulty was overcome in time, and the later studies were better planned. Though the project had the effect of emphasizing the importance of metropolitan areas and the need for planning their defense upon an area-wide basis, it did not devote as much attention to the governmental aspects of the problem as would have been desirable.

On examining the whole civil defense program, one can only conclude that it has been feeble in its handling of the major problem, metropolitan areas. In part the reason for this is that the program has been built from the beginning on a federal-state basis. A realistic program would establish some kind of government machinery for metropolitan areas that would facilitate working relations in civil defense between the federal government and these areas. There are few indications, however, that, short of war, such a realistic program will be put into operation. At best, there probably will be some increase in federal activities, together with somewhat, but not significantly, larger appropriations for grants-in-aid. Congressional hesitation to increase expenditures in this direction, and the Eisenhower Administration's interest in federal-state relations rather than direct federal-local relations, will militate against a large civil defense program in the near future. The FCDA has been headed by former governors from some of the least metropolitan states, rather than men from large urban areas. Though one may concede that rural areas and small towns will have problems in a decentralization of industry and population, one may question whether the United States could survive as an effective fighting force if the major metropolitan areas were destroyed, since most of the nation's industrial potential is in these areas. The Office of Civil and Defense Mobilization must recognize the importance of metropolitan areas in national civil defense planning and make up its mind what to do about them.

Highways

If it is true that the "basic problem of metropolitan areas is not the way we move but the way many must live," then it may follow, as one of the country's leading transportation authorities concludes, that "the new highway program, as it now stands, may wind up attacking the transportation problem in a vacuum." [101] The program is isolated by law from the rest of the transportation system and from the urban areas it is designed to serve. Thus, it may intensify rather than alleviate the difficulties of metropolitan areas. The result of the program may be to compound congestion and to retard the development of better communities.

The Federal-Aid Highway Act of 1956 [102] authorized $25 billion for the Interstate Highway System, and more than $10 billion has been appropriated for the four fiscal years 1957–60 inclusive. Federal funds are to be matched by the states on a 90 per cent federal to 10 per cent state basis. The details of the whole road-building program need not be described here. The most significant fact about it is that a major portion of the funds will be spent for highways in urban areas. Indeed, the original proposal was in terms of a highway network to join the nation's metropolitan areas, but the bill as passed by Congress entitled the new program the System of Interstate and Defense Highways. Even so, it might more correctly be called the Intercity Highway System, because people want to go in and out of cities, not in and out of states. The new system is really a trunk line, linking together 90 per cent of the cities in the United States having a population of 50,000 or more. These roads are expected to carry not only long-distance traffic, but also a vast number of suburban and urban commuters.

The administration of the new program at the national level was confided to the federal Bureau of Public Roads. The Bureau started as a small unit in the Department of Agriculture in 1893, and was primarily concerned with rural roads during the first forty years of its existence.[103] The first aid bill for highways was passed in 1917 and provided $5 million for farm roads. The following year the authorization was doubled, and then it was increased to $75 million for each of the next twelve years. During the depression, the regular federal aid for highways was supplemented by large grants for emergency and public works programs. Very little of this money, however, was spent in cities.

The federal aid program for city highways virtually started in 1944. Before that time, a few states paid a portion of the costs when a road which was part of the state primary system was located in a city. The decision in each case rested with the state, and the federal government was not directly concerned. The Act of 1944,[104] however, specifically provided grants for roads inside cities. It authorized 45 per cent of federal aid to be expended for primary roads, 30 per cent for farm-to-market roads, and 25 per cent for primary roads in urban areas. The 1954 Act [105] expanded this to include secondary roads in cities where they connect with secondary roads outside. Though no exact data are available on how much of the money under the 1956 Act will be spent in metropolitan areas, it is estimated that considerably more than half the total amount will be used there. This would mean a total expenditure in the neighborhood of $13 billion to $15 billion in metropolitan areas.

As of the end of June 1959, it appeared that the new highway program was in danger of being temporarily stopped. The 1956 legislation required that the program be financed on a self-liquidating basis and that all construction grants be made from trust fund revenues derived from a federal motor fuels tax. In 1958, during the recession, an emergency appropriation was borrowed from the fund, which must be made up before further expenditures can be made. Costs have risen, and revenue has not come in fast enough to keep the fund replenished. Increased gasoline taxes to provide the necessary revenues were proposed by the Administration, but Congress has been cool toward the proposal.

Piecemeal Approach to Urban Highway Problems

All formal contacts of the Bureau of Public Roads are with state highway departments, and state highway departments traditionally have been rurally oriented. This is partly because state legislatures have been dominated by rural constituencies and partly because originally roads were chiefly of concern to farmers, who had to get their produce to market. The mere fact that the federal Bureau of Public Roads was originally placed in the Department of Agriculture is evidence enough that the rural orientation was carried even to the federal level. It was not until 1939 that Public Roads was moved to the new Federal Works Agency, and in 1949 it was moved to the Department of Commerce. For one short period in recent years, the Bureau even had an Urban Highways Branch in its headquarters organization. Unfortunately, this unit was abolished in a reorganization of 1957 which placed the Bureau on a functional basis, and for a time urban matters were handled piecemeal in a series of branches devoted to research, operations, engineering, and so on. In January 1959 a new Urban Division was established which took over many of the functions formerly performed by the Branch.

The Bureau has endeavored to encourage state highway officials to work more closely with cities, and in general it has had considerable success. One device used has been to require the state departments to hold public hearings before undertaking new construction. All cities through which a proposed highway will pass or around which it will be built, the Bureau reports, must be given an opportunity to express their views. Transcripts of these hearings are sent to the Bureau of Public Roads, and projects submitted by state departments are rejected unless the transcripts indicate that the cities concerned have been consulted. There is some evidence, however, to indicate that in practice this device is sometimes by-passed. In Reno, Nevada, when a freeway through the city was under consideration, it was charged that the "so-called public hearings were a farce." Inadequate notice was given to the city officials concerned, and the meeting was run so as to favor the requirements of a particular plan supported by the State Highway Department.[106] Nevertheless the federal-state relationship is defended as the only practical system possible,[107] and it is argued that direct relations between the federal government and the cities would be difficult for many reasons. Many smaller cities do not have engineers of broad competence, and it is only in the state highway departments that sufficient trained manpower for long-range planning of highways is found. A co-ordinating committee composed of state and local representatives in each metropolitan area, the Bureau suggests, is the best way to obtain a sound highway plan. In the Detroit area, for instance, there is a Design Committee composed of state, county, and city engineers and representatives of general planning groups at all three levels.[108] The Bureau's district engineer sits with the Committee as an observer. Though no Canadians are included in the Committee—one of the instances where an international boundary through a metropolitan area makes handling of a common problem difficult—informal contacts are maintained with appropriate Canadian highway officials. To be sure, this type of co-ordinating committee will be satisfactory only where metropolitan planning machinery exists.

Highway Planning Isolated

Mayor Taft of Cincinnati, testifying before a congressional committee, pointed out one case of poor planning that may have been repeated many times in other parts of the country. "For instance, we have a new bridge coming across the Ohio, which is going to be built under the interstate highway program. The approaches on the Ohio side, in the middle of Cincinnati, are 60 acres, and they run through our absolutely worst slums, and they are overlapping our present major redevelopment project which covers 450 acres that include the 60 acres. There the interstate highway and the urban renewal, urban redevelopment programs, should be operated as a unit in planning and acquiring property." When land is purchased by highways, whole city lots are acquired, said the Mayor. Frequently a highway runs diagonally across an area. Thus uneven amounts of land remain on both sides of the highway in various odd shapes. "It would make a great deal more sense if the urban redevelopment people bought the entire ground and sold back for highway purposes only the right-of-way for highways. They would then manage all these little odd pieces that go along the side of the highway right-of-way." [109]

There is evidence, too, that not only does the Bureau of Public Roads sometimes proceed without adequate local consultation, with consequent poor planning, but also that it is over rigid in its requirements. Perhaps the most amusing—but nonetheless serious—example of this is Wyoming's experience with her yellow lines. The Bureau requires that *all* center lines on interstate highways be white; violation of this requirement results in denial of federal-aid funds. Wyoming is a state with a great deal of snow, however, and white lines on snow-swept highways are clearly next to useless. Therefore she attempted to use yellow lines, to the dismay and disapproval of the Bureau of Public Roads. The issue was resolved in the state's favor, but, as Representative Thomson of Wyoming told the House, this incident makes it quite obvious that federal funds, at least as far as interstate highways are concerned, certainly mean federal control. [110]

New highways in urban areas usually involve taking land now used for residential or industrial use. Unfortunately, the 1958 Act makes no provision for relocation of persons who will be forced to find new homes. Nor, indeed, does the Bureau of Public Roads. As the mayor of Portland, Oregon, commented recently, "I can find no evidence that [the Bureau] assumes any responsibility for helping people displaced by freeways to find other places to live." [111] The question of moving people never was discussed in the hearings on the bill. Though some testimony was presented in support of the idea of compensating public utilities that would be required to move, nothing was said about people. Finding new housing in already overcrowded cities will be a major problem, and it is a problem the highway program leaves in the laps of local authorities. In this respect, the Highway Act is in strange contrast to the Housing Act of 1949, which does require that in order to qualify for federal loans or grants, a local urban renewal agency must show evidence that "not generally less desirable" housing is available for those who must be relocated. Without such a provision in the highway law, local authorities are free to do as they please, and most have done precious little.

Highways attract industrial and residential development. Along the New York Thruway, industry had located $150 million worth of new plants, employing 30,000 workers, even before it was completed.[112] Another example may be found in the belt-line Route 128 around Boston. Industrial plants manufacturing products ranging from sewing machines and greeting cards to frozen foods and electronic items have sprung up all along the route. Property values have increased from $50 and $100 an acre to $5,000 and $10,000 an acre. There can be no doubt that this same attraction for industry exists along all major highways across the country. Suburbs move with highways; inevitably metropolitan area development thus follows highways.

Another problem which has arisen in connection with the highway aid program is the effect participation in it has on many of the smaller states' secondary road systems and state highways. In Virginia, for example, it was reported that "the Virginia Department of Highways [found] itself forced to slice $5 million off the secondary road fund" because in attempting to match federal funds to finance her share of the interstate highway system, the state was forced to expend "56.8 per cent of all the department's money." Building the interstate system, at least in Virginia, costs over $1 million a mile. Such expenditures seriously drain a state's highway budget, even if it is required to meet only one-tenth of the cost. The result is inevitably neglect of the state roads. "Of Virginia's total highway system of around 51,000 miles, about 1,100 miles are in the Interstate System. So, the Virginia Highway Department is being forced, under the program, to spend 56.8 per cent of all its money on only 2 per cent of its total highways." [113] This is particularly a matter of concern to metropolitan areas, where much of the traffic flows on state-built roads. It is of even more concern in the growing suburbs, where in many areas farm roads are still the only means of access.

The very isolation of highway policy making has made it impossible to develop a broad over-all transportation policy which would include all forms of mass transportation. Still more, the consideration of road building apart from the general development of a whole area may make conditions of urban living worse rather than better. Unless the needs of areas that produce traffic, that is, residential suburbs and industrial locations, and areas that absorb traffic, that is, the central city, are brought into balance, the mere construction of highways will be of little value. Although familiar with the situation, highway planners to date have paid very little attention to these sociological factors which are already intensifying the problems of government in metropolitan areas.

The chief defect of the federal highway program is that it deals with only one part of an integrated problem of land use. The first step in transportation planning [114] is land use planning. Highways, consequently, should be closely tied to urban renewal, slum clearance, and the development of recreational areas. Even highways are only part of the total transportation problem. Urban mobility depends not only on trucks and passenger automobiles, but also on all forms of rapid transit, including railroad and air facilities. For many car owners, the problem is not simply how to get into the city, but finding a place to park. Highways that bring more autos into an area without additional parking facilities will do little to make moving about in an urban center easier.

Effective solution of the urban traffic problem depends, in the last analysis, upon a major replanning and redevelopment of the metropolitan area. This involves much more than highways, although highways are one of the most important tools by which a sound plan may be made effective. Most metropolitan areas, however, do not have comprehensive plans, and, worse than that, many do not even have a planning organization. The federal government should insist that metropolitan communities first put their own houses in order before they can receive grants for new highways. The role of the federal government ought to be to encourage metropolitan areas to establish adequate planning organizations. Moreover, there are inconsistencies in federal programs themselves. Thus, the Bureau of Public Roads deals with state highway departments, while the Housing and Home Finance Agency, in administering the public housing and urban renewal programs, deals directly with cities, and neither of them gives much thought to metropolitan areas. Even at the federal level, integrated planning would yield substantial dividends.

Air Pollution Control

Air pollution is another problem of increasing importance in many metropolitan areas, yet here too an adequate federal policy is lacking. Air pollution is a concomitant of the industrial and motorized age, and it is in the nation's large metropolitan centers that its effects are most evident. Already some areas—notably Los Angeles, Pittsburgh, and St. Louis—have had to act in the face of the menace to public health presented by air pollution. As nuclear energy becomes more common, a great many other areas will be faced with the same necessity. As an official of the World Health Organization has pointed out, "It is apparent . . . that with the development of nuclear energy for industrial purposes, the whole subject of the dispersal, monitoring and control of radioactive effluents" will become of overriding importance, and effective action "on the legislative and administrative levels" will be necessary to deal with it.[115] Although Congress passed an Air Pollution Research and Technical Assistance Act [116] in July 1955, and a National Advisory Committee on Community Air Pollution was subsequently appointed by the President, hearings held by the Subcommittee on Intergovernmental Relations of the House Committee on Government Operations in 1957 and 1958 indicated that the federal program had not been nearly so effective as it should have been. The Subcommittee was told that federal activities largely duplicated state and local programs and that the federal government had not given the latter any substantial amount of assistance.[117]

Early in the Eighty-sixth Congress, bills were introduced in both houses (S. 441 and H. R. 2347) to extend the duration of the 1955 Act (which authorized federal activity for five years only) for another four years and to raise the annual amounts to be made available under it. The Senate has approved its bill, hearings have been concluded in the House on its version, and final action will probably be favorable. It is worth while to comment, however, that even should the amount be expanded from $5 million to $7.5 million a year, as seems probable, this will be but a drop in the bucket. All it permits now is a limited program of investigation, research, and personnel training, and another $2.5 million would not make a very appreciable difference. Yet according to the Assistant Surgeon General, 10,000 communities—most of them integral parts of metropolitan areas, it might be added—"have an air pollution problem of some kind, but only 250 have active, operating programs." [118] Because air pollution is a problem which defies "company, community, county, and State boundaries," its control will not, it has been pointed out, "be achieved unless the Federal Government continues and increases its efforts." [119] Indeed, the day may not be too far distant when regulatory action, which is now the responsibility of state and local agencies, may have to be entrusted to federal hands. For "states and localities cannot control pollution which originates outside the limits of their jurisdictions, nor do they have the resources necessary to solve some of the more difficult technical problems of air pollution control." [120]

The federal government alone seems able to solve this kind of air pollution problem. Inevitably, as it moves into this field, it will have an influence on government in metropolitan areas.

Recreation

Another area in which the federal government is becoming more and more involved is recreation. National parks, national forests, and reclamation projects all are being used increasingly for recreation. Automation and the broader use of atomic energy will give Americans even more leisure time. Since the majority of American people live in metropolitan areas, this is a metropolitan problem. Already it has been found that additional facilities are needed to accommodate the 59 million visitors who annually visit national parks and the 68 million visitors to national forests each season.[121] The bulk of these visitors are temporary refugees from the summer unpleasantness of one or another of the nation's metropolitan areas. For example, statistics indicate that of the thousands of people who come to Yosemite National Park each year, most come from the Los Angeles and San Francisco metropolitan areas. Yet in the National Park Service's Mission 66—the long-range plan for the development of national parks—there is little recognition of the role that national parks should play in meeting the recreational needs of metropolitan America.

In 1958 Congress established for three years an Outdoor Recreation Resources Review Commission. In the act creating the Commission, Congress set forth three specific goals:

1. To preserve, develop, and secure accessibility for all American people of present and future generations such outdoor recreation resources as will be necessary and desirable for individual enjoyment, to assure spiritual, cultural, and physical benefits that such outdoor recreation provides.

2. To inventory and evaluate the outdoor recreation resources and opportunities of the Nation and to determine the types and location of such resources and opportunities which will be required by present and future generations.

3. To make comprehensive information and recommendations leading to these goals available to the President, the Congress, and the individual States and Territories.

Unfortunately, few of the Commission's members are from metropolitan areas. Even so, in its three-year study the recreational needs of residents of those areas will no doubt be emphasized, and the final report may very well contain recommendations to meet them. In any case, the potential impact of its recommendations on metropolitan areas is great.

Federal Programs and Metropolitan Areas

Virtually every other federal program—crime prevention, grants for health, education, and welfare, payments in lieu of taxes—may and probably does have a demonstrable effect on metropolitan areas. For example, the hundreds of millions of dollars spent each year by the federal government on rivers and harbors and port development have an impact on the in-. ternal growth of any given metropolitan area, besides affecting the relative position of one metropolitan area as compared with others. Again, every time the Interstate Commerce Commission alters freight rate schedules, it may affect the competitive position of metropolitan areas as well as the internal development of a given area. For example, a rate differential between Jersey City and Brooklyn may alter the pattern of industry in both communities. Indeed, the decisions of any federal regulatory agency may cause reactions on the economic growth of metropolitan areas, and eventually may have political and social effects. The impact of a good many of these actions is hard to measure objectively because of the lack of adequate statistics with which to work.[122]

It becomes clear as one examines one federal program after another that the approach of the national government to urban problems has been not only piecemeal but, with few exceptions, through the cities. Unfortunately some of the most difficult and complex urban headaches cannot be relieved by working through cities. The new pattern of urban settlement is the metropolitan community, and it is only through using a metropolitan approach that real progress can be made.

The whole problem of federal-metropolitan relations and of devising action programs to assist in solving metropolitan area problems is complicated by the fact that metropolitan areas, with rare exceptions, have no corporate existence. The federal government, particularly under President Eisenhower, has been inclined to emphasize state relations, and many states have been laggard in creating suitable governmental devices for metropolitan areas. Thus while cities, counties, and *ad hoc* governmental units *within* metropolitan areas can receive federal grants directly, since they are all public corporations, entire metropolitan areas cannot, with the sole exception of small grants for planning under recent housing acts. And, having no legal existence, metropolitan areas have no over-all governmental organizations which can be used for spending grants. At first glance, it would appear that this is an almost insuperable problem, outside the realm of federal government. But, in fact, the federal government can assist in solving the problem. It has already taken a few positive steps in this direction by providing for planning grants in metropolitan areas under the housing program.

This is a general difficulty, but there are a number of specific difficulties as well. A lack of co-ordination between one federal program and another is one of them. For example, the highway and housing programs are not tied together, either in planning or in execution. In addition, the timing of federal programs fails to take into account the limited resources of local governments. Sometimes too many temptations are dangled before urban officials for them to make an intelligent decision among them.

Furthermore, federal administrative agencies rarely have units representing city interests, to say nothing of metropolitan interests. On the contrary, most federal agencies have long been oriented toward rural problems. Nowhere in their administrative organization is anybody charged with the responsibility for presenting the urban, metropolitan point of view. This lack has been particularly serious in the Eisenhower Administration, in which so many appointed agency heads have been former governors from states with few large cities within their borders.

Complaints about the detailed and cumbersome requirements of federal programs have been numerous. Any large-scale governmental program is necessarily complex, but it is always valid to inquire whether the government has done all it can to minimize red tape and simplify procedures. The foregoing cursory examination of major federal programs in urban areas would lead one to conclude that there is still much room for improvement.

More than by anything else, one is impressed by the lack of information all the way up and down the line. Nobody in the federal government or out of it knows what the total impact of all these federal programs upon metropolitan areas is. There are a great many *ideas* of what the total impact is, but no one really *knows* because no serious attempt has ever been made to find out. Even the impact of single programs has never been analyzed in terms of their effects on whole metropolitan areas. The result is that despite large expenditures of money and a great deal of activity by the federal government, no one is sure whether in the long run all this will be good or bad for metropolitan areas. The billions that are being spent for urban housing and highways are freezing the pattern of metropolitan communities for generations to come. Yet the pattern may turn out to be far from ideal. Whereas intelligent use of land in the metropolitan area as a whole should be the goal, federal programs are built upon individual functions of government, which may or may not lead to better land use. Consequently, individual federal programs may make things worse in particular areas. The tragic part of it all is that no one seems to be concerned about finding the answer.

The extent of the federal government's commitment in metropolitan areas today is clear proof that the states and local communities have not been able to act effectively alone to meet metropolitan needs. And those needs become greater every day. Already, the federal government has become involved in meeting needs for housing, urban renewal, water supply and pollution control, and airports, among other things, because the problems to which they give birth have been recognized as national problems. Reluctantly, step by step, the federal government has been pushed more and more toward the center of the metropolitan stage. It is too late now for it to retire to the wings. The whole cast now depends upon its playing an effective role of leadership. Indeed, the overriding influence of the national tax system is well on the way toward making a single economic unit out of the whole nation. There are good grounds for believing that local and state tax differences are being evened out as a result of the impact of federal income taxes on everyone, no matter where he lives in the United States. This being so, the federal treasury in one way or another will have to bear a substantial portion of the costs of the nation's adjustment to "the day of the metropolis."

As the federal government has become involved, it has proceeded on an *ad hoc* basis, its many parts moving independently most of the time and without any attempt at coordination. There is little doubt that its efforts have on the whole been extremely worth while. But there can be equally little doubt that in all its activity, Washington has not made as large a contribution as it might have to the government of metropolitan areas.

It is the purpose of this study to dissect, if it can, the various strands which go to make up federal policy—or contribute to its lack—toward government in metropolitan areas, and to find ways by which the federal government can

(1) co-ordinate and strengthen existing programs in metropolitan areas so that each separately and all together will make their maximum contribution toward desirable metropolitan development;

(2) identify and properly assist in solving new problems in governing metropolitan areas;

(3) be of the greatest assistance to governments in metropolitan areas as they seek to attack their problems.

Since the federal government will have to lead the way, it is of paramount importance that the relation between it and the governments of the nation's metropolitan areas be clarified. Such a clarification can be made only within the framework of the American political system. Leadership from the federal government, and an intelligent and organized expression of their needs by the people most concerned—in this case, the residents of metropolitan areas—are both necessary for successful action. Has there been any such expression of metropolitan needs? Have metropolitan interests been adequately represented in Washington? What steps have been taken to understand the problems of government in metropolitan areas and to give co-ordinated leadership in solving them? Have Congress, the White House, and the administrative agencies furnished the leadership that might have been expected? Have they organized themselves so as to be able to provide leadership most effectively? These are the kind of questions which should be asked and which must be answered if the federal government is to play the role for which the emerging nature of American society has cast it. The chapters which follow will attempt to suggest answers to these questions.

2

REPRESENTATION OF
METROPOLITAN INTERESTS
IN WASHINGTON

THOUGH there are thousands of pressure and interest groups in the United States today, none is specifically directed toward presenting a clear and persuasive picture of the problems and needs of metropolitan areas. As a result, the problem of government in metropolitan areas in all its magnitude has not been brought sharply into focus for either members of Congress or administrative officers. Many individual urban problems are spelled out for Congress, but by many different groups which often conflict with one another in their presentations and demands. Metropolitan needs have no such spokesmen. They are garbled in transmission through a variety of pressure groups, which differ greatly in background, make-up, purposes, and functions, or they are simply ignored altogether. Thus Congress or an executive department is often persuaded to take action here and action there, as urged by one or more interest groups, in the belief that such action is helpful. Often it is, at least in a partial way. But more often than not, such action only serves to complicate the problems of the larger metropolitan areas. Since those problems are not presented with equal force, their solution is neglected or overlooked entirely.

There are many reasons for the lack of a unified metropolitan voice in Washington. Unlike the farm bloc, for example, metropolitan areas do not have a single interest; rather, they have a composite set of interests. Thus they have no spokesmen for the same reason "the public" does not. In addition, metropolitan areas are geographic units, whereas farmers, labor, railroads, and so on, are economic units, and pressure groups are geared to the latter, not to the former. Indeed, although metropolitan areas are frequently called economic areas, they may largely be artificial ones.

In any case, what is needed is not spokesmen in Washington for each metropolitan area in the nation, in the sense that states have senators to speak for them, and districts have congressmen. Such representation would only add to the babel of voices on Capitol Hill. What is needed instead is an organized group, or groups, concerned about the broad problems brought about by the development of the metropolis in the United States and especially about their solution. In a political system such as ours, which responds chiefly to the overtures of articulate pressure groups, the lack of such a group is serious.

There are, to be sure, a number of pressure groups in Washington which speak for urban citizens. It is the purpose of this chapter to examine the degree to which they represent the broader metropolitan interests of those citizens. Do these groups speak also for the interests of the metropolitan areas in which their supporters live? To what extent are they concerned about the problems of government of those areas? What are their programs for the solution of those problems? How effective has been the presentation of their case? Only after such an examination can a judgment be made as to the quality of metropolitan representation in Washington.

American Municipal Association

One group which would be expected to speak for metropolitan areas is the American Municipal Association. AMA, however, represents primarily small and middle-sized towns. The oldest of the municipal pressure groups in the nation, it was created in 1924 as a federation of state leagues of municipalities, and today represents over 13,000 municipalities. In addition, many larger cities maintain individual memberships. It maintains two offices, a headquarters office in Washington, and a research office at 1313 East 60th Street in Chicago. The constitution of the Association gives it four principal objectives:

(1) the perpetuation of the Association as an agency for the cooperation of state leagues of municipalities and municipalities in the practical study of all questions pertaining to municipal administration;

(2) the holding of annual and other conventions for the discussion of current municipal affairs;

(3) the furnishing of information and services to the state leagues of municipalities and to municipalities in order that assistance may be rendered such leagues and municipalities in performing their functions;

(4) the safeguarding of the interests, rights, and privileges of municipalities as they may be affected by federal legislation.

In meeting the first three objectives, the Association has developed extensive information and research services. Through them, member cities can seek the collective advice and experience of other cities and draw from a common reservoir of information to assist them in solving their own problems.

But it is in connection with the fourth objective, to safeguard the interests of cities under federal legislation, that the AMA is important as far as the subject of this study is concerned. It was not until 1932 that that objective was translated into the language of pressure groups. At the 1931 annual meeting, Harold D. Smith, then director of the Michigan Municipal League, suggested that the Association become a "super-organization of cities," and urged the delegates to consider the merit of the AMA as "an organization to deal with the federal government." [1] But no action along these lines was possible until the next year, when for the first time, thanks to a grant from the Spelman Fund, the Association was able to employ a full-time secretariat. Then it publicly oriented itself toward Washington and became "the spokesman for our American municipalities, large and small, and thereby spokesman for the needs of half of our population." [2] In 1936, a Washington office was established by the Association "for aiding the federal administrative officials to better integrate their activities and to present local needs to the attention of the federal government." [3]

The Association's first efforts to "present local needs" were successful, with the result that its orientation in that direction became fixed. Its pressure on the federal government to come to the rescue of urban dwellers with relief and public works programs in the early days of the depression, for example, were at least partly responsible for that action's being taken. A few years later the Association led the way in getting the federal government to recognize air transportation as a national problem, deserving federal financial assistance as much as highways and waterways. Since then it has taken positions on many municipal problems and exerted pressure both on Congress and on administrative agencies to have them solved its way.

Today the Association makes no bones about its purpose. In an open letter printed as a part of the AMA's 1956 brochure, Patrick Healy, Jr., the director, remarked that he thought that mayors should know "that we in AMA have come to feel more strongly each year that municipalities throughout the nation must have an organization through which they can speak with the full force of their combined influence. Too often in the past we have had the discomforting feeling that in speaking for our individual cities we were merely small voices in the wilderness." Elsewhere the same brochure emphasizes AMA as the "Washington representative" of municipal governments, carrying "the cause of municipalities to Washington, with the weight of its membership behind its position."

The "cause of municipalities" is agreed upon each year at

the annual congress of the Association, at which a National Municipal Policy is adopted. The Policy "sets forth the aims and purposes of municipalities. It suggests broad areas of responsibility for municipal, state, and federal authorities on matters affecting localities." [4] Recent Policy statements have contained, among others, sections on the following topics: home rule; municipal association movement; international municipal association; intergovernmental relations; municipal career service; economy in local government; financing America's municipalities; municipal credit and federal tax immunity; payments in lieu of taxes; traffic and transportation; highways, roads, and streets; parking; mass transit; airports; civil defense; shelter; water and air pollution control.

Because the National Municipal Policy makes the Association's position clear on such topics, and because the Association's staff buttresses each position with appropriate facts and figures, and because the statement on each topic seems to represent the consensus of all the constituent cities and state leagues, and so presumably of a large number of important state and local party officials, Congress and agencies of the executive branch have become accustomed to asking representatives of AMA to be present and testify at hearings on any of the topics on which it has taken a position. AMA has been quick to respond, and in recent sessions of Congress it has presented oral or written testimony on over two hundred bills a session, besides making frequent appearances to explain one position or another before the President and officials of executive departments. Although the Association's point of view is of course not always accepted, it very often is, especially by vote-sensitive Congress. Certainly AMA's batting average on Capitol Hill is above .500.

In addition to presenting the case of the cities to Congress and the appropriate executive agencies, the AMA works in other directions as well. It helps Congress on many occasions, as it did, for example, in connection with the passage of the Water Pollution Control Act of 1956. The director of AMA, acting through the leagues of municipalities in 18 states, queried cities with regard to their interest in pollution control legislation. He reported back to Congress that 330 cities were interested. As a result, Congress felt it was in a much better position to enact legislation. AMA also helps officials in the executive branch, as it did in the early days of the New Deal, when the Reconstruction Finance Corporation solicited AMA's help in clarifying its loan program to city officials so as to enable them to make quicker use of it. In the first stages of planning for World War II, President Roosevelt drew upon AMA for advice and suggestions. Later, representatives of AMA were appointed to a number of defense boards (the Board for Civilian Protection and OCD, for example). Today AMA is represented on a score or more of advisory committees to federal agencies in all areas of urban concern. In another direction, AMA keeps the mayors of direct-member cities, the executive directors of the state municipal leagues, and members of AMA committees informed about legislative developments in Washington which affect cities, through its regular publication, *American Municipal News*, through frequent special releases and communications, and through the National Legislative Bulletins. The latter are designed to form a *National Legislative Manual*, a permanent reference tool to facilitate action by local officials in support of the national program of the AMA as set forth in the National Municipal Policy. "The purpose of all national legislative communication is to present up-to-the-minute information on legislation as it affects municipalities. It is up to local officials to follow through. If there is informed support for the national legislative program at the local level, success is assured." [5]

The Association thus serves as a two-way channel of communication between cities and Washington: to carry the demands and suggestions of the former to the Capitol and the White House; and to report on actions by the latter which are of interest to the cities, and stimulate local officials into action in their own behalf. There is hardly a subject in which city officials are interested on which the Association has not taken some kind of action or other. As the trade association of the nation's cities, it performs invaluable services for its constituents.

Developing Concern for Metropolitan Areas

But if AMA has a long record of serving as the Washington representative of its constituent cities, it has been slow to speak in behalf of metropolitan areas. Nor is this surprising. Not only is the Association's approach to the matters of its concern a functional one (it was, after all, the need for help with regard to specific problems—traffic, housing, parking, for example— that brought it into being and is still felt by its constituent mayors), but the very nature of its membership works against an over-all approach. Cities join the Association or the state leagues of municipalities as cities. Their representatives at Association meetings are mayors of cities. They pay their fees to the Association as cities. The rules of practical politics being what they are, it is the problems of cities as such with which the Association consequently deals. As yet, metropolitan areas are organized politically only in a scattering of places. They thus can send no emissaries of their own. Of necessity, the metropolitan problem must be broken up into parts which can be fitted into the existing scheme of things.

Even so, the AMA has begun to demonstrate some concern for metropolitan areas. Enough interest had been aroused by 1956 so that a section on "Metropolitan Problems" began to be included in the National Municipal Policy, and it has been included ever since. It notes briefly the nature of the problem and applauds some of the actions local governments have already taken to meet it, particularly the "intelligent and timely use of the annexation device." In addition, in recognition of the "seriousness of the metropolitan problem," the Association has pledged its full support to an early solution of the problem. To that end, in 1956 it authorized the appointment of a Metropolitan Area Committee, "broadly representative of the major geographical sections of the country and of the different types of metropolitan areas," and gave it the following assignment:

(a) To assist the officers and staff in maintaining contact and mutually beneficial relationships with other nationally recognized organizations and groups conducting research on or otherwise actively concerned with the metropolitan problem.

(b) To evaluate the recent and current experimentation throughout the nation looking to solution of the metropolitan problem, including the relationships between metropolitan areas and state and federal governments, and to make . . . a summary report of its findings and recommendations to the member leagues and cities.

The section also notes that state and federal governments are involved in solving metropolitan area problems, and declares that "the federal government must be concerned with metropolitan areas which cross state borders and with the problems of coordinating civil defense." The final resolution of the section in the 1956 statement favored a new federal Cabinet post for urban affairs. Although the resolution was couched in terms of cities only, there can be little doubt that AMA believed that such a department, if created, would ultimately be involved in the solution of metropolitan area problems.

Elsewhere in the 1956 National Municipal Policy, the Association's awareness of the special problems of metropolitan areas is manifest. In a number of sections, such as those on "Mass Transit" and "Civil Defense," it urges action on a metropolitan basis.

In addition, AMA joined in 1956 with the American Association of State Highway Officials to plan for better co-ordination between state and local officials in the development of plans for the location and design of highways in and around urban areas under the expanded highway program. Although a number of meetings have been held in the ensuing three years, the specific problems of metropolitan areas, particularly those of interstate metropolitan areas, have not been tackled as such.

By 1957 the Association evidenced further interest in metropolitan areas. Not only did a number of the subject-matter sections of the National Municipal Policy adopted that year contain recognition of the implications of the metropolitan explosion, but the section on "Metropolitan Problems" incorporated in the previous year's Policy was retained and expanded to include a statement on federal aid. "The metropolitan areas of the nation," the statement declared, ". . . continue to be severely shortchanged in the various federal grant-in-aid programs." "City-based institutions and installations such as hospitals and airports which serve great metropolitan areas have not received the funds to which they are entitled because federal funds have been distributed according to the population of the city in which the institution or installation is situated, rather than the population of the area served."

In addition, two new sections were added, devoted to specifically metropolitan problems: a short section on "Depressed Urban Areas," which called for federal aid to "cope with basic problems" in such areas, and a longer section on "Urban Policies of the Federal Government." The latter section called for the President and Congress to create a Council of Urban Advisors, a presidential agency empowered "to conduct continuing research and make recommendations on urban problems . . . to coordinate all federal programs affecting urban areas," and to develop a federal urban policy based on its study of urban problems. It also called on Congress to appropriate each year the full amount authorized for each grant-in-aid program affecting urban areas. This time, the Association was not quite so sure it wanted a federal Cabinet post for urban affairs; in the resolution proposing the Council, it suggested merely that the Council should "specifically review the suggestion for a new federal cabinet post for urban affairs."

The Association also took a dim view of the recommendations of the Joint Federal-State Action Committee that functions now financed by the federal government be turned back to the states, and that the federal government withdraw from certain fields of taxation, leaving them to the states. Indeed, the Association maintained, "In many cases the metropolitan areas stretch across state lines into two or more states. Future state legislatures cannot be bound to continue programs which are transferred to their jurisdiction. There will be no uniformity regarding the use of federal revenues released to the states, and no assurance that revenues would be applied to programs which have been abandoned by the federal government."

The 1958 and 1959 congresses of the Association devoted still more attention to metropolitan problems.

Though AMA has reached a definite turning point in its interest in the metropolitan area problem, this does not greatly alter the fact that the Association still speaks for cities and their problems first and foremost. The Policy section on "Metropolitan Problems," for example, is in no way integrated with other sections of the Policy statement. Such important parts of the over-all problem as transportation, highways, roads, and streets, mass transit, airports, civil defense, and the like, are still dealt with in entirely separate sections, and nowhere are all these various aspects of the metropolitan problem as a whole brought together under one roof. Moreover, the subject-by-subject approach to urban problems results in a number of contradictions or at least incompatibilities between the several sections.

Even the special Metropolitan Government Committee authorized by the 1956 annual congress has not reflected the emphasis the resolution calling for its creation seemed to suggest. It has not directed its attention toward the delineation of the metropolitan area problem as a whole. Although, according to Mayor Richardson Dilworth of Philadelphia, a former chairman, "the purpose of the committee is to develop what might be considered a national policy for the AMA with regard to metropolitan government and in doing so to take into consideration the many and varied problems in all sections of the country," [6] its interest has largely been confined to the structural aspects of government in metropolitan areas. It has concerned itself with the pros and cons of annexation, county-city consolidation, and a federal local government like Toronto's. It has not been concerned with the larger problems of intergovernmental relations. It is understandable why the Committee chose such an orientation. It was, after all, set up alongside a great many existing subject-matter committees—on airports, civil defense, highways, parking, urban renewal, for example— each of which is concerned with another aspect of the over-all problem. The new committee was not given authority to pull all these various threads together, and of course jurisdictional disputes between committees cannot be allowed to arise.

Before AMA can become the voice of metropolitan areas before Congress and the executive branch, it must overcome certain difficulties. It has no representatives of metropolitan areas as such among its members. Indeed, its membership, built as it is on state leagues of municipalities, tends to be oriented toward small cities. To be sure, those which are suburbs of larger cities should be very conscious of the metropolitan problem, but unfortunately many are hostile to a metropolitan approach. AMA still must pull the many parts of the problem together and by looking at it as a whole enable others also to see it as a whole.

If AMA is to be of assistance to the federal government in directing its attention to the solution of the problem, the Association must go farther than it has in defining the federal government's role. Already, as one authority has remarked, AMA has shown its awareness "that problems of metropolitan areas are the concern of all levels of government—municipal, county, state and federal—and that their solution is dependent in large measure upon a variety of adjustments in intergovernmental relations." [7] But AMA's recorded position does not yet suggest how to bring about such readjustments. By and large, the Association takes two positions: inclusion of metropolitan areas in the federal grant-in-aid programs in an ever wider circle of activities, and the creation of some kind of governmental unit within the federal structure to bring about better co-ordination of the many federal programs in metropolitan areas. Like the federal government itself, AMA should pay close attention to the way in which federal grant-in-aid programs complement one another, to the end that they be better co-ordinated. Also, it might concern itself with the fragmentation of federal grant programs among individual municipalities within metropolitan areas. It must also decide what type of federal administrative structure is best suited to meet the needs of metropolitan areas. Although the American Municipal Association has gone a long way down the road since 1956 in the direction of assuming the position of national spokesman for metropolitan areas, it still has a way to go before it can speak in a voice which will be clear and meaningful to Congress and the executive branch

United States Conference of Mayors

The United States Conference of Mayors is the second big national organization of municipal officials. It is organized on a different basis from that of the American Municipal Association. Its membership is open only to cities of over 50,000 population, with the proviso that the Executive Committee may accept cities in the 30,000 to 50,000 population range. In addition, it has been proposed that, in view of the rapid rise of metropolitan areas, the population basis for membership be somewhat modified to make metropolitan area representation possible. As yet, however, no action has been taken on that proposal. In 1959, over 300 of the major cities in the United States were members of the Conference, including all of the 20 largest cities.[8] Indeed, "over 95 per cent of all American cities over one hundred thousand in population are represented in the Conference membership. The combined population of the cities comprising the present membership of the . . . Conference . . . is over 52,000,000—or about *one-third* of the total population of our Nation." [9] Thus USCM is the national spokesman for the big-city point of view, and one would think that it might also speak for metropolitan areas.

USCM's roots lie in the large cities' concern over the problems each faced as a result of the depression. "The United

States Conference of Mayors came into existence," it was noted in the foreword to the first volume of the Conference's proceedings, "because of the emergence of certain governmental problems (such as unemployment relief, municipal finance, etc.) in our cities, the solution of which clearly pointed to *national* action." [10] The then mayor of Detroit, Frank Murphy, called a meeting of representatives of the larger cities in Detroit in June 1932. The same invitation was sent to the American Municipal Association, but AMA did not respond as an organization on the ground that its constitution required it to be an association of *leagues* of municipalities and of service to them. The result of AMA's failure to respond was that a Committee on Permanent Organization was appointed in Detroit, and at Washington the following February (1933) the USCM was established as a permanent organization "to establish closer cooperation, make a careful study of municipal problems and keep before the government and the people of the nation the vital interest of municipal government." [11] AMA generously loaned USCM a staff member, Paul V. Betters, to serve as its secretary. Mr. Betters later became the core around which USCM built its program, and his brother, Harry R. Betters, still serves as executive director. He is assisted by a small staff which works in the Conference's offices at 1707 H Street, N. W., in Washington.

At first, USCM was concerned chiefly with securing federal action to solve the unemployment problems in the large cities and to bring relief to the millions of jobless citizens. It was the first body of public officials to urge a major public works program to get people back to work, and throughout 1933–35 President Roosevelt and the Congress paid USCM close attention. Most of the big-city mayors at the time were Democrats, and so it was easy and natural that a spirit of co-operation should develop between them and officials of the federal government. President Roosevelt regularly sent messages to the annual meetings, and in 1935 he invited the Conference to the White House. Secretary of the Treasury Morgenthau, Secretary of Labor Perkins, Attorney General Cummings, Harry Hopkins, and Senator Wagner all appeared before the delegates that same year.

Perhaps no organization has ever started off with such initial success. USCM had the advantage of offering municipal solidarity at a time of crisis and was directed from the first to securing and facilitating federal action. It did not then have the service orientation of AMA. It could thus devote itself exclusively to working the Washington front during the critical depression years, while AMA had to divide its efforts between Washington and the state and local fronts. The Conference met in Washington regularly at first and still meets there frequently.

The constitution of the Conference of Mayors makes its purposes broader, however, than merely serving as the Washington representative of the big cities. Part of the constitution declares:

The objects of this organization . . . shall be the general improvement of every branch of city government by the following means: First, the perpetuation of this organization as an agency for the cooperation of mayors and municipal officials in the practical study of all municipal questions; second, the holding of annual and other meetings for the discussion of current city problems; third, the furnishing of information to the municipalities in order to enable them to better perform their functions; and, fourth, the safeguarding of the interests, rights and privileges of municipalities as they may be affected by legislation.[12]

In operation, USCM performs many of the same services as AMA. It provides a variety of informational services to its member cities. It sends to the mayors of its member cities free prints of all bills affecting cities pending before Congress, amendments as they are introduced, and testimony delivered at hearings. As bills are passed, member cities are notified, and the legislation is explained. Items of municipal interest are sent on occasion, as are regulations and reports of departments and agencies of the executive branch. During the first part of January 1958, for example, USCM supplied both a brief summary of and detailed excerpts from the President's budget message concerning matters of urban interest; a statement concerning the hearings held by the Housing Subcommittee of the House Banking and Currency Committee, along with the remarks of Mayor Wagner of New York on behalf of the Conference before that Subcommittee; and copies of the Census Bureau's report on *Local Government in Standard Metropolitan Areas*, accompanied by a brief analysis of the report. These were in addition to the issue of the *United States Municipal News*, which is sent out regularly as a report on news items of current interest from Washington and from other areas of the country.

But perhaps the chief emphasis of its activities is on fostering "proper and adequate relationships on mutual problems between the government of the United States and the cities." [13] The mayor who is serving as president of the Conference, other mayors on the Executive Committee and Advisory Board, and the executive secretary make direct contacts both on Capitol Hill and on Constitution Avenue as the need arises. So frequently is the executive director invited to appear or make statements before Congress that more than once a member of Congress has expressed his appreciation, and when Paul Betters, the late director of USCM, passed away, Representative Rains, chairman of the Subcommittee on Housing of the House Committee on Banking and Currency, took pains to note that he had been "a great deal of help to us." [14] If it is decided that more than a single appearance or statement is necessary, an appeal by letter, telegram, or telephone is made to strategically placed member mayors to contact Congress or the particular executive agency (on occasion, even the President) themselves. For example, when it became known in 1954 that an amendment had been proposed to the basic housing legislation which would have removed the constitutionally recognized exempt status of public housing securities, the USCM immediately prepared a memorandum to Sherman Adams, President Eisenhower's administrative assistant, and to Albert M. Cole, head of the Housing and Home Finance Agency, telling them that the amendment must be deleted or virtually every city in the nation would request its representatives in Congress to oppose the whole bill. USCM followed this action up by preparing a memorandum for distribution to its members pointing out the threat of federal taxation to municipal bonds and urging each mayor to write or call every member of the House Ways and Means Committee in protest. For convenience' sake, the names and addresses of every such member were listed. Needless to say, the Committee deleted the objectionable amendment shortly thereafter. Through such means, the Conference believes that it has generally been, as its constitution requires it to be, a guardian of the major municipalities of the nation, carrying forward an aggressive program on their behalf in Washington.

USCM has been much slower to espouse the cause of metropolitan areas than it has the cause of big cities. It is indicative of USCM's detachment from the larger problem that it did not participate in the National Conference on Metropolitan Problems called by the Government Affairs Foundation in East Lansing, Michigan, in the spring of 1956, as did the American Municipal Association, which was represented in force, and a host of other agencies. Both because of its structure, representing as it does cities as such, and because of the way it is financed, each city appropriating funds out of the city treasury for the services USCM provides, it has been difficult for USCM to move into the broader area. The situation will no doubt be altered when and if the present population basis for membership is changed to permit metropolitan area representation, but until that time the Conference, of necessity, must represent cities *qua* cities rather than the larger metropolitan areas in which these cities are situated.

Even so, USCM has begun to evidence interest in the overall problem of metropolitan areas. At its most recent annual conferences, a number of speeches on metropolitan problems have been delivered, which were given considerable attention in USCM's own reporting of the conferences. Two of the resolutions adopted at the 1957 conference in particular showed concern for the problem. Under the topic "Highways," it was resolved that "the Federal law be amended so as to require state highway departments to create urban divisions qualified to handle the special problems of planning, design, and project execution peculiar to areas of dense population," and under the topic "Water," it was resolved that USCM "encourage the Federal Government and the state governments to study and investigate our water resources as related to the possible future scarcity of water for the greater urban centers of population."

At its 1958 conference in Miami, USCM went even farther in demonstrating its interest in the metropolitan area problem as a whole. Its resolution on "Urban Redevelopment" phrased the need for continued slum clearance and urban renewal assistance from the federal government in terms of "the welfare and prosperity of the more than 110 million Americans now living in metropolitan areas," and its resolutions on "State Highway Urban Divisions" and "Bureau of Public Roads Urban Division" were couched in terms of "urban areas." Even more important, it devoted an entire resolution for the first time to "Metropolitan Developments." The bulk of the resolution merely sought to describe the metropolitan area problem in general terms, but, prefaced by the reminder that "the United States Conference of Mayors is established to facilitate the exchange of ideas and experiences on such problems," the resolution concluded: "Be it resolved . . . that a standing committee of the Conference be established to consider ways in which the Conference can and should assist in the exploration of solutions to metropolitan problems in the period immediately ahead, the Committee to report its recommendations to the Executive Committee for consideration and presentation to the next Annual Conference." The Committee was not appointed until early in 1959, and its first meeting was held at the 1959 conference in Los Angeles in July.

USCM also labors under difficulties imposed by its functional approach. In its resolutions, it continues to approach each problem not only from the point of view of individual cities, rather than from that of whole metropolitan areas, but also as a separate and distinct problem, not part of a larger whole. Thus its resolutions on "Airports," "Public Transit," and "Civil Defense" not only are adopted individually but are solely from the point of view of cities and municipal officers rather than that of metropolitan areas. Even the resolution it adopted in 1958 on "Intergovernmental Relations" was confined to requesting the Eisenhower Administration "to invite the participation of local officials responsible for municipal policy determination and execution to all future discussions involving Federal-State-local relations." The Conference must demonstrate that it understands the scope of the over-all problem before it can provide Washington with the help it needs in evolving its program for metropolitan areas.

As spokesmen for cities, the American Municipal Association and the United States Conference of Mayors can be well satisfied with what they have accomplished. They can point with pride to the much larger role the federal government has come to play in the lives of their constituent members and the resulting improvements which have come about in the many areas of their interest. Together, they are influential in determining what federal policy toward cities will be. Although the Eisenhower administrations have been less responsive to large cities than the preceding administrations, Congress has continued to respond to their demands.

Since these organizations are so effective, and since they render very much the same kind of services to their constituents and perform the same functions in relation to Congress and the executive branch, the possibilities of their combined action with regard to the metropolitan area problem are great. The two organizations frequently join hands and appear together to protest or suggest. Very often, at a congressional hearing, for example, a spokesman for AMA is immediately followed by one from USCM, and very rarely are there significant differences in the approach or testimony of the two. Sometimes the same person appears as spokesman for both groups. The staffs of the two groups co-operate freely with each other, and together they form a phalanx of municipal interests to which the federal government pays close attention. Indeed, so closely do they parallel each other and so obvious is their combined strength that a number of proposals have been made that the two organizations merge. At the 1957 annual conference of USCM, the Executive Committee and Advisory Board of that group, acting in response to a proposal advanced by AMA that the two merge, resolved that "the United States Conference of Mayors continue in being and not merge with the American Municipal Association, but that the incoming President of the United States Conference of Mayors appoint a committee to confer with a similar committee of the American Municipal Association to explore possibilities of a suitable, mutually beneficial working arrangement between both organizations." [15] If the interest both have already demonstrated in metropolitan area problems is further developed and broadened, as seems probable, and if the two work together to develop a suggested program, there can be little doubt that their recommendations will be heeded.

National Association of County Officials

The American Municipal Association and the United States Conference of Mayors are not the only organizations which are concerned with one or more problems in metropolitan areas and which thus might assist the federal government in developing an adequate policy toward those areas. The National Association of County Officials, organized in December 1935 and recently revitalized by the appointment of an executive director and another full-time professional staff member with offices in Washington, and the launching of a broader publication and service program, has become interested in metropolitan area problems and in their solution. The very first declaration in its most recent policy statement was devoted to metropolitan and urban area problems: "County government has a decisive role to play in so-called metropolitan or urban area problems. Counties should take the lead in providing services in metropolitan areas where exploding populations have made it impossible for incorporated and unincorporated areas to provide an adequate level of vitally needed services. The National Association of County Officials will devote a very large proportion of its efforts in the coming years to the solution of these pressing problems." [16]

In its policy statements on many of the individual problems counties and county officials face—airport construction, public works planning, air pollution, urban renewal, for example—NACO likewise showed its increasing interest in the broader problem. In a background paper prepared in 1957 for members of NACO's committees, the executive director commented at some length on the metropolitan problem. He noted that in many cases "the county is the key to the solution of the problem" and suggested that NACO pledge its full co-operation with all interested persons for its early solution. The Association has even taken a position on the question of how to organize the federal government so as to co-ordinate its various urban programs more effectively. Unlike the American Municipal Association, however, which at least showed original enthusiasm for a federal Department of Urban Affairs, NACO has consistently opposed such an idea "on the grounds that it would further weaken the states and would tend to create an unwieldy bureaucracy of the type found in many foreign countries." [17] "Whenever possible, dealings with county and other local governments by the federal government," it has asserted, "should be channeled through an appropriate state agency." [18]

Converting principle into practice, NACO sponsored in March 1959 the first Urban County Congress as a means of bringing county officials together "to exchange ideas and to find practical solutions to . . . urban area problems." [19] Over 1,000 delegates attended the congress, and discussed general approaches to the better government and administration of urban counties, the problems of urban transportation, health, education, and welfare, water pollution control, airports, and long-range county planning and development for the future. If a judgment is made on the basis of the tenor of the remarks made at the congress and of the enthusiasm of NACO's staff, this organization will exert considerable influence in meeting the challenge of metropolitan growth.

NACO, too, is handicapped, however, in moving toward effective representation of metropolitan needs. Its chief support comes from the forty-three state associations of county officials, the majority of whom still serve in nonmetropolitan counties. Just as AMA and USCM must heed the interests of their constituents first, so must NACO. Moreover, NACO is an individual membership body. Its members thus tend to speak for themselves or for their particular interest in county government rather than for the county as a whole. To many of them, the transition of NACO to a position of leadership in formulating a metropolitan area policy for the federal government would be difficult to make. In addition, NACO has to date been severely limited in its program by the fact that its only source of revenue has been the individual membership fees of $6.00 a year from its approximately 6,000 members. Although the Ford Foundation awarded NACO $160,000 (to be administered by a separate corporation set up by NACO) over a five-year period beginning in 1958 to bolster its shaky financial position, the Association will have to demonstrate that it can carry on the expanded activities after the grant has expired.

Service and Professional Groups

Another organization which seemed to have great promise at the outset as a spokesman for metropolitan areas, but which evidently was unable to proceed much beyond the organizational stages, was the Council of Metropolitan Regional Organizations. Formed in 1952 of metropolitan planning groups and public authorities, it seemed to be just what was needed. Its basis was official metropolitan bodies, and thus it promised to represent metropolitan areas as such. It was unfortunate that certain federal officials failed to see the possibilities of such a group and discouraged its activity. Though the Council has remained in being, it has been largely inactive in recent years, and, as a result, the interest of the original members of the organization has almost died out.

There are many other groups which represent one or more municipal, and thus often metropolitan, interests before the federal government. For the most part, these organizations are primarily service and research groups and professional societies. Though many on occasion adopt pressure tactics, that is not their principal aim. None of them, moreover, are representative of metropolitan interests as such. There are, for example, twenty-two organizations of municipal officials alone, including the well-known International City Managers Association and the Municipal Finance Officers Association of the United States and Canada. In addition, there are a number of organizations of county officials, such as the National Association of County Engineers and the National Association of Treasurers and Finance Officers. The Urban Land Institute carries on studies and conducts an extensive publication program in the field. The Section on Municipal Law of the American Bar Association is concerned with the legal aspects of urban problems. The Council of State Governments has devoted considerable attention in recent years to metropolitan problems. The National Municipal League, which dates back to 1894, has long served as a clearinghouse for information on state and local government and a focal point for research in the field. Recently its interest has turned toward metropolitan areas, and beginning with the November 1957 issue of its publication, the *National Municipal Review* (now the *National Civic Review*), special reporting of news developments in metropolitan areas is given in a separate section on "Metropolitan Government." The Government Affairs Foundation and the Institute of Public Administration in New York City both conduct research in the field.

A number of these organizations, along with the American Municipal Association, the United States Conference of Mayors, and the National Association of County Officials, have joined in establishing a continuing Conference on Metropolitan Area Problems, to serve "as a cooperating agency for groups and organizations concerned with metropolitan problems; to encourage and cooperate in such research; and to prepare and cooperate in the preparation of such publications and to hold such national, regional and other meetings as may further the objectives of the conference." [20] The Conference has been organized under the chairmanship of Frank C. Moore, president of the Government Affairs Foundation, and has begun publication of *Metropolitan Area Problems News and Digest*, a bimonthly report of activities in the field. In the fall of 1959 it became a part of the Institute of Public Administration, at 684 Park Avenue, New York. Though it may make some contribution to the final solution of many metropolitan area problems, it probably will not give Washington the kind of help it needs in acting to meet the problem as a whole.

Indeed, the multiplicity of organizations which from time to time speak on one aspect or another of the metropolitan area problem only adds further to the confusion. Several of these groups have established good working relations with Congress and agencies in the executive branch, and in their particular areas their recommendations are listened to with respect. But because none of them are primarily interested in the metropolitan area problem as such and because they are concerned with only one part—or perhaps several parts—of the problem, rather than the whole problem, they are of little service to the federal government in conceiving its own policy. Actually, they may be a hindrance in developing a unified policy. Certainly neither Congress nor officials of an executive agency can be blamed for lopsided or incomplete thinking with respect to the larger problem when they hear about it so seldom.

One of the most respected of these groups is the American Planning and Civic Association. Begun as the American Civic Association in 1904, it is primarily concerned with parks, conservation, and natural resources. According to its statement of purposes, it is dedicated to "the education of the American people to an understanding and appreciation of local, state, regional, and national planning for the best use of urban and rural land, and of water and other natural resources; the safeguarding and planned use of local and national parks; the conservation of natural scenery; the improvement of living conditions and the fostering of wider educational facilities in schools and colleges in the fields of planning and conservation." [21] Throughout its existence, it has shown a pronounced interest in the impact of metropolitanization on the need for parks and planning and has been an earnest advocate of comprehensive metropolitan planning. It has also supported a coordinated watershed program and has been active in recommending steps for the better development of Washington as a fitting national capital for the American people. The Association does not take a stand on all issues, even within the realm of its interests, and when it does, it usually takes its stand on principle. Its officers and board of trustees include some of the nation's most distinguished planners and conservationists, however, and when it does appear for or against something within the range of its interests, it is listened to with courtesy and respect. There is little doubt that it has been an important influence through the years in the development of national parks and conservation policy, but it has not yet broadened its concern to include the metropolitan area problem in its entirety.

Another such group is the National Planning Association, whose interests range widely across the American scene, from agriculture, business, and labor to international policy. Though its reports have won wide acclaim, the NPA is less interested in exerting continuous pressure than in its research function. Recently it issued a thoughtful statement under the title "A

Ten Year Program for Metropolitan Areas."[22] It proposed a White House Conference on Metropolitan Development, to be followed by a series of regional conferences, in the course of which an adequate ten-year program might be developed. It did not attempt to define the role of the federal government in relation to the larger problem. So broad are its interests and so slim are its resources that it is unlikely that NPA will be able to do much more than this about metropolitan areas.

Effective in another area is the National Association of Housing and Redevelopment Officials (NAHRO). Founded in 1933, it is one of the "1313 group" of professional societies, which provides a home for persons engaged in community rebuilding, slum clearance, public housing, and the like. It acts as a service agency for its members, reports on current events that influence administrative decisions in the fields of its interest, testifies before congressional committees, holds national and regional meetings, and counsels with federal agencies on questions of national and local policy. It maintains a Washington office especially for the latter purpose, and its record speaks for itself. As early as 1934, it developed a comprehensive housing program for the United States, which, along with its later recommendations on slum clearance, housing for low-income families, and maintenance of an adequate housing supply, is reflected in every housing act passed by Congress since the historic Housing Act of 1937. Its staff is competent and experienced in the forceful presentation of its point of view. The great help it has given the federal government in formulating housing policy must be acknowledged by any student of the field. Although it did endorse the idea of a Department of Urban Affairs, NAHRO has not broadened its interests sufficiently to be of help to Congress in the wider field.

NAHRO is but one of a great number of groups with interests in housing. Congress has learned to listen as well to the National Association of Home Builders, the National Association of Real Estate Boards, the National Housing Conference, and the American Council to Improve Our Neighborhoods

(ACTION). Labor unions and business groups likewise make presentations in the housing field, as they do in many others. Indeed, the Chamber of Commerce of the United States in its annual *Policy Declarations* is concerned with national policy in a great many areas, ranging from business and government relations to foreign commerce. And the Chamber's Construction and Civic Development Committee has devoted considerable attention to what it calls "the complex of urban problems" and has published an *Urban Development Guidebook* for the use of civic leaders in attacking problems of growth and development. In December 1958, the Chamber sponsored a National Conference on Metropolitan Growth in Washington.

The list of pressure groups which have the ear of Congress in many of the fields which constitute parts of the metropolitan area problem could be extended indefinitely. Each group has been of greater or lesser assistance to the federal government over the years as it has formulated policy in each area. But none of these groups was organized to see the whole metropolitan problem. Their purposes are much more particular. Although federal policy in many an area derives in some degree from the actions of one or more such groups, no such group has attempted to present Congress or an executive agency with recommendations far beyond its own narrow field. Even if it should, it is doubtful whether Congress would be much persuaded by the presentation of a total program for action on the metropolitan area problem by representatives, for example, of the National Association of Real Estate Boards. Its advice Congress may accept at face value as it relates to land use; but Congress would probably take broader advice from NAREB at a heavy discount.

Representation of Individual Cities

Not all contacts between Washington and the nation's urban areas are channeled through interest groups. Complicating the picture even further is a great deal of individual action and representation of cities and towns before Congress and the executive branch. Indeed, the individual approach is the oldest and still the most common method cities have utilized in presenting their demands to Washington. Even before 1932, especially during World War I, the mayors and other elected officials of at least the nation's largest cities began to make the trek to the capital city. Harold D. Smith has described the situation in 1917–18:

Complete confusion developed during . . . World War I when the officials of individual communities attempted to express their points of view to officials in Washington. The situation created was impossible. Individual local officials came to Washington in droves. Busy Federal administrators, absorbed in the war effort, could not give [them] a hearing. Under such circumstances, the point of view of local government simply could not be adequately represented in national thinking. Even while the national government was placing great burdens on local units these local units had no way to get the ear of the national government.[23]

The Armistice removed many of the problems for the solution of which mayors turned to Washington, and during the 1920's there was considerably less traffic between municipal centers and the Capital. The onset of the depression, however, and the quick discovery that state aid simply would not be forthcoming, brought about a tremendous increase in the number of pilgrimages to Washington. "A common passion" stirred the heart of every visiting municipal official, noted one observer. "What made each and every mayor anxious was the fact that his municipality was . . . dangerously long on joblessness requiring relief and unfortunately short on cash to meet that requirement. What each and every mayor was in Washington for was to get money, more money and still more money out of the Federal Treasury." [24] Not only did municipal officials seek to develop a closer relation with the federal government "as a means of avoiding . . . the unsympathetic and, at times, uninformed consideration of urban problems by state legislatures of a dominantly rural character," but, as representatives of the people most often hardest hit by the economic difficulties of the times, they felt that they had a definite and necessary "contribution to make in formulating and planning national policies . . . as they related to munici- palities." [25] It became very common for many a mayor, as well as members of his official family, to spend as much time in Washington as in their offices at home.

To all intents and purposes, cities and city officials became lobbyists, each for their own beleaguered citizens. They were tremendously aided in their cause by the fact that Franklin D. Roosevelt had designed his program for the benefit of the "forgotten man," millions of whom were residents of urban and metropolitan areas. It was the essence of good politics for the President and the Democratic Party to recognize the pleas of the urban forgotten man's representatives and to act upon them. For if "Democratic strength began in the Solid South . . . it burgeoned into national majorities in the metro- politan and urban areas." [26] Municipal "lobbyists" soon learned that they could use the number of voters each represented to quite as good advantage as any other lobbyist. The myriad of relief projects for city dwellers which were enacted in the early days of the New Deal were the proof of the pudding, and the pattern was set for the future.

World War II, with its many effects on municipal govern- ment and development, accentuated the pressure activities of individual cities, and the years since 1945 have seen no slackening of the pace. Indeed, so natural has it become for individual cities to try to win governmental attention that "it's a rare day when dozens of city officials from all points of the compass don't descend on Washington to plead for more money to solve such problems as slum blight, airport develop- ment, water and air pollution, and so forth." [27] Mayor Ben West of Nashville, Tennessee, like most of his fellows, goes "to Washington . . . about once a month, unless Congress is in session, [then he goes] oftener." [28] At least one city, Philadelphia, found the presentation of its claims before Congress and the many administrative agencies around Washington had simply become too much to put on the shoulders of the city's elected officials, and so it took the next logical step and hired for a while a firm of professional lobbyists to present its case in Washington.

Washington is now well used to the "tincup parade," and for political reasons at least has accommodated itself to the procession. In addition to representatives of AMA, USCM, NACO, and other organized groups, mayors of important cities are invited both by congressional committees and by executive agencies to testify individually. Virtually every congressional hearing on an urban topic has one or two such mayors present by request. The story they present is much the same. Each mayor is convinced that his city is in crisis and that only particular federal action will save it. It is revealing to read through the hearings of any of the congressional committees which are concerned with one or more urban programs and to get an insight into the typical "crisis approach" of most municipalities. Testifying before the Subcommittee on Housing of the House Committee on Banking and Currency, the mayor of Los Angeles, for example, recently declared that "we have some unique problems" in Los Angeles. "Our problem is so much different from many other areas because the people have different habits here. . . . So our problems cannot be compared with the other large cities of the East." [29] Mayor Poulson was sure that Los Angeles' plight must be presented separately, lest the peculiar needs of his own area be lost sight of in whatever general legislation might follow in the wake of the hearings. All his fellow mayors share his conviction. And certainly Congress has not been immune from such blandishments in enacting urban legislation over the years. If it has not been willing to enact special legislation to fit each city's particular plea, the legislation it has enacted has nevertheless been *ad hoc*, passed in any fields in which the persuasion of the municipal pleaders has been strong enough to convince Congress. Surely no system is better calculated to produce inconsistent and unco-ordinated results.

In all this individual municipal lobbying, however, no one represents the metropolitan areas of the nation. Each mayor speaks for his municipality only, as he properly should. He owes nothing, politically speaking, to residents of outlying communities, and is in Washington on the city treasury only to advance the cause of his own constituents. It may well be that the same congressional committee or executive official will hear directly conflicting testimony from representatives of adjoining municipalities, and no testimony at all from other municipalities in the same metropolitan area. Thus even if lobbying "pays off" for individual cities, it may do nothing toward solving the larger problems in the metropolitan areas in which many of the cities are situated, and indeed often results in further complicating and aggravating these problems. Since neither in Congress nor in the executive branch is there a mechanism for dealing with metropolitan area problems as such, it is difficult if not impossible to counteract the atomistic effects of municipal lobbying on program formulation and execution.

Since individual lobbying continues to yield a high return on the investment of municipal time and energy, it will probably continue to be relied on. Washington is crowded every day with throngs of mayors, each acting independently of every other, each pleading his own particular cause, each working both Capitol Hill and Constitution Avenue. All the while, activities of the many organized groups are being carried on simultaneously. The effectiveness of all this pressure cannot be denied. But with regard to the solution of the metropolitan problem as a whole, it does more harm than good. Both the activities of the various organized groups and those of individual mayors emphasize the partial attack, the *ad hoc* solution. In many cases, the result is the adoption of contradictory and conflicting policies. The pressures for partial action have compartmentalized the machinery and procedures of

Congress with regard to city problems and have caused urban programs to be entrusted to a great variety of executive agencies for execution. Or it may be because the existing legislative and executive machinery was not built to take account of urban problems as such that these pressures have been fitted to the existing pattern and have therefore been unrelated and partial. In any case, the fact that the cause of cities has been presented in Washington as it has, has caused the federal government to see only the trees and not the forest. Yet only by seeing the forest as a whole can the work on each tree have any value in the long run. Until the piecemeal approach is replaced by a strong and unified voice, an orderly and coherent federal program for metropolitan growth and evolution will not be developed, and the metropolitan area problem will not be solved. Washington needs help in developing such a program. Metropolitan interest groups can go a long way toward providing that help.

3

CONGRESS AND
METROPOLITAN AREAS

ALTHOUGH Congress has paid considerable attention to a number of individual urban problems over the past twenty years, it has done so only haphazardly. It has ignored the problems of metropolitan areas as such. Unlike the farm problem, for example, which is a major legislative item in virtually every session of Congress, the metropolitan area problem has been on the periphery of congressional interest. In a sense, this is understandable, because there is a fundamental difference between the kind of one-interest situation that exists in the case of agriculture and the many-interest situation that exists in metropolitan areas. The political power of the farmers is, to be sure, the result of their overrepresentation in legislative halls and their effective political organization, but even more, it is the result of the fundamental unity of their particular interest. In metropolitan areas, there are a great many interests, many of which are opposed to one another. Consequently, perhaps one should not be shocked that congressmen do not have deep convictions about a problem which is not a single cohesive whole in the sense that the farm problem and most other domestic issues are. But it did surprise the authors when it was revealed in the course of interviews with a cross section of the members of the Eighty-fifth Congress that a majority of the members interviewed did not have any convictions, general or particular, about the problem at all.

The feelings of most congressmen about metropolitan areas have probably been similar to those of a member of the House from a New England district. When questioned, he admitted to some awareness of the problem in general, but he did not see how it bore any relation to his work in Congress. "Hell," he said, "I have so much to do now that I can't get caught up with what I have, to say nothing of tackling new problems!" And he was sure this was true of Congress as a whole.[1] The congressman had not even had time to read the bills then before Congress for the creation of a study commission on metropolitan problems and for the establishment of a Department of Urban Affairs. The only suggestion he had to offer was that if someone thought federal action was desirable in attacking the metropolitan area problem, public interest must be aroused and political pressure—the only kind Congress understands—brought to bear by the people. Then, he thought, Congress would acknowledge the problem and come to grips with it.

Another congressman put the same point quite bluntly. He told the authors that Congress never goes out of its way to tackle new problems. It responds to demand for action and does not itself often take the initiative. If there is no overwhelming popular sentiment in favor of a particular action, Congress will not usually act. Instead, it will let sleeping dogs lie and devote its attention to the demands of its most articulate constituents. Since there is no metropolitan constituency as such, Congress will, as the congressman put it, leave metropolitan areas to solve their own problems. Most members of recent Congresses would probably have agreed with his dictum.

Congressional Inaction

If this view of what prompts congressional action is correct, Congress can perhaps be excused for failing to recognize the governmental problems of metropolitan areas and to act to help solve them. Congress, after all, developed as an action-minded body, not a research-minded one. It has become accustomed to taking short-range thrusts in the direction of resolving urgent issues rather than evolving long-range strategy to prevent them from forming. Its committees are in the main designed to facilitate the passage of legislation. Though each has a staff, in no case is it possible for its members to devote themselves primarily to research. Each committee and each member can be concerned only with those problems their constituents and the President present for their action. To date, no President has exerted himself in behalf of an attack on metropolitan problems, and neither have any large number of constituents. For, to a large extent, an awareness of those problems has not yet come over the horizon of public interest. Thus a vote by the public on the most important issues before the nation today, as recently reported in a national weekly magazine, did not show a metropolitan problem even among the first ten, to say nothing of listing the larger problem of governing metropolitan areas.[2] The people in metropolitan areas are not conscious themselves of the problems their very presence creates, and thus have not yet begun to push their representatives, even at the local level, for a solution, much less to push the President or their representatives in Congress for federal help in solving them.

Rural Interests Dominate Congress

There are other explanations of Congress' failure to act. Traditionally, Congress has been the organ of rural interests, in part perhaps because of the lingering potency of the myth that the farm is the citadel of virtue while the city is the den of iniquity, but more probably because, politically speaking, "the urban majority is . . . a minority, and the rural minority dominates the polls." "The failure of our governments to respond to the problems of the cities," Senator John F. Kennedy has remarked, "reflects this basic political discrimination." [3] It is a well-known fact that state legislatures uniformly gerrymander congressional districts to favor the rural voter, leaving city dwellers underrepresented and outvoted. The author of one recent study of rural versus urban political power even goes so far as to contend that the lower house of Congress ought more correctly to be called the "House of Misrepresentatives." [4] Nor is the situation in the Senate any better. The 10 most heavily populated states, containing over half the nation's population, have only 20 senators to the 80 left to the other states. Twenty states with 40 senators have a total population less than that of the Philadelphia or New York metropolitan area alone. The voters in the great cities may be the major factor in electing the President, and the cities may be the centers of the nation's financial power, but they do not count for much in Congress, "where their voting power is felt by only a minority of the membership." [5] That minority can do little else, one senator has declared, than ask for "tolerance" and hope that "the needs of . . . urban communities will receive sympathetic attention from [members of Congress] who come from the less densely settled areas." [6]

"While there are some exceptions, the 'safe' constituencies for each party are usually rural," [7] and since the seniority system gives preference in committee assignments and chairmanships to the senior members of Congress, who have almost invariably been representatives of rural districts and thus "last longer" than their city brethren, the leadership of Congress reflects even more sharply than the membership as a whole the bias in favor of the farmer. The result of such disproportion is that Congress has been more inclined to consider rural problems than urban.

Thus in the Eighty-fifth Congress the House was quick to hold hearings on a bill proposing a commission on country life,[8] but completely ignored a bill to create a commission to study metropolitan area problems.[9]

The difference in Congress' approach to farm and urban problems lies also in the fact that farmers have been used to speaking with strength and volume through their four big pressure groups: the American Farm Bureau Federation, the National Farmers Union, the National Grange, and the National Farmers' Organization. The Grange and the Farm Bureau are old hands at successful lobbying. The Grange dates from 1867 and the Farm Bureau from 1919, and their representatives are well entrenched in the Capitol.[10] It has become a truism that if these four unite on any particular stand, "they can get almost anything out of Congress short of guarantees of good growing weather." [11] And when the Big Four "are not applying . . . heat in Washington, flying columns of prune growers, raisin, citrus, wool, apple, peanut, potato, cane sugar growers will execute [their own] giant pincer movement on the Capitol to attain the ends they desire." [12] Congressmen who owe their seats to rural voters have become used to responding to these pressures and have come to rely heavily on spokesmen of the various groups for advice and even for proposed legislation. There have been no such loud and united voices of metropolitan interests.

To be sure, as has been demonstrated earlier, Congress has taken its eyes off the beaten rural path long enough to establish a number of programs with impact on metropolitan areas and to create agencies to administer them. But, taken together, the many urban activities launched by Congress do not constitute a program for metropolitan areas in the same way that farm legislation, say, is packaged into a farm program. Urban programs are created as isolated units and are administered in isolation from one another. The result is a jungle of disconnected programs and projects, strewn among a variety of administrative agencies. A typical example of the way Congress failed to see the metropolitan forest in its hurried selection of urban trees is the new highway program. As noted above, in establishing that program Congress gave no consideration at all to the impact of highway construction on metropolitan areas. It did not, for example, require any co-ordination between the highway program and the urban renewal program in the areas affected. The highway program emphasizes only one aspect of the whole transportation problem in metropolitan areas. Thus, as one congressman put it, "The big, new multi-billion dollar Federal Highway Program . . . is likely to intensify and accelerate" the metropolitan problem, since it left unresolved "who will decide where the new . . . and essential highways will go . . . [and] what community values shall be conserved and which sacrificed to make way for progress." [13] Congress as a whole, however, evidently did not share his concern.

Procedural Difficulties

The legislative process as it exists today adds to the difficulty. Congress is faced with much more legislation than it can consider in detail, and thus is forced to paint with a broad brush. Much of the housing, urban renewal, airport construction, and other urban legislation, like bills on any other subject, is set forth in general terms, leaving to the administrative agency charged with its execution the power to make detailed regulations. In exercising this rule-making authority, each agency, in the absence of specific congressional instructions to the contrary, concentrates on its own program, often to the virtual exclusion of related programs. And because they have to justify their actions to Congress, the agencies frequently tend to keep too tight a rein on program activities and not permit the leeway which may be necessary for the most successful operation of the program.

To use housing as an example, the Senate Banking and Currency Committee discovered in its 1955 review of the housing programs established by Congress that whereas "Title I of the Housing Act of 1949 provided a large degree of flexibility to cities and local public agencies undertaking urban renewal projects to permit them to exercise initiative and ingenuity in devising new or different means for accomplishing their objectives, the Urban Renewal Administration tends to impose rigid requirements which discourage the exercise of this initiative and ingenuity on the part of cities and local public agencies." [14] The 1956 housing investigation conducted by the House Banking and Currency Committee cited additional examples "of administrative policies and decisions which tended to frustrate programs enacted by the Congress." [15] In one instance, discussing the co-operative housing program under section 213 of the Housing Act of 1954, the Committee reported flatly that "section 213 projects" could not go forward on a large scale in the face of "the administrative roadblocks set up by FHA policy formulators." [16] The administration of the complex civil aeronautics program is another excellent case in point. The basic legislation is virtually lost in operation by the Federal Aviation Agency's own elaboration of the details of policies and procedures. Thus, not only is the Constitution what the Supreme Court says it is, to cite Justice Hughes' famous remark, but aviation law is what the Federal Aviation Agency says it is. Without a *cause célèbre* forcing it to act, Congress does not investigate the degree of accuracy with which operating details match basic principles.

It would appear from these examples that congressional intent has often been lost in administrative elaboration, and, indeed, no doubt it has. On the other hand, Congress has never made up its own mind about what it wants in the way of a metropolitan program, as the vagueness of much of the legislation it has enacted shows. Yet the basic legislation is all administrative officials have to go on. To complete the vicious circle, Congress has necessarily been vague because it has not understood the metropolitan problem as a whole. Thus we are back where we started.

Nor does the committee system help Congress much in obtaining information on which to base an integrated approach to metropolitan area or any other problems. The limitations of what is primarily a division of work among committees on a functional basis means that no over-all review is ever possible of all federal programs that affect a single geographic unit such as a metropolitan area. Urban programs are divided among 18 separate standing committees in the two chambers and again subdivided among 25 subcommittees, and each committee jealously guards its own jurisdiction. Even the District of Columbia, which has congressional committees of its own, contrary to the usual functional pattern of committee organization, can run into trouble. For example, when the House Committee on the District of Columbia proposed legislation to create a study commission concerned with interstate transportation in the Washington metropolitan area, Representative Wolverton of New Jersey told the House: "I will not object at this time to the bill . . . but I do wish to point out that the Committee on Interstate and Foreign Commerce has jurisdiction of the subject-matter under the rules of the House. . . . It will be assumed by our committee . . . that if . . . [the proposed bill] is passed . . . the result of the study so far as it relates to interstate transportation will be referred to the Committee on Interstate and Foreign Commerce, which is the only committee that has jurisdiction of both transit and transportation affecting . . . Maryland and Virginia in connection with the District of Columbia." [17] Representative Wolverton served notice, in other words, that the Committee on the District of Columbia could not have the final word even on a plan certainly within its general area of interest.

Finally, an over-all congressional approach to urban policy is made even more difficult by Congress' habit of dividing a single function, such as housing, among several different committees. This was illustrated during the Eighty-fifth Congress when Representative Albert Rains, the chairman of the Subcommittee on Housing of the House Committee on Banking and Currency, which was charged with trying "to get more and better housing for the people of the country," [18] was forced to admit that when it came to Veterans Administration loans, his committee "doesn't have that jurisdiction." [19] This matter lay instead with a separate Veterans Committee.

One might assume that the reports of each of the committees and subcommittees concerned with some aspect of urban and metropolitan affairs are available and are read by the members of the other committees of Congress also concerned with urban problems. But congressmen are busy men, and the amount of time they can devote to these things is limited. Interested members of one committee sometimes attend and even testify at hearings of other committees, so there is some cross-fertilization, and occasionally one committee will make a recommendation to another on a particular aspect of a problem. The House Committee on Banking and Currency, for example, recently offered "the suggestion" to the Committee on Appropriations that, in the light of the information elicited during hearings held by the Banking and Currency Committee, the Appropriations Committee "might want to take testimony" with regard to staffing and operating the Housing and Home Finance Agency which would result in a more flexible budget system.[20] Whether a committee will take action at the suggestion of another is, of course, problematical. In any case, the organization of Congress into firmly independent and jealous committees, each assigned a functional area, makes little provision for the development of broad programs, in metropolitan areas or elsewhere. Agriculture is perhaps the single and fortunate exception. Even the most extensive hearings and investigations by one committee or subcommittee, though they may result in legislation affecting one particular aspect of the problem, do not guarantee that Congress will apply the lessons learned there to other aspects of the metropolitan area problem or to the problem as a whole.

Congress and the Washington Area

Even in the one situation where Congress has had ample opportunity to provide a good example and to exercise leadership in attacking the problems of metropolitanization, it long failed to grasp it. In its treatment of the District of Columbia, Congress always proceeded without defining any over-all policy of metropolitan development within which to operate. Although the Constitution gives Congress "power to exercise exclusive legislation in all cases whatsoever over . . . the seat of the government of the United States," Congress preferred to exercise its power in an off-the-cuff, *ad hoc* manner rather than in accordance with an orderly concept of growth. The chief responsibility for congressional action has been devolved upon the District of Columbia committees of the two houses. The membership of these two committees, like that of the body of Congress itself, is usually largely representative of rural areas, and in neither house has an assignment to the District of Columbia Committee usually been considered very desirable. Neither circumstance is calculated to produce a thoughtful and considered program for attacking the District's metropolitan problems. Even those two committees do not have the sole responsibility for the affairs of the District, because public works, highways, and housing, for example, lie partly within the cognizance of other committees. Thus the responsibility the Constitution vests in Congress is diffused at the outset and is often lost altogether in the political shuffling which constantly goes on.[21]

Furthermore, although Congress has provided an organizational framework for the government of the District, it is a wholly inadequate form of government, lacking an effective executive and unduly cumbersome in its operations. Nor has Congress been willing to give the District Commission full authority. "Nominally the city's top administrators are three Commissioners appointed by the President," but "by patchwork interference" Congress has authorized more than a score of federal agencies and local boards and commissions to operate independently of the Commissioners.[22] Thus parks in the District are not administered by the government of the District of Columbia, but by the National Park Service of the Department of the Interior, and, all told, some seventy governmental agencies have a finger in running Washington.[23] Moreover, Congress frequently interferes by enacting detailed legislation in the very fields in which it has empowered the

Commissioners or one of the agencies or boards to act for it. During the first session of the Eighty-sixth Congress, for example, bills concerned with such minor items as renaming the Fourteenth Street bridge, licensing dentists in the District, exempting certain property of the United Spanish War Veterans, Inc., in the District from taxation, and authorizing fees to be collected for transcripts of birth certificates were all on the congressional agenda. The result of all this is that no coherent policy on any subject can easily be developed for the District, much less a single comprehensive plan for metropolitan area government.

Yet Washington had become by 1959 the center of the ninth largest metropolitan area in the nation and the second fastest growing area in the United States. The problems present there are common to all metropolitan areas. Transportation in the Washington metropolitan area, for example, has been growing increasingly snarled ever since World War II; downtown Washington's sewage is one of the chief causes of pollution of the Potomac River; the area's airport facilities are rapidly becoming inadequate for the air traffic the growing metropolitan region requires; the number of houses deteriorating into slums increases steadily, and urban renewal has only begun. In addition, the Washington area is plagued by a number of problems peculiarly its own: its rapid residential expansion since 1945, "spurred by National Capital functions"; the slight industrial tax base upon which local governments in the area may rely; and the tax-free status of the major employer and landholder in the area, the federal government itself.[24] Washington thus offers Congress a signal opportunity to assume vigorous leadership and to make a significant contribution not only to the solution of the District's problems, but also, by example, to the solution of similar problems in every other metropolitan area.

Except for providing for water supply and creating a metropolitan park system, which it did quite early, it has been only very recently that Congress has taken steps at all commensurate with the possibilities of developing the Washington area as a whole. But if there are now indications of a newly acquired determination to seize the opportunity, Congress still hesitates where it counts the most—in the area of finances. Indeed, in recent years, despite the increasing number and severity of problems in the area on the one hand and inflation and a higher cost of living on the other, Congress has not been willing to assume a larger proportion of the budget even for the District of Columbia than it has been accustomed to carry, to say nothing of taking over a share of the responsibility in adjoining areas. Indeed, the proportional share of the budget of the District which Congress has been willing to bear has declined over the years. In 1917, the federal government bore 50 per cent of the District's budget; forty years later, it bears much nearer 25 per cent.

To be sure, congressional efforts to deal with the problem of the Washington metropolitan area as a whole are handicapped by the fact that the area encompasses parts of Virginia and Maryland. Both states have long insisted on independence in matters concerning the areas adjoining the District, and indeed have protested any attempt on the part of the federal government to "encroach" on their powers in these areas. A recent display of the states' attitude in the matter was given by Senator Richard B. Russell of Georgia, who, in the course of a Senate discussion of the desirability of establishing a joint congressional committee specifically to study the problems of the Washington area as a whole, protested that it seemed odd to him "for a joint committee of the Congress to be investigating areas within the province of the State of Maryland or the State of Virginia." [25] Before Senator Harry F. Byrd of Virginia would permit the bill to be voted on by the Senate, he took elaborate pains to clear the measure with county officials in near-by Virginia.

There is no doubt that the complications of the federal system compound the difficulties Congress encounters in tackling the problems of the Washington metropolitan area. But as early as 1937, the Urbanism Committee of the National Resources Committee pointed out a way to get around those complications. It recommended that "as an experiment, the Federal Government should cooperate with the States of Maryland and Virginia and make use of the unique opportunity to devise a complete scheme of integrated metropolitan government for the District of Columbia and the urbanized outlying areas within the metropolitan district." [26] The possibilities of the interstate compact method suggest themselves as well. But only recently has Congress begun to try to surmount the difficulties of the federal system.

To a large extent, Congress did not try to exert itself with regard to the Washington metropolitan area because it was long unaware that such an area existed and because it had not grasped the idea that the seat of government had become in reality a 1,500-square-mile metropolitan region rather than a city confined within the 70 square miles entrusted to Congress' care by the Constitution. Traditionally regarding the federal system as an absolute barrier to its assumption of leadership in developing policy for the metropolitan area as a whole, Congress kept its interests confined solely to the District of Columbia proper.

The failure to conceive of Washington as a single metropolitan area was particularly obvious in the physical realm. Congress permitted federal agencies to be scattered around the suburbs of Washington—agricultural research facilities in Beltsville, Maryland; the Bureau of the Census at Suitland, Maryland; numerous defense installations in both Maryland and Virginia—without giving adequate consideration to the impact of their location on the area as a whole and often without making any attempt to help local communities adjust to them. Throughout the area, the federal government was the principal builder, yet Congress did not require such federal programs as slum clearance, highway construction, housing, and airport construction to be applied with consistency inside the city of Washington and outside it in the Greater Washington metropolitan area. It has long been a recognized fact in many places outside of Congress that the impact of federal activities puts severe strains on local facilities and services, and that, if Congress continues to allow vital decisions about federal installations to be made without prior consultation with the local governmental units concerned, the situation can only be made worse. Congress' long failure to consider outlying areas has resulted in the loss of the opportunity to make a more efficient and more attractive total community out of the nation's capital area. If the Washington area is ever to be made the "efficient and aesthetically pleasing metropolitan region" it should become, Congress must see to it that the policies of the federal government are "properly co-ordinated" [27] among themselves and particularly with those of the surrounding state and local governments. This it has been slow to do.

Although Congress had established a National Capital Park and Planning Commission as early as 1924 [28] and had authorized it to act in conjunction and co-operate with whatever representatives the states of Maryland and Virginia might designate in carrying out its functions, it endowed the Commission with advisory powers only, and those, as the Commission's title suggests, only in terms of planning. Through the years, the Commission made and revised plans which it hoped would "guide not only development and redevelopment within the District itself," but also the "new growth throughout the National Capital metropolitan region." [29] Though the Commission recognized "the need for cooperative attack upon interdependent metropolitan problems by independent local and state governments, the District Government, and Congress," [30] Congress itself did not attempt to give any of the various plans the force of law. Indeed, as the Commission pointed out in 1950, "In the end, accepting and building this plan is up to the people of the area and to Congress. Theirs is the final authority, and also the immediate responsibility." [31] The people of the area were inarticulate, however, and Congress hesitated to take the responsibility.

Even in 1952 when it replaced the old National Capital Park and Planning Commission with the National Capital Planning

Commission,[32] Congress went no farther. The new Commission was made, like its predecessor, merely an advisory planning agency. It was given the duty of preparing and maintaining a "comprehensive, consistent, and coordinated plan" for the National Capital region. In order to provide for representation of the planning interests of the Maryland and Virginia parts of the metropolitan area, the National Capital Regional Planning Council was established. But if Congress stated its aim in creating the two agencies in terms of a truly regional approach, it failed to follow through by allocating either the Commission or the Council power or money enough to achieve the aim.[33] As the situation stands today, Congress still deals with the Washington area as it always has.

Congress has, however, at last taken steps which will give it the opportunity of tackling the problem of the entire metropolitan region. In 1953, it passed a bill to create a Commission on the Area Problems of the Greater Washington Metropolitan Area.[34] That bill was vetoed by President Eisenhower, and Congress did not attempt to rewrite the bill to meet his objections. As originally conceived by its sponsor, Representative Joel T. Broyhill of Virginia, it would have created a commission to study the traffic and transportation problems of the Washington area. The Senate, however, amended the House bill by providing for two commissions instead of one: one, a regulatory commission to regulate public interstate transportation in the District and the adjoining counties of Maryland; the other, the study commission proposed by the House. President Eisenhower was unwilling to permit the bill to become law on the dual grounds that failure to include the adjoining counties in Virginia within the jurisdiction of the regulatory commission, forcing it to deal with only a part of the metropolitan area, was a fundamental deficiency; and that the proposed study commission would conflict unduly and unnecessarily with the National Capital Planning Commission and National Capital Regional Planning Council.

After two years had elapsed, Congress decided to assign the

Commission and the Council the job of making the transportation study called for in the Broyhill resolution. Congress appropriated $400,000 to the two bodies to finance the study, and their final report was made in July 1959. It recommends the establishment of an interstate transit authority and an integrated system of subways, suburban railroads, express buses, freeways, and parking facilities. Congressional hearings will no doubt be held on the proposals, and President Eisenhower will probably submit his own recommendations based on the study and report. In this field at least, Congress now has a sound basis upon which to act from the point of view of the whole metropolitan area.

The third and most recent step Congress has taken—and indeed the longest step so far—in the direction of dealing with the over-all problems of the Washington area was its passage, September 3, 1957, in the last days of the first session of the Eighty-fifth Congress, of House Concurrent Resolution 172. That resolution created a six-man joint committee to "examine, investigate, and make a complete study of any and all matters relating to (a) the problems created by the growth and expansion of the District of Columbia and its metropolitan area, (b) how and with what degree of success such problems are handled and resolved by the various agencies and instrumentalities of the government which are charged with the duty of resolving them, and (c) how the resolution of such problems is affecting the affairs of the District of Columbia." An original appropriation of $50,000 was made to finance the Committee, and it was instructed to make an interim report to Congress by January 31, 1958, and a final report by January 1959. Early in the Eighty-sixth Congress, the life of the Committee was extended to September 30, 1959, and an additional $30,000 was authorized for its use. With the Committee's report now before it, Congress has for the first time a comprehensive analysis of the problems of the whole metropolitan area, including traffic strangulation, slum clearance, mass transportation, streets, water supply, sewage disposal, air pollution, and airport needs,[35] and thus, as Senator J. Glenn Beall of Maryland remarked, should at last be able to "legislate properly" on the subject.[36]

Not only does the Committee's report enable Congress to deal better with the problems of the Washington metropolitan area, it also provides information Congress needs to help other metropolitan areas solve their problems. Indeed, House Concurrent Resolution 172 was offered by its proponents as a pilot study, as a way to develop new tools to help solve metropolitan problems anywhere in the nation. Representative DeWitt Hyde told the House when he introduced the bill, "Actually what we are proposing will serve as a pilot study for the use of urban centers throughout the United States. That is . . . one of its real purposes." When the idea was first discussed, Mr. Hyde reported, "it was thought that we should . . . study urbanization throughout the United States, but then it was thought that we might get more definitive answers of real value in trying to solve the problem if we confined the study to just one particular metropolitan area; and, of course, the most logical place for a joint committee of Congress to make the study is the metropolitan area of the District of Columbia." [37]

The Bible Committee, as the Joint Committee on Washington Metropolitan Problems has been tagged, consisted of Senator Alan Bible (D) of Nevada, chairman, Representative DeWitt S. Hyde (R) of Maryland, vice-chairman, Senators Wayne Morse (D) of Oregon and J. Glenn Beall (R) of Maryland, and Representatives John L. McMillan (D) of South Carolina and Howard W. Smith (D) of Virginia. In the Eighty-sixth Congress, Representative McMillan replaced Mr. Hyde as vice-chairman, and Representative Joel T. Broyhill (R) of Virginia was added. All the members were appointed from the District of Columbia committees of the two houses. Representative Smith is also chairman of the powerful House Rules Committee, a fact which may serve to give the recommendations of the Joint Committee stature, at least in the House of Representatives.

In the words of Senator Bible, "The main focus of interest of the committee might be described as institutional and organizational. We do not aim to solve technical problems in a technical way, but to make sure that the conditions for solution are met in terms of policy, powers, organization, jurisdiction, money and in other ways. . . . Our metropolitan problems are continuing problems; not to be solved by any single action. Hence, we are interested in establishing the needed framework of metropolitan agencies, equipped with suitable powers, and able to command the funds needed to meet the needs of our rapidly expanding greater Washington." [38] As its first action, the Committee submitted a questionnaire to sixty-eight local, state, and federal officials in the Washington metropolitan area, asking them to list what seemed to them to be the most serious problems created by the growth and expansion of the Washington area. The responses ranked the problems deserving the Committee's attention as follows:

> Mass transportation
> Highways
> Recreation
> Water supply
> Sewage disposal
> Stream pollution
> Zoning and land use
> Planning powers and organization
> Education
> Hospitals
> Taxation and assessments
> Public housing
> Parking
> Taxicab regulation
> Character of the National Capital area

From among those listed, the Committee decided to concentrate at the outset on the interrelated problems of water, transportation, and economic development. Under the direction of Frederick Gutheim as staff director, a number of consultants were employed to prepare working papers for the Committee's consideration, "summarizing existing research and data, providing a background for hearings, and leading to a clearer understanding of specific legislative remedies" which might be needed.[39]

All the staff papers prepared for the Committee stressed the need for greater federal action and leadership in solving the area's metropolitan problems. Only federal action, they all agreed, could make the region the efficient, livable, and economically sound urban area it must and should be. All the papers emphasized the unique role of the federal government in the economic life of the area. As one study put it, "The widespread decentralization of Federal agencies throughout the metropolitan area has broadened the original concept of the Federal City to a larger Federal region." As the largest employer in the region, now and in future, as well as the largest landholder, the federal government, the study concluded, is chiefly responsible for the establishment of an orderly development pattern for the region. "In carrying out this unique role, the Federal Government can help make the Federal region as well as the Federal City a model for all America."[40]

All the staff papers recognized the problems of the District and those of its surrounding suburbs as parts of a single whole and urged Congress to assume a larger role of leadership in meeting them. In addition, they suggested a number of specific actions Congress might take. One suggestion was for the inauguration of a program to acquire vacant land outside the District of Columbia but within the metropolitan area, through the use of which the federal government could effect long-term planning and development in the area and set the standards for the future development of the area as a whole. Another staff paper recommended that the federal government assume a larger share of the financial burden imposed by the growth of the area as a national capital, in order to achieve a better financial balance and to compensate urban communities for the tax losses which the spread of the federal establishment has brought with it. Still another recommended better co-ordination both among the programs of the various federal agencies in the area and between their programs and the projects of local governments, and particularly urged a co-ordinated program of water use, water resource development, and conservation, as well as the development of a comprehensive transportation policy.

The Committee's final report, submitted on January 31, 1959,[41] did not incorporate all the suggestions made in the staff papers. The Committee took a more cautious view and contented itself with the declaration that "the immediate governmental need of the metropolitan region [is] to create a network of regional public works and services to support the estimated metropolitan growth." It based its specific recommendations on existing institutions in the area and recognized the need to deal with established local governments, which could continue to exercise the operating functions now assigned to them. Thus it did not recommend that the federal government attempt to become heavily involved in operations, but instead urged a "combination of local initiative and federal assistance."

As "the voice of the region," the Committee recommended that the National Capital Metropolitan Conference, now a loose, voluntary, and largely informal grouping of local government officials, be strengthened, and perhaps be given limited taxing power, and eventually some elected members. The Committee felt, however, that the initiative for so doing ought to be left with the Conference itself, "although some initial Federal assistance is appropriate if desired." Planning for public works in the region as a whole the Committee recommended be undertaken by a Regional Development Agency, a federal agency to be established by Congress, supported by federal appropriations, and its members appointed by the President, on nomination of the local governing bodies in the area. The Agency would "succeed to the co-ordinating role of the National Capital Regional Planning Council." To provide a uniform factual basis for decisions affecting the metropolitan area, a Regional Statistical Agency would be created as an operating arm of the Development Agency. The Committee further recommended the establishment of a Regional Sanitary Board "to co-ordinate planning, operations, and construction" of water supply and sewage disposal facilities in member jurisdictions. In the field of transportation, it noted that "some regional agency will clearly be required." No concrete recommendations were made with regard to the transportation agency, however, pending the Committee's review of the report of the Transportation Survey.

Other recommendations included specific declaration of the federal interest in the co-ordinated development of the National Capital region by Congress, broadening the jurisdiction of the House and Senate District of Columbia committees to include federal interests in the metropolitan area as well as in the District itself, creation of a Co-ordinator for National Capital Affairs in the Executive Office of the President, adding a comprehensive planning department to the government of the District of Columbia, and the creation of a Metropolitan Fiscal Agency to finance regional public works. The latter agency, like the Regional Development Agency, would be established by Congress and given power to issue bonds on the credit of the United States and to make loans to the operating agencies as needed.

As the *Washington Post and Times Herald* pointed out editorially, "Such a limited federation of Washington area local governments, built around a more broadly expressed Federal interest in the region, is certainly not a radical program. No overnight miracles would be worked." [42] But the Committee's recommendations do at least provide a basis on which the Washington area problem can be approached as an entity.

Congress began to respond to the Committee's recommendations in July 1959, when a joint resolution [43] which set forth a declaration of congressional policy enjoining all parts of the federal government and the District of Columbia government to work together for the achievement of co-ordinated regional development was introduced and passed by the Senate. The resolution was not, however, passed by the House. Whether such a "best endeavors" directive would have any effect is an open question. How Congress will react toward the other recommendations remains to be seen. It will probably take a good deal of jostling to shake Congress loose from its long devotion to the limited concept of the District alone. In the meantime, the problems of the area will be growing worse.

Portents of Change

There are a number of factors which indicate that the Eighty-sixth and subsequent Congresses may be more receptive to the assertion of positive leadership in developing a federal policy on metropolitan problems than any of their predecessors. One straw in the wind is that in the Eighty-sixth Congress a committee hearing was called on the proposed metropolitan problem study commission almost as early as a hearing was held on the country life commission bill.

It is not hard to find reasons for the change. Perhaps most important is the increased trend toward urbanization each year's census figures reveal. By the fall of 1959, less than 20 million out of the approximately 179 million people in the United States lived on farms. In 1920, 30.1 per cent of the population lived on farms; today, the percentage has probably dropped below 10. Not only has farm population declined absolutely, but more and more persons living on farms earn part or all of their income from non-farm activities. "There is a steady increase in commuting by farm residents. . . . Even the farmers are becoming urbanized to some extent in their politics." [44] As a result, politicians are rapidly awakening to the fact that "the farm vote no longer is as important as it once was and that it is becoming less important every year. . . . Congress in the future is going to listen increasingly to urban and suburban votes." [45]

The change has been most startling in the traditionally rural

South, from which so many congressional committee chairmen have come for so long. In 1900, only 15.2 per cent of the South's population was urban; in 1930, only 32.1 per cent; in 1940, only 35.1 per cent. But by 1950, the proportion had jumped to 42.9 per cent, and it is still increasing. It goes without saying that a "region with only 15 of each 100 of its people in cities is a distinctly different kind of . . . entity from one with 43 of each 100 in urban places." [46] Even more significant is "the degree to which the urban South has shifted from small town to city in its essential character." [47] By 1950, over 40 per cent of the urban population of the South lived in or on the urban fringes of cities of 100,000 or more, as compared with less than 18 per cent in 1900. [48]

It is the general consensus that urbanization produces mutation in politics. Voter participation is usually higher in urban than in rural districts,[49] and in the long run, the demands of the new urban voters can be expected to be reflected in the votes of Southern members of Congress. Eventually, though probably not so quickly, the population shift in the South and in the nation as a whole will open the way toward reapportionment and thus toward a more equitable relation of urban to rural seats in the House of Representatives. As Congress comes closer to representing urban dwellers more fairly, it will take up the problems that urban living poses, including those of metropolitan areas, much more readily.

Indeed, the number of urban spokesmen has increased in recent Congresses. Only a few, however, seem so far to have transcended the boundary lines of the urban districts they represent to assume leadership in behalf of metropolitan areas. There is always a turnover in the representation of urban districts in the House of Representatives. By midway in the Eighty-sixth Congress, however, a number of representatives had asserted active leadership in behalf of some aspect of the larger metropolitan problem, including: Harold C. Ostertag (R) of New York, Albert Rains (D) of Alabama, J. Arthur Younger (R) of California, Dante B. Fascell (D) of Florida,

Martha W. Griffiths (D) of Michigan, John A. Blatnik (D) of Minnesota, L. H. Fountain (D) of North Carolina, Florence P. Dwyer (R) and Hugh J. Addonizio (D) of New Jersey. Few of these representatives belong to the leadership of the lower chamber, but several of them are senior or ranking members of important committees. As population changes come to be felt, the number of members who are willing to accept responsibility for metropolitan areas will probably increase, and before too many sessions, the Rayburns and the McCormacks will probably find it necessary to take this cause under their wings.

In the Senate, even the top leadership seems to be moving in the direction of concern about the metropolitan problem. Senator Lyndon B. Johnson, the majority leader, included "a bold housing program," "a re-examination of our airport program," and a "courageous urban renewal program" among his proposals for the Eighty-sixth Congress,[50] and several times during the first session of that Congress, he went out of his way to demonstrate his concern about the over-all problem. For example, when Senator Joseph Clark was introducing his bill (S. 1431) for the establishment of a Commission on Metropolitan Problems, Senator Johnson asked him to yield and announced, "I assure him of my support." This is "an extremely important field," Senator Johnson went on, and "anything that [I] can do to bring about early action on the bill" he promised to do.[51] The number of Senate members concerned about metropolitan problems has also increased significantly during the past three or four years. Among that group in the Eighty-sixth Congress were Senators Joseph Clark (D) of Pennsylvania, Hubert H. Humphrey (D) of Minnesota, Jacob K. Javits (R) and Kenneth B. Keating (R) of New York, Warren G. Magnuson (D) of Washington, Wayne Morse (D) of Oregon, John J. Sparkman (D) of Alabama, Paul H. Douglas (D) of Illinois, John F. Kennedy (D) of Massachusetts, Philip A. Hart (D) of Michigan, Alan Bible (D) of Nevada, J. Glenn Beall (R) of Maryland, Thomas H. Kuchel (R) of California, and Edmund S. Muskie (D) of Maine. Some of these senators held important chairmanships, and several occupied important subcommittee posts. In future sessions of Congress, these positions can be used as springboards for action on the metropolitan area problem.

Another factor which may make it more likely that future Congresses will develop a policy for the federal government to follow in attacking the metropolitan problem is that Congress now has, at least on the House side, a unit which could direct its attention to that area. During the Eighty-fourth Congress, the Committee on Government Operations of the House established a Subcommittee on Intergovernmental Relations. That Subcommittee, headed since its creation by Representative L. H. Fountain of North Carolina, has undertaken a general exploration of the whole field of intergovernmental relations, using the report of the Commission on Intergovernmental Relations (Kestnbaum Commission) as its point of departure. The bulk of the Subcommittee's interest has so far been directed to grants-in-aid.[52] But the Subcommittee has concluded that "particular attention should be directed to the effects of Federal grant-in-aid policies on our urban communities and metropolitan areas." [53]

The subject of federal-state-local relations is so broad and the possibilities therein are so numerous that it is very probable the Subcommittee might eventually recommend some action with regard to the metropolitan area problem. It is at least interesting to note that of the six members of the Subcommittee in the Eighty-sixth Congress, four are representatives of districts either entirely within a standard metropolitan area or including such an area. Certainly the questionnaire to state and local officials from which the Subcommittee gathered its basic data and on which it held hearings across the nation during the fall of 1957 provided ample opportunity for presenting metropolitan problems. It asked state and local opinion on the federal programs most important in their areas, and specifically sought to elicit feelings as to the adequacy or inadequacy of those programs in meeting local needs. The questionnaire also asked for comments and suggestions as to what additional fields federal action might be appropriate in. Both the replies received from the questionnaires and the testimony at the hearings revealed a great deal of interest and concern about metropolitan area problems.[54] Thus the Subcommittee quickly discovered that "the intergovernmental programs attracting the most attention among the municipalities were highways, public housing and urban renewal, civil defense, [and] airports,"[55] all of which are aspects of the metropolitan area problem.

The replies to the questionnaires and the hearings also made it obvious to the Subcommittee that on the whole, municipal officials are happy with the present situation in regard to federal grant programs, and that if they have any complaint at all, it is that more federal leadership in solving their problems is desirable and necessary. Almost unanimously, city people testified that the big stumbling block in the way of attacking their own problems is their state government. Only because urban problems get short shrift at home do they turn for help to Washington. The Subcommittee does not work under either the geographic limitations of the Joint Committee on Washington Metropolitan Problems or a time limitation. Thus it could become a focal point for developing a federal policy for metropolitan areas.

Possibilities for Future Action

Both the Bible Committee and the Fountain Subcommittee have been steps in the right direction. But there are still other steps Congress might take. Perhaps the most obvious is to follow several recommendations of the Commission on Intergovernmental Relations (Kestnbaum Commission) relating to metropolitan areas, which it has so far largely ignored. The Kestnbaum Commission recognized that, although the states are clearly responsible for assuming the main burden of leadership in solving metropolitan area problems, the federal government has nevertheless "an obligation to facilitate State action with respect to metropolitan problems." [56] It also suggested several ways the federal government might act upon the obligation. Thus, it recommended better co-ordination between federal and state policies and programs in metropolitan areas. To date, congressional legislation has paid very little attention to this problem. The Commission also recommended that the federal government "carefully scrutinize its grants-in-aid and other expenditures policies to make sure that it does not improvidently prolong the lives of local units that have no excuse for being, or inadvertently add to the complexity of the existing patchwork of overlapping local jurisdictions." [57] Grants-in-aid have normally been granted without such consideration by Congress, with the probable result that the governmental machinery in a number of metropolitan areas is more complex and duplicatory than it needs to be. If Congress were to remove the incentives for many of these local units, they might cease to exist.

In addition to its general recommendations, the Kestnbaum Commission made recommendations on a number of subjects of direct concern to metropolitan areas.[58] With regard to airports, the Commission recommended that Congress modify the federal aid-to-airports program in one important respect, "namely, the stimulation of airport development on a regional basis." [59] Though Congress subsequently did authorize the Federal Aviation Administrator to exercise a greater amount of discretion in allocating certain funds for the construction of such airports,[60] it has extended this authority so far only through fiscal 1961.

Another kind of action Congress ought to take to assist in the solution of metropolitan area problems is to do all it can to facilitate interstate approaches to specific metropolitan problems. Interstate boundaries are major barriers to a unified approach to a single metropolitan area. There are a great many co-operative devices, both informal and formal, that the states can use in developing such an approach. Congress could offer incentives for their development. As far as compacts, the most formal of interstate arrangements, are concerned, Congress could make them easier to use. Under Article I, section 10, of the Constitution, congressional approval is needed in most cases for a compact among two or more states. Congress has established a precedent by giving its permission in advance to the states to negotiate compacts in the fields of forest conservation and civil defense. It could follow that precedent farther by enacting a simple resolution granting states permission in advance to enter into compacts with each other to solve metropolitan problems. The Kestnbaum Commission recommended this procedure,[61] and the Forty-ninth Annual Governors' Conference urged it.[62] Indeed, Congress itself has already recognized the utility of interstate metropolitan planning agencies by its willingness to permit federal funds to be appropriated to them. It could now clear the way for the broader use of such agencies by granting its consent-in-advance to interstate compacts for metropolitan development.

Congress should also simplify its procedure for granting its consent to completed compacts. Under its present practice, a bill to grant consent to an interstate compact may be stalled in Congress for several years, as was the bill to consent to the Tennessee River Water Pollution Control Compact. Such delay is unnecessary. Congress should pass the Interstate Compact Procedure Act, which has been introduced in the last two sessions by Senator Bible of Nevada. Senator Bible's bill provides an optional procedure for Congress to follow in approving compacts. Under its terms, a copy of any compact formulated and approved by the states would be transmitted to the President and Congress. Unless Congress as a whole, or either house thereof, passed a resolution denying its consent within ninety days of continuous session thereafter, the consent of Congress would be deemed to have been granted. The Association of Attorney Generals has endorsed the bill, and it should be passed.

In addition, Congress might well study the necessity for approving all compacts.[63] The Southern Regional Education Compact never received congressional consent, yet the Southern Regional Education Board has been accepted and utilized as a valid compact agency by the states party to it. There is reason to believe that the constitutional requirement is interpreted too rigidly and that as a result the use of the compact device is made more difficult. Only Congress has the power to lay down the rules. A thorough study of the kinds of compact possible and of the record of existing compact agencies might produce evidence that congressional consent need be sought for only a minority of compacts. The rest would then be launched by the states as are any other enterprises set afoot by state law. Unless Congress itself takes the first step, however, virtually every compact will continue to be submitted to it. The delay which results is harmful in all areas, but is a special handicap in the solution of pressing metropolitan problems.

Still another step Congress can take if it intends to assume the leadership in attacking metropolitan area problems is to take action with regard to the District of Columbia. If it continues to be impossible, as it has been in the past, to give the District home rule, Congress can at least simplify its own procedures for handling District of Columbia business. Bills to accomplish this purpose by creating a Joint Committee on the District of Columbia, to replace the existing separate committees in the two houses, were introduced late in the first session of the Eighty-fifth Congress.[64] The Joint Committee proposed would consist of 18 members, 9 from each house, and would be authorized to act on all District matters, including appropriations involving the spending of District tax revenues. The Appropriations committees of the two houses would continue to have authority only over federal payments to the District. The sponsors expressed their conviction that the proposed arrangement would result in a considerable saving of members' time (only 18 members would be involved instead of the present 34) and make for more efficient use of committee staff. Thus the larger problems such as those of the metropolitan area, which are now beyond the abilities of the staff to study, might be given more adequate consideration. A joint committee has been successfully employed in the efficient management of atomic energy, proponents point out, and the same advantage ought to be secured for the District of Columbia. If a joint committee arrangement is politically feasible, a similar bill should be reintroduced in the Eighty-sixth Congress and receive adequate consideration by both houses. Indeed, the new committee's jurisdiction might be extended to include the surrounding metropolitan region.

If nothing else, Congress should strengthen the present District of Columbia government and give it broader and more independent powers. This would probably entail a change from the commission form of government and might be resisted by vested interests in the District, but it may well be the necessary condition to any constructive action in the future.

Congress has an excellent opportunity to exert its leadership at once in solving at least one problem in the Washington metropolitan area. In 1956, the Interstate Commission on the Potomac River Basin, an agency created in 1940 by interstate compact among the four states in the Basin, the District of Columbia, and the federal government to fight pollution in the Potomac River, engaged Dr. Abel Wolman to prepare a plan for achieving a clean Potomac. Dr. Wolman's report recommended the construction of a silt barrier upstream from Washington and a number of added terminal and outfall facilities for sewage in the Basin. More important, it emphasized the extent of federal responsibility in the matter and insisted that the expenses for the construction of the new facilities be borne by the federal government. "The District of Columbia, [and] the Virginia and the Maryland communities tributary to the Potomac should continue their financial responsibility for lateral sewers, interceptors and treatment plants. Beyond these fiscal responsibilities, supplementary works should be financed by the Federal government as part of the development and protection costs of the Capital of one of the major countries of the world." [65] The report recognized the difficulties that have been encountered in the past in bringing all the diverse governmental units in the Basin together in a single plan of action, and it recommended that, instead of again attempting "any such time-consuming and embattled steps," the initiative should be seized by Congress and action launched under its aegis to attack existing pollution conditions. Here is a clear-cut challenge to Congress not only to recognize the financial stake of the federal government in solving this particular metropolitan problem, but also to recognize the problem itself as one for which it has primary responsibility and to act upon that recognition. Bills to make federal action a reality were introduced early in the Eighty-sixth Congress by Representatives Richard E. Lankford, Joel T. Broyhill, John A. Blatnik, and John R. Foley, but at the end of the session, no action had been taken on them.

Although Congress can use the recommendations of the special Joint Committee on Washington Metropolitan Problems and depend on such occasional special reports as the Wolman report to supply it with the facts needed to tackle the Washington problem, to rely solely on such partial and *ad hoc* studies would be to prejudice the possibility of Congress' fully understanding the over-all problem. Basic to any congressional action in the years ahead is information on the many aspects of metropolitan problems, information that can be acquired only from a whole series of broad analyses. What might seem to be the easiest way for the Congress to accomplish this would be simply to create a new standing committee on metropolitan problems in one or both of the chambers. To create a new standing committee of Congress, however, is difficult. Quite properly, both houses have shown a strong aversion to making additions to the committees provided for in the Legislative Reorganization Act of 1946. Thus the Senate still refuses to create a counterpart to the Veterans Committee of the House of Representatives, and despite the many convincing arguments for the creation of a standing Committee on Administrative Procedures and Practice in the House, directed to exercise continuous supervision over the independent regulatory agencies of the federal government, a resolution to accomplish this was not acceptable to the House.[66]

Possibly a more feasible method of approach might be a select committee of one or the other of the two houses, created without a termination date. The Senate Small Business Committee might serve as an example. Under this arrangement, it is possible to employ a staff and engage in long-range operations without making a permanent change in the organizational pattern of either house. A Select Committee on Metropolitan Problems, created after this pattern, could be assigned the continuous function of studying metropolitan problems and recommending solutions to them until such time as Congress might consider its usefulness at an end. Or, if it seemed best to tackle the problems one at a time, separate select committees might be established as needed. Representative William S. Mailliard of California proposed the creation of one such committee to the Eighty-fifth Congress. He suggested the formation of a seven-member select committee of the House to study "the existing and the probable future mass transportation problems in the large metropolitan areas of the United States" and to report on the following:

1) which metropolitan areas have now or will have in the future mass transportation problems;
2) what progress local authorities are making toward solving these problems, and if progress is not being made, what impedes it;
3) the need for federal technical assistance and coordination of mass transportation studies, and if the need is demonstrated, what form federal action ought to take; and
4) what federal financial aid is necessary to assist in solving these problems.[67]

The Committee on Rules, to which the proposal was referred, however, did not act on it during the Eighty-fifth Congress, and it has not been reintroduced in the Eighty-sixth Congress. The creation of the Joint Committee on Washington Metropolitan Problems may, however, be an indication that Congress favors that type of approach. The precedent set there could of course be followed in studying the broader metropolitan problem.

There is still another possibility. Congress might refer the matter to a specially created commission for study and recommendation after the pattern of the Commission on Intergovernmental Relations or the more recently created Outdoor Recreation Resources Review Commission. Congress has made frequent use of such temporary study commissions in recent years, and the complexity and multiplicity of the problems of metropolitan areas seem to many to make such a commission appropriate here. A separate commission, properly financed to enable it to employ a suitable staff, and given a long enough lease on life to enable it to do a thorough job, could, it is argued, supply a basis of fact and a program of action which Congress could then adapt to its own procedures and act upon as it saw fit.

Indeed, it may be argued by some that the new Advisory Commission on Intergovernmental Relations [68] whose members were announced by President Eisenhower on December 8, 1959, is intended to be just such a study commission. Though it is entirely possible that the Commission may provide new light on metropolitan problems, it nevertheless seems clear that its mission is primarily concerned with federal-state relations, as was that of its predecessor created two years earlier by the Governors' Conference at the President's suggestion. Certainly big-city problems are sufficiently urgent to justify a special study. There have been such proposals.

During the first session of the Eighty-fifth Congress, Representative Harold C. Ostertag of New York submitted a bill calling for the establishment for two years of a Commission on Metropolitan Problems and Urban Development, with the double purpose, as he told his constituents, of concentrating attention on the problem and suggesting "guidelines for its solution within and among the states and localities." [69] The bill provided for a commission of 25 members, 15 to be appointed by the President, 5 by the Speaker of the House, and 5 by the President of the Senate. It would have been charged specifically with studying and investigating "the problems of metropolitan expansion, with special reference to the needs, in terms of adequate governmental structure, to make suitable provision for land use, planning and zoning, industrial and residential development, housing, transportation, water supplies, air and water pollution control, civil defense, recreational, social, and educational services." [70] It would have been further charged with studying the usability of such devices as cooperative planning, consolidated city-county planning, federative structures, and intergovernmental contracts or compacts. On the basis of its studies, the Commission would have submitted to Congress findings and recommendations "as to the necessary and desirable steps to be initiated at the national, state, and local levels, to insure sound and orderly metropolitan growth within the framework of our traditional patterns of responsibility and control." [71]

No action was taken on Representative Ostertag's proposal, but he reintroduced his bill early in the Eighty-sixth Congress.[72] Senator Clark introduced a similar bill, as did a number of other members,[73] and under pressure from Senator Clark, committee hearings were held in the Senate. No action, however, had been taken by the end of the session. The American Municipal Association and the United States Conference of Mayors have gone on record in support of the idea, and the proposal has much to recommend it. It recognizes the need for the federal government to exert leadership in solving metropolitan problems, and provides it with a mechanism for doing so, while at the same time it avoids both the hostility with which Congress faces an alteration of its own internal structure and a commitment to positive action which such an alteration might logically be interpreted to mean. Not only would it provide Congress with data on which to base its actions, but it might also go far beyond House Concurrent Resolution 172 in providing assistance to the states and cities in planning for action in their respective spheres. It would result in a broad over-all study of the entire problem by experts, free from political pressures, on the basis of which all future planning might take place.

In large measure the Advisory Commission on Intergovernmental Relations was a compromise which senators and representatives from urban states accepted on the principle that half a loaf was better than none. Its assignment is so broad that metropolitan problems will have little chance of receiving the detailed attention they so desperately need. At this time, however, a study of intergovernmental relations at all levels was all that could be agreed upon. Thus in an endeavor to please everyone, no one was completely satisfied.

Even if Congress decides to improve its own fact-finding mechanism, there is little likelihood of effective action in the long run unless leadership is exerted from the White House. For by now, it has become obvious that Congress needs presidential guidance if it is properly to perform its role as the national legislative body. In establishing an adequate federal policy for metropolitan areas, as with any other policy, Congress is not apt to act without the stimulus of presidential leadership. Accordingly it is the purpose of the next chapter to examine the President's role, and particularly the means by which he can be made more effective as a leader in helping Congress and the federal government to solve metropolitan problems at the national level.

4

PRESIDENTIAL LEADERSHIP

ALTHOUGH the metropolitan problem has been rapidly approaching the crisis stage during the past two or three decades, no recent president has shown any appreciable interest in it. The sole reference to metropolitan problems in President Herbert Hoover's *Memoirs* is a comment on the fact that he helped the municipalities in the Los Angeles area obtain a loan from the Reconstruction Finance Corporation to construct the gigantic aqueduct system to bring water from the Colorado River. Hoover's comments, however, indicate he was more impressed by the engineering aspects of the undertaking than he was by its implications for metropolitan development.[1] His successor, President Franklin D. Roosevelt, had a continuing interest in city *people* and their problems, but little interest in the government of cities as such. At certain points in his career he seemed to imply that large cities were an evil to be avoided, and preached the virtues of rural life.[2] He was concerned about unemployment, social security, poor housing, water resources, all of which affect people in metropolitan areas, but nowhere in his published papers is there any indication that the problem of government in metropolitan areas seriously troubled him. And so much of President Harry Truman's attention was given to demobilization, the Korean crisis, and foreign affairs generally that he too seems to have ignored the problem. Not once in his *Memoirs* does he refer to it.

The Eisenhower Administration and Metropolitan Areas

By the time President Eisenhower took office, there was a growing demand for reappraisal of the federal system in general. The Governors' Conferences, the first Hoover Commission, and various civic and academic bodies were urging an intensive study of national-state-local relations. Acceding to their pressures, Eisenhower in a message to Congress, March 30, 1953, recommended the creation of a commission "to study the means of achieving a sounder relationship between Federal, State, and local governments." The act subsequently passed by Congress creating the Commission on Intergovernmental Relations (Kestnbaum Commission),[3] however, instructed the Commission to study "the proper role of the Federal Government in relation to the States and their political subdivisions." On the basis of this assignment, the Commission was primarily concerned with the "proper division of labor and authority between the Nation and the States" as the key to "maintaining the federal nature of our system of government." [4] Thus it was only incidentally concerned with urban and metropolitan problems. But it did recognize their importance. Though it concluded that it was "the responsibility of the States to assume leadership in seeking solutions for the problems of metropolitan government," the Commission believed that the "National Government has an obligation to facilitate state action with respect to metropolitan problems." [5]

President Eisenhower seems to have accepted wholeheartedly the first part of the Commission's conclusion without paying much heed to the second. Indeed, in his 1955 Economic Report he urged the states "to study the problems of metropolitan areas" and recognized that "for some of our larger metropolitan areas, interstate action is indicated." "The metropolitan problem," he declared, "is both a challenge and an opportunity." Though he continued to be interested in intergovernmental relations, his interests have been concentrated on those between the federal government and the states. In his major address on the subject, before the 1957 Governors' Conference in Williamsburg, Virginia, he admitted that "the needs of our cities are glaringly evident" and that unless action is prompt and effective, "urban problems will soon almost defy solution." He recognized that metropolitan areas, in which citizens were clamoring for adequate services, "ranged far beyond city boundaries," but he was "earnestly hopeful" that the task of furnishing these services would be assumed by the states and not by far-off Washington. Unfortunately, though he thus recognized the existence of major metropolitan problems, he lost sight of them in his greater concern to reduce the role of the federal government in relation to that of the states. Both in the conclusion of his Williamsburg speech and in later actions he indicated his fear that the federal government had "improperly invaded the rights and responsibilities of states" and his hope that "some adjustments in revenues and functions could be made." To this end, he suggested that the Governors' Conference join with his administration in creating a task force to make a searching examination to designate the functions being performed wholly or in part by the federal government which the states were willing to assume.

Joint Federal-State Action Committee

As a result of the President's suggestion, a Joint Federal-State Action Committee was set up, consisting of seven federal members and ten state governors,[6] under the co-chairmanship of Robert Anderson, Secretary of the Treasury, and Lane Dwinell, Governor of New Hampshire. Taking his cue from the President, Secretary Anderson, in opening the first session of the new Committee, stated that the Committee was gathered together for "the single purpose of restoring our Federal system to balance." "For a long time," the Secretary continued, "this system of ours . . . has become more and more out of balance as power has shifted from State Capitols to Washington, D. C."[7] The Committee had been appointed, the Secretary said, "to provide the means by which we can reverse that trend" by returning both functions and sources of revenue to the states.

In a series of later meetings, the Committee reviewed memoranda prepared by its staff on a number of specific functions and recommended a reduction of the federal role in matters so vital to metropolitan areas as the construction of municipal waste treatment plants, slum clearance, and urban renewal. To compensate for federal withdrawal, and with the assumption that the states would provide the requisite financial support, the Committee recommended that certain additional revenue sources be made available to the states which are now being utilized by the federal government. The Committee did identify metropolitan problems among the emerging problems which might be studied, but if it follows the policy it has established in its earlier recommendations, it can be expected to urge further reduction of federal activities which have hitherto been regarded as essential in meeting metropolitan needs. Indeed, in considering emerging issues at its Chicago meeting in October 1957, the Committee discussed areas of action where "the need for federal intervention" could be minimized.[8]

Though the Committee noted, in considering these areas, that consultation with representatives of various municipal groups might be necessary,[9] evidently the need did not arise. For, as the United States Conference of Mayors noted as late as September 1958, when it met in its annual conference, "local governmental representatives have not been invited to participate in [the Committee's] discussions."[10] Thus, not only has the Committee de-emphasized the federal role in solving metropolitan area problems; it seems to have reached this decision without consulting the people who are most familiar with these matters.

So completely has President Eisenhower agreed with the Joint Committee's conclusions and with the philosophy behind them that in a letter to Speaker Sam Rayburn, dated May 13, 1958, he urged Congress to discontinue federal grants to cities for the construction of water treatment facilities under the

Water Pollution Control Act, despite the insistence of many members of Congress and the strong arguments of municipal officials that more, not less, federal aid was needed. Evidently a year later he had not changed his mind, for at his direction the Bureau of the Budget transmitted to Congress a draft of a bill to discontinue federal grants for waste treatment facilities. Similarly, in his message to Congress explaining his 1958 veto of the legislation increasing federal aid for airport construction, he said that the time had come to turn over airport financing to the cities and states. Despite the fact that slum clearance and urban renewal programs have met with wide approval throughout the country, President Eisenhower continues to urge a substantial reduction in federal expenditures both with regard to the total funds to be made available and with regard to the formula for federal participation.

The action of the Joint Committee gives further evidence that its attention will be confined, as its title indicates, to federal-state problems to the exclusion of those of metropolitan areas. The agenda for a recent meeting, for example, included items on state activities in the peacetime use of atomic energy, work being done in the states to handle increasing college enrollments, migratory labor, problems of the aging population with special attention to its medical needs, forestry grants to the states, and a proposal to provide better liaison between the Council of State Governments and the White House. If the Committee continues to keep strictly within its narrow frame of reference, it will not be of any help to President Eisenhower in developing a positive approach toward metropolitan problems.

Indeed, it may be that the Committee was never intended to be more than a device for manipulating symbols. As such, its purpose would have been to give psychological comfort to the conservatives, not to guide policy changes. If this is the case, one should not expect the Committee to come up with helpful ideas on government in metropolitan areas. At best, the Committee is a poor substitute for the kind of staff assistance the President needs to help him formulate policy on that problem.

For by now it is a well-established principle that a president needs assistance in developing public policy in the broad fields of governmental action. Until well into the twentieth century, presidents had only a secretary and executive clerks. Later the number of secretaries was raised to three and the White House was departmentalized. On occasion, especially in the early days of the New Deal, it was necessary to borrow staff members from executive agencies. When the President's Committee on Administrative Management made its study in 1936, it devoted particular attention to the need for presidential staff assistance. It discovered then that the "normal managerial agencies designed to assist the executive in thinking, planning, and managing, which one could expect to find in any large scale organization, [were] either undeveloped or lacking" in the federal government.[11] From the operations of this Committee came the proposal, which was later adopted, for the six presidential administrative assistants with a "passion for anonymity." This marked the first major expansion of the permanent White House staff. World War II and the recurring crises since have seen a steady growth in White House staff assistance. In 1949, the first Hoover Commission in its thorough review of the organization of the executive branch commented that "the wise exercise of authority is impossible without the aids which staff institutions can provide to assemble facts and recommendations upon which judgment may be made and to supervise and report upon the execution of decisions." [12] The Commission reported, however, that despite improvements since 1936, the presidential staff set-up was still not so effective as it should be.

White House Staff for Intergovernmental Relations

The Kestnbaum Commission, reporting in 1955, found that staff assistance was particularly lacking in the field of intergovernmental relations. One of its recommendations concerned the problem of continuing attention to interlevel relations. To this end, it urged that "there should be a special assistant in the Executive Office of the President to serve with a small staff as the President's chief aide and adviser on State and local relationships." [13]

The President accepted the Commission's suggestion and, in the spring of 1956, named Howard Pyle, former Republican governor of Arizona, as his special assistant for intergovernmental affairs on the White House staff. According to the executive order establishing his office, [14] Pyle was to form study groups at the federal level as might be required to meet emerging problems, to examine the possibilities of establishing regional boards of intergovernmental relations such as formerly existed on the Pacific coast, and to work with federal departments and agencies in fostering better relations between and among all levels of government. Furthermore, he was to co-operate with such groups as the Council of State Governments, the American Municipal Association, the United States Conference of Mayors, and the National Association of County Officials.

However broad his assignment, Governor Pyle played a fairly limited role. As a former governor of Arizona, a state not particularly plagued with metropolitan problems, Pyle was much more concerned with federal-state than with federal-local relations. He emphasized his "staff relationship to the President," and felt that his role should be to deal only with those intergovernmental problems that found their way to the White House. [15] As a matter of principle, he believed that local groups which had complaints about federal action or which wanted something from the federal government should work through their congressional delegations. Until cities had decided what they wanted and had cleared it with their congressmen, any interference on his part, he believed, would simply add to the confusion. He warned the American Municipal Association in a speech at their 1956 congress that they must exhaust possibilities for action through their congressmen before coming to the White House. His Western background was reflected in his belief that most state and city relations would be with the Department of the Interior. If that Department could solve the difficulties, so much the better. Only when an appeal came to the White House, supported by a congressional delegation, did he feel that he should become involved. Then his task, as he saw it, was to aid in working out a solution satisfactory to all concerned. In a word, he functioned as a trouble shooter and sought to relieve the President from the political and administrative worries that intergovernmental problems brought to his office.

Three examples can be given of the kind of situation involving cities that Governor Pyle's office was effective in solving. He assisted in the preparation of a revised bill granting the consent of Congress to the Great Lakes Basin Compact. He helped the city of Cleveland to obtain a special grant of $5 million from the federal government to enable it to be host for the Pan-American Games. He helped the city of San Diego in a conflict over airports with the Navy Department. On occasion, he aided cities in obtaining the information that they needed in order to file applications for urban renewal funds. He also drafted letters for the President, arranged interviews, briefed him on problems, and aided him in preparing speeches and public announcements in the field of intergovernmental relations.

Governor Pyle devoted himself to his job with dedication. Within a limited area, he provided the President with effective staff assistance, but whether he had any influence on federal programs as they affect metropolitan areas is another question. Mayor Ben West of Nashville, Tennessee, president of the American Municipal Association, in testimony before the Fountain Subcommittee on Intergovernmental Relations, speaking of Pyle's office, thought not: "They have set up a thing up there, you know; Governor Pyle is supposed to be—I don't know what his title is—anyway, he is supposed to be the man to look after the local governments. Well, we get lectures on various subjects when we go see Governor Pyle, and he is a nice gentleman and a fine man, but we just don't get results. By the way, he is a former governor, not a local official at all." [16] Probably the principal reason for the lack of success of the operation as a whole was the failure to recognize that there were really two jobs to be done. One was the usual personal staff relationship with the President, at which Governor Pyle did quite well. The other was an institutional role to be played by a staff agency with broad powers of co-ordination over federal policies and programs affecting metropolitan areas. It was in this aspect that the program broke down. There was some discussion in the White House about appointing an inter-agency co-ordinating committee and an *ad hoc* committee on metropolitan problems, as recommended by the Kestnbaum Commission, but neither discussion bore fruit.

Such institutional direction as has been given to intergovernmental relations has come from the Bureau of the Budget, which is not particularly suited to handle this function. The assignment was given to the Bureau in the first place partly because of the happy circumstance that Robert Merriam, a former city councilman in Chicago, was at that time assistant director of the Bureau. Accordingly, he was given the assignment of "backstopping" Pyle's office. In that capacity, he tried to act as a bridge between various municipal groups, the White House, and the federal administrative system generally. His role, as one would expect, was more administrative than Pyle's, but nevertheless it, too, had political overtones. He was at least conscious of the crucial nature of metropolitan problems, and tried to spell out in his speeches before municipal groups an over-all pattern of relations between the federal government and the nation's great urban areas. In particular, he voiced his conviction that the problem of metropolitan areas "is and must be one of concern to the Federal Government." But he did not bring forward any concrete proposals for action. Rather, as Merriam himself once said, he and Governor Pyle continued to feel their "way slowly towards the techniques and procedures best adapted to accomplish the mission . . . at all times taking into account the views of State, county and local officials." [17] Indeed, he could do little more, for he had a full-time schedule of other duties in the Bureau and was thus unable to give as much time to intergovernmental relations as they required. To be sure, Merriam was assisted by Dr. Thomas Graves of the Bureau staff, a trained political scientist and a civil servant of wide experience, but Graves too had other assignments all along.

Governor Pyle's appointment and Merriam's designation to help him indicate that the White House realizes the importance of the problems of intergovernmental relations in general, if not those of metropolitan areas in particular, and of the need for staff assistance in meeting them. But it is not clear that the need for clear thinking, careful planning, and intelligent leadership in attacking either set of problems has yet been felt. The progress which has been made was chiefly because of two individuals, both of whom were political appointees and have since moved on. Merriam has been assigned to other duties in the Executive Office of the President, and Pyle has resigned. There is a definite need to institutionalize these staff relations in a much more permanent form if metropolitan problems are to be handled at all adequately. The problem here is part of the larger problem of the need for presidential staff assistance. This whole matter needs rethinking.

Presidental Staff Agencies: The Lessons of Experience

So far as metropolitan problems are concerned, what is needed is a focal point in the White House where all the multiform data about metropolitan areas will be collected and analyzed and from which the facts about metropolitan problems will flow into the planning stream at the top staff level and from there on to Congress. A permanent staff agency should be created, whose job it would be to furnish the President with the information he needs on metropolitan matters to permit him to build a balanced program of action. Such an agency can be successful only if established in the Executive Office of the President, where it can operate as an equal with the other staff agencies. Its establishment would not make unnecessary a personal staff assistant in the general area of intergovernmental relations, or even in the narrower area of National Capital regional relations, as recommended by the Bible Committee. The greater need, however, is for a Council on Metropolitan Areas to give concentrated attention to metropolitan problems, whose findings can then be woven into the development of the Administration's thinking and from there into a concrete action program.

Working closely with the other agencies in the Executive Office and with the White House staff, such a council would not only collect data and provide a point of contact with metropolitan research and governmental units across the country, but would also be a means by which the conclusions of sound thinking about metropolitan problems could become the basis of effective planning to solve them. A staff agency on metropolitan areas would have to face the same problems that every specialized staff agency must meet. The experience of presidential staff agencies in other areas can serve as a guide to its success, by illustrating the kinds of problems that have handicapped their functioning and by enabling it to proceed at once to give the President the staff assistance he so sorely needs in the field of metropolitan area problems. Consequently, a brief examination of the organization and operation of some of the principal presidential staff agencies may be helpful.

Bureau of the Budget

One of the most successful presidential staff agencies is the Bureau of the Budget. The Bureau has operated now for nearly four decades. It was established by the Budget and Accounting Act of 1921,[18] which provided for sweeping budgetary reforms on the national plane, following extensive state and local pioneering and experimentation in that field. The outstanding feature of the Act was the fact that it supplied the President for the first time with the services of a staff agency, the Bureau of the Budget, headed by an officer chosen at his discretion, to bring together at one point budgetary, management, and congressional liaison services. During the first fifteen years of its existence, the Bureau remained a small agency. In 1935 it had less than forty employees, whose attention for the most part was devoted to routine budgetary activities. The hearings on the original bill, however, had made much of the benefits the Bureau was expected to bring about by making possible greater economy and efficiency in the administration of the federal government through detailed management studies.[19] Though these objectives were largely ignored for many years, President Roosevelt began to use the management potentials of the Bureau soon after he took office. Both the President's Committee on Administrative Management and the Brookings Institution in their recommendations for administrative reform in 1937 stressed the need for a reinvigoration of the Budget Bureau. Both emphasized the Bureau's possibilities in the field of program administration and as a management research and analysis agency. In President Roosevelt's acceptance of these recommendations, the Bureau was returned to the goals that the sponsors of the 1921 Act had established. Thus what seemed to be an innovation when the Bureau was reoriented in the late 1930's was in fact merely a reaffirmation of its original purpose.[20]

Today, the Bureau's biggest activity in terms of the number of staff assigned to it is still the preparation of the budget and the examination of the estimates of the executive departments. Management research and analysis has been increasingly emphasized, however, until it has become a major activity of the Bureau. The clearing of legislation desired by administrative agencies is the third main area of the Bureau's activity. Finally, it carries on some over-all economic forecasting as a basis for budgetary planning. The Bureau, particularly in its management work, has often been used as a seedbed for the germination of programs which have later been transferred elsewhere, and it may well serve this purpose with regard to metropolitan areas. But the Bureau's main activities remain fiscal planning, administrative management, and legislative liaison.

With the tremendous growth in the size of the federal budget, the Bureau has inevitably had to concentrate on fiscal matters. "Charged with tasks that border on the highly dynamic sphere of joint legislative-executive actions . . . the Bureau of the Budget is compelled to place a premium on good working relations with Congress." [21] Economy and efficiency in the budget have always been popular "catch phrases" on Capitol Hill, and Appropriations committees tend to demand that the Bureau justify its activities in terms of demonstrable savings. For example, in 1957, when the budget of the Bureau itself was before the House Appropriations Committee, Representative Cannon said: "As I understand it, for 1956 the Bureau of the Budget staff cost us $3,559,000; for 1957 $3,935,000, and for 1958 the estimate is $4,400,000; so there has been a steady increase for the last three years in the cost of the Bureau of the Budget." He also pointed out that the Bureau's staff had increased from 422 in 1956 to a requested 470 in 1958. Said Mr. Cannon, "Will you tell us briefly, Mr. Brundage, what you have been able to accomplish with this increase in money and employees?" [22] Mr. Brundage, the Bureau's director, replied that these additional employees had been assigned to management studies and estimates analyses, activities which would not produce immediate savings but which would have satisfactory long-term results. The Budget Bureau must always expect this kind of pressure, as long as the nation operates with a budget the size of recent ones. Good management may, as the President's Advisory Committee on Management notes, require "program staff support for executives and a readiness to invest money to that end," but action to secure such support is "often a target for economizers complaining of unnecessary overhead." [23] Thus, although the Bureau is free to germinate ideas, it runs into trouble when it attempts to expand its activities greatly.

The Budget Bureau has been a very successful presidential staff agency, notwithstanding occasional tiffs with Congress and with some executive departments. Its success is due partly to the fact that it was established by an act of Congress. Not only did it begin its life with congressional approval, but its purpose was thrashed out and its course charted in extensive committee hearings and debates on the floor of Congress. Furthermore, although closely attached to the President, as one of his "principal management arms," [24] the Bureau has served Congress in much the same way. It supplies committees with a vast amount of fiscal data, information from management surveys, and other information upon request. The director and his principal subordinates testify freely and frequently before congressional committees. Thus the Bureau has usually been able to maintain harmonious relations with congressional leaders of both parties.

However successful it has been, the experience of the Bureau of the Budget makes it clear that it is not the proper presidential staff agency for metropolitan areas. It is too busy with its primary responsibilities, and Congress is properly unwilling to let it deviate from this path. Any substantial undertaking in metropolitan area research would require either the addition of new employees or the shifting of present employees from budgetary and management duties. Congress would not welcome such an assignment.

Nor would assignment of the metropolitan problem to a general staff agency like the Bureau give it the focus or the public attention which it deserves. What is needed instead is a more specialized staff agency of narrower scope, able to direct its full attention to the problem assigned to it.

Better models for a staff agency on metropolitan areas than the Bureau of the Budget are the National Resources Planning Board, the Office of War Mobilization, and the Council of Economic Advisers. All three of these agencies were concerned with planning. The National Resources Planning Board was charged with consideration of social, physical, and economic factors in national planning, and the Office of War Mobilization was given somewhat similar functions when it was created upon the demise of NRPB. The Council of Economic Advisers was endowed with responsibility for broad planning for full employment by the statute which created it, the Employment Act of 1946. Thus all three are examples of specialized presidential staff agencies, assigned in general the kind of role in their areas of activity that a Council on Metropolitan Areas would be given in its field. Moreover, they differ in organization and methods of operation, and thus their experiences, taken together, provide a virtual text of lessons for the new agency.

National Resources Planning Board

The first suggestion of a planning agency as a staff aid to the President was made by President Hoover's Committee on Recent Social Trends, which suggested in a report in 1933 the possibility of a "National Advisory Council" to consider basic questions of a social, economic, and governmental nature, both in their interrelations and in the light of trends and possibilities. The recommendation came too late for President Hoover to act upon it, but shortly after President Roosevelt's inauguration, the National Planning Board was established as part of the Public Works Administration. Its members were Frederic C. Delano (President Roosevelt's uncle), Wesley C. Mitchell, Professor of Economics at Columbia University, and Charles E. Merriam, Professor of Political Science at the University of Chicago. The latter two had been chairman and vice-chairman, respectively, of the Social Trends Committee.[25]

The next year, 1934, was marked by the first of a series of changes in title and membership of the Board, although there was little change in its primary function. The National Planning Board was converted into the National Resources Board,[26] with Secretary of the Interior Harold Ickes as chairman and the secretaries of Agriculture, Commerce, and Labor, as well as Harry Hopkins, the Federal Emergency Relief Administrator, added to the three members of the old Board. Later Beardsley Ruml and Henry S. Dennison were added to the Board, and the name was changed once again, to National Resources Committee. In each case, the change in name and membership was accomplished by executive order, and the only statutory recognition of the Board's existence was given in appropriation acts. In 1939, the name was changed to National Resources Planning Board, and that agency was made part of the Executive Office of the President. In 1943, the Board was abolished, when Congress refused to vote appropriations for it and specifically enjoined the President from using other funds to continue it in existence.

All the Board members had other positions and gave only part of their time to the Board's work. Apparently the Cabinet members met only rarely with the group after the first years. Thus, in effect, during the ten-year period, the agency was run by the staff, with the non-Cabinet members of the Board meeting, on an average, once a month for two or three days. Charles Merriam was the leading figure in the Board's activities during all the Board's life, but unfortunately he frequently did not see eye to eye with the Board's full-time director, Charles Eliot III, who was much closer to Delano. Thus personality difficulties contributed their share to the difficulties the Board encountered.

The Board submitted reports to the President, and he transmitted them to the Congress. There was no single congressional committee on planning, however, and thus there was no machinery to ensure that the Board's recommendations would be considered by Congress. To be sure, the regular standing committees usually studied the Board's reports and sometimes held hearings. The Board itself felt that there should be a single congressional committee to which the reports could be referred, and it made several recommendations urging the creation of such a committee, but Congress did not act on them. The lack of adequate congressional liaison was at least partly responsible for the Board's unhappy demise.

One would assume that the Board's relations with President Roosevelt, on the other hand, would have been close, frequent, and informal, particularly in the light of Merriam's concept of the Board as the planning arm of the Chief Executive. There is considerable doubt, however, whether this was true.[27] The President never saw fit to use the Board as his principal planning agency, and, as John Millett has said, "No administrative arrangement can alter the fundamental convictions of a chief executive. . . . Planning leadership . . . in the last analysis must always depend upon the personality of the chief executive." [28] The Board saw the President occasionally, but not often, and it never established continuous contacts with him. Apparently, when the Board did see the President, the conversation was general and friendly, but reminiscent and indecisive. Except for plans for certain public works, the President did not as a rule refer his problems to the Board. He seems to have regarded the Board chiefly as a useful means of stimulating discussion on public policies, a role that did have educational value. Indeed, this was probably the major accomplishment of the Board.

At first, NRPB concerned itself primarily with preparing reports on national problems requiring long-range planning, including public works, power and transportation, land and water use, housing, the structure of the national economy, the development of national resources, and urbanism. After 1940, it began to prepare quarterly reports to the President on general economic trends. As the war approached, the Board endeavored to adjust its program to war purposes, but all-out production with little regard for long-range consequences was a far cry from its original concepts. The Board found that the War Production Board and the military services occupied the center of the stage. The Board was able to advise these agencies on a number of matters, but its role was not a vital one. During the last two years of its existence, it became interested in demobilization planning, particularly in planning for the return of military personnel to civilian life. It had considerable to do with laying the groundwork for what came to be called "the G. I. Bill of Rights." According to Merriam, the Board's idea was that if the United States could buy what it made, "industry and labor [could] be stabilized and the standard of living raised notably, perhaps in the ratio of one-third to one-half." Operating from this premise, the Board concluded that the federal government should stand ready to "(1) undertake full employment for all employables; (2) guarantee a job for every man released from the armed forces and the war industries at the close of the war, with fair pay and working conditions; and (3) guarantee and, when necessary, underwrite equal access to security, equal access to education for all, equal access to health and nutrition for all and wholesome housing conditions for all." [29]

All this was well and good, but the attention of the President and Congress was fixed at the time on winning the war. The Board unfortunately does not seem to have realized that its timing was bad until it submitted its request to Congress for an appropriation for fiscal 1944 nearly twice that of the preceding year. When Congress came to consider the request, it revealed its annoyance with the broad "post-war agenda" of the Board, which ran a wide gamut from plans to encourage private initiative and develop river basins to education, improvement of the condition of low-income groups, and control of working conditions, and beyond, to over-all fiscal policy and international economic development.[30] Even the *New York Times* was profoundly disappointed in the Board and called its agenda largely "an exercise in rhetoric." [31] In the end, the House Appropriations Committee refused to appropriate any funds at all to continue the Board, and since the Senate did not bail it out this time as it had in the past, NRPB was in effect abolished.

As long as the Board's interests coincided with those of President Roosevelt—and in the early years of the New Deal both lay in public works, water resource planning, and the like—its contributions were effective and appreciated. But when the war came along, the President, as was his wont, created new and more specialized agencies to tackle the problems of industrial mobilization, and naturally enough his interests turned in that direction. NRPB thus lost the spotlight of presidential interest, and when it tried to move into postwar planning, its work was thought to be "visionary" and duplicatory of the work of other agencies.[32] Indeed, Representative Taber charged that the work of the Board was "useless" and "a menace to the country,"[33] and Representative Dirksen declared that planning ought to be brought back to Congress where it belonged.[34] President Roosevelt himself indicated that he too had doubts about the Board,[35] and when it came under congressional attack, he remained aloof from the battle. For their part, the NRPB members felt that the President should not be asked to undertake a fight with Congress when its support in the war effort was a critical necessity, and so they did not ask for his intervention. Thus the Board could only defend itself, and, as it turned out, its self-defense was not enough.

Although NRPB was abandoned, its experience is full of lessons for a presidential staff agency on metropolitan areas. It certainly demonstrates the necessity of close relations with Congress and especially with the Appropriations committees for successful functioning. But other lessons are to be drawn from the personality difficulties the Board experienced within itself, its failure to limit the scope of its activities to the interests of the President, who was preoccupied with other matters, and finally the nature of the Board's postwar plans themselves.

Office of War Mobilization

The experience with NRPB made it very clear that "a central planning board appointed by the President and responsible to him, and, on the legislative side, of a joint congressional committee on planning" were national necessities. "There was more than coincidence in the fact that the first Congressional post-war planning committee was established in the Senate two days after the publication of the [final] NRPB report. . . .

The appearance of the NRPB report seemed to galvanize the Senate into action."[36] President Roosevelt himself turned almost at once to the establishment by executive order[37] of a successor agency, the Office of War Mobilization, more suited to his immediate needs and directed toward the nation's most pressing problems. In many ways the Office of War Mobilization was a striking contrast to the National Resources Planning Board. Established in May 1943, it was charged with the task of developing unified programs and policies for the maximum use of the nation's natural and industrial resources, for effective use of manpower not in the armed forces, and for the maintenance and stabilization of the civilian economy. Though OWM was not at all concerned with metropolitan areas, and though it was established for short-term purposes, its experiences have important lessons too.

Functionally, OWM emphasized day-to-day policy co-ordination and short-range planning. It met problems as they arose, and long-range planning was the exception rather than the rule. It dealt primarily with problems the President and Congress felt were of immediate importance. Unlike the NRPB, the Office of War Mobilization was little concerned with educating the public. Its quarterly reports were available to the public, but for the most part it worked behind the scenes. This did not prevent the Office from being criticized, particularly regarding its policy of relaxing government controls. It is important to note that the agency, rather than the President, was attacked, a fact which seemed to indicate that it makes little difference how close the planning agency is to the Chief Executive or how careful it is to be anonymous, it will still be held responsible for the advice it gives the President.

Unlike NRPB, OWM was headed by a single individual, who devoted his full time to this work, rather than by a board composed of citizens giving part of their time. All the directors of the Office carried political weight with the President, and much of its success was due to the rapport they established with the

White House. James F. Byrnes, the first director of the Office, saw the President daily. Though he helped with program planning, particularly planning for the termination of war contracts and the relaxation of government controls over prices and production, he gave most of his time to settling disputes between operating agencies. The same pattern was followed by his successors, Fred M. Vinson, John W. Snyder, and John R. Steelman. Their task was primarily that of a management aide to the Chief Executive. They were first and foremost policy co-ordinators for war agencies. In large measure, they were "vice-presidents in charge of production," and they usually had the last word on all matters affecting the home front.

Moreover, all the directors stood well with Congress. Byrnes and Vinson had been leaders in Congress, so that their relations with Capitol Hill were close and friendly. Indeed, OWM had more trouble with other administrative agencies than it did with Congress. As a result, its efforts in policy co-ordination were not always successful. Despite an occasional failure, however, OWM must be considered an administrative success. At the end of the war, its mission accomplished, OWM was abolished.

Council of Economic Advisers

If it did nothing else, the work of the National Resources Planning Board and the Office of War Mobilization attested to the need for specialized staff agencies in the White House. With concern about postwar economic conditions growing more acute as the war progressed, the problem was to design a permanent structure that would satisfy both the President and Congress. Some thought that the Office of War Mobilization ought to be continued, not only to give direction during the period of transition to peace, but also to deal with longer-range economic planning. Congress, however, decided to separate the two functions, and in 1946 passed the Employment Act of 1946,[38] which pledged the government to the policy of "assuring continuing full employment." To aid in carrying out the terms of the Act, Congress established the Council of Economic Advisers to be a part of the Executive Office of the President, and a Joint Committee on the Economic Report, composed of seven members from each house, to be a part of its own organizational framework.

The Council of Economic Advisers is perhaps the closest model for a Council on Metropolitan Areas. Therefore it is worth while to discuss its origin and history in considerable detail. The kinds of problems it has faced will be the same that a staff agency on metropolitan areas would have to face. To be sure, the statute creating such an agency could provide the general framework within which it would work, and deal with such things as its size, membership, and organization. But only the agency itself could hammer out its day-to-day operational pattern. The Council of Economic Advisers had to do the same thing after its creation in 1946. Thus its experience as a specialized staff agency will be particularly helpful.

The Employment Act spelled out in some detail the national economic objectives which should guide the Council. Among them were the attainment of "conditions under which there will be afforded useful employment opportunities, including self-employment, for those able, willing, and seeking to work," "maximum employment, production and purchasing power," and the promotion of "free competitive enterprise and general welfare." These were broadly defined aims, but the important thing was that they were fixed by Congress itself.

Originally proposed as an amendment to the Budget and Accounting Act of 1921, the Employment Act went through many stages from conception to final passage. "The drafters of the bill were agreed that analysis of economic conditions and the planning initiative for a full employment program should be the responsibility of the President rather than of Congress. Furthermore, it was agreed that that part of the Executive Branch best equipped to help the President handle such duties was the Bureau of the Budget." [39] Thus the bill, as originally prepared, lodged the planning function in the Bureau. So far as relations with Congress went, the original draft provided that there should be a Joint Committee on the Budget.

The idea of entrusting the economic planning function to a specialized staff agency rather than to the Bureau of the Budget seems to have been first put forward during hearings of the House Expenditures Committee in 1945.[40] Representative Whittington of Mississippi, who was largely responsible for drafting the House Committee's version of the bill, was the father of the idea of having a Council of Economic Advisers. During the hearings, Whittington said: "I want to supplement the joint Congressional committee . . . by the establishment of a permanent agency devoted to one thing and one thing alone . . . to give to the President of the United States the best available expert advice of the leading economists, the leading thinkers, the soundest planners of the country, that will enable them to make sound recommendations to the Executive and then to Congress." [41]

Whittington's first draft of this section provided for an Economic Council to be nominated by the President and confirmed by the Senate. Members were to have five-year overlapping terms. The Council was to be required to make available to the congressional Joint Committee at the option of the Committee copies of all studies, reports, and recommendations made by the Council to the President. Secretary of the Treasury Fred Vinson, among others, objected to these provisions as unwise limitations on the President's power and altogether too rigid to succeed.[42]

In conference, the provision for the Council of Economic Advisers in the House draft was accepted but with some important modifications. The section requiring overlapping terms was dropped, as was the requirement that Council reports to the President be made available to the Joint Committee if requested; and the Committee's name was changed to Joint Committee on the Economic Report.

From the extensive hearings on the Act emerges clear evi-

dence that Congress had conceded that planning was an executive function, thus ending the doubt whether Congress should
keep the function for itself. It was also clear that Congress considered and rejected the idea that the Council should be an
economic Supreme Court, divorced from executive control. It
is equally clear that its intention was to provide the President
with a professional economic staff. Congress did not make it
clear how it expected the Council to advise Congress while
still preserving its confidential relation with the President. Time
was to show that this was one of the problems that the Council
had to face in its work. Nor did Congress settle what would
happen if the Council and the President disagreed about the
economic health of the nation. This was an intriguing question,
especially to an English observer who remarked, "In the American governmental system even staff agencies do not necessarily
rotate around a single sun: the gravitational pull of Congress
is also generally apparent." [43]

The statute provided that members of the Council should be
nominated by the President and confirmed by the Senate. It is
somewhat unusual for presidential staff officers to require Senate confirmation.[44] Appointment to the position of director of
the Bureau of the Budget, for example, does not need Senate
confirmation. Council members serve at the President's pleasure, and thus there is nothing to prevent the President from
appointing a new Council whenever he wishes.

The first Council of Economic Advisers was composed of
Edwin G. Nourse, chairman, John D. Clark, and Leon H. Keyserling. Disputes soon developed among the members concerning the Council's goals and procedures. In the course of the
argument about how it should operate, the Council had to
consider whether it should regard itself as an independent professional agency or as part of the Administration. Did it have
the obligation of supporting the President's political policies
in its annual reports and in testimony before congressional committees? Or was it free to follow its own political lights? Indeed, should its members appear before congressional com-

mittees at all, or should they confine themselves to preparing reports for the President? These arguments eventually did a good deal to clarify the Council's role, but they also led to Dr. Nourse's resignation. He was succeeded as chairman by Keyserling, who served for the remainder of the Truman administration. When Eisenhower became President, he appointed as chairman Arthur Burns, who has since been followed by Raymond J. Saulnier. The other two members at present are Joseph S. Davis and Paul W. McCracken.

Nourse's ideas on how the Council should work vis-à-vis the President were set forth in a paper which he read before the American Philosophical Society in Philadelphia in April 1950.[45] This question is important because a staff agency on metropolitan areas would be faced with the same problem. Nourse thought that the Council of Economic Advisers should make the economic analysis of proposed policies, and the President the political synthesis, the Council's analysis to be based strictly upon the "criteria of economics as a social science," the President's to combine economic considerations with others, including the political, that could not be ignored.

In dealing with the President, Nourse thought that the Council "should undertake to show him the agreements and disagreements among qualified economists and experienced business, labor, and agricultural leaders and the grounds on which these disagreements arise." [46] In other words, Nourse thought of the Council as a nonpartisan professional body. He even recommended that Council members be put above the vicissitudes of politics and retained so long as they met high professional standards. Nourse's colleagues on the Council, Leon H. Keyserling and John D. Clark, seem to have had somewhat different ideas. They thought the Council should come up with a single definite conclusion, reached by majority vote, and attempt to "sell" the President on it, and that thereafter they should vigorously support their recommendation, both before Congress and before the public generally. In considering a proposal, they believed, it was fruitless and improper to draft analyses whose conclusions were at variance with the President's known policies.

Nourse felt it was neither proper for members of the Council to appear before congressional committees nor necessary, since the Joint Committee on the Economic Report had employed its own staff and had ample funds on which to operate. As Nourse saw it, to appear before Congress would be a

course . . . mischievous and fatal to the Council's unique character as a staff arm on which the President could rely for politically disinterested or colorless analysis and advice. If a member of the Council exposes himself to merciless questions in the political and partisan atmosphere of Capitol Hill, he faces a dilemma of a sort intolerable to an economist of professional training and scruples. Shall he accept the role of economic attorney and, by rhetorical agility, make the most plausible case he can for someone he serves as a mouth piece? Such a following of the "party line" would not only be repugnant to professional standards, but also self-defeating in the case of anyone who had previously contributed to serious economic literature.[47]

Was it possible for a Council member to testify simply on economic trends and their consequences?[48] Or did Council members have the duty of expressing their personal opinions in testifying before congressional committees? Keyserling maintained that this was the intention of the 1946 Act. While Arthur Burns was chairman of the Council, he appeared before the Joint Committee in executive session, and no record was published of his testimony. One may assume, however, that even if future Council members could persuade the Committee to continue this policy, they still would have to be in agreement with the Administration on major policies. Leaks about testimony in executive sessions of congressional committees are frequent.

Nourse also was unhappy about the lack of opportunity to sit down with the President and discuss the Council's reports. He found President Truman always pleasant and friendly when the Council submitted a report. Invariably the

President would thank the Council and say, "I'll take this home with me or down to the *Williamsburg* and read it with great care. Then we can discuss it further." [49] But the opportunity for further discussion never came. The Council's only way of knowing whether the President accepted their advice was to watch his public statements and the legislation he supported.

There is strong evidence, however, to indicate that President Truman placed a great deal of reliance on the Council and did not feel that debate was necessary. The President had great respect for Nourse and actually accepted his diagnoses of the economic health of the nation without question. Unfortunately, the President never seems to have made this clear to Nourse.

Essentially, members of the Council have no different problem from members of any presidential staff agency. It is always possible for a conflict to arise between what a professional person sees as his responsibility as a staff officer and his professional integrity. As economists, the members of the Council of Economic Advisers have responsibilities to their profession, and as staff officers of the President, they owe loyalty to the President. Should they ignore what they consider to be sound economic principles in order to support presidential policies? Science obviously has to be coupled with value judgments in the political realm. It is impossible for any of the President's staff on economic matters or metropolitan problems to be wholly aloof from political questions. This does not mean, however, that staff members must compromise their integrity. In case of differences between them and the President, stemming from fundamental disagreements over values, the course of any staff officer would seem clear: he should resign. It would be naïve to expect that economics is so exact a science that there would be no grounds for different conclusions regarding public programs. But if the Council is to be a satisfactory staff aid to the President, it must be in agreement with him on broad fundamental policies.

The character of the annual report was another point upon which Nourse had differences with his colleagues. During the first two years of the Council's existence, the only reports issued bore the President's own signature, and thus he took sole responsibility for them. This is what Nourse believed to be the proper way for such a report to be made.[50] In 1948, however, "A Review of the Economic Situation" was begun, and these reviews were signed by the Council members and represented their own opinions. Nourse had some misgivings about the wisdom of this plan, but went along with it. A staff arm to the President, he felt, which should not appear before Congress, ought not logically to issue statements to the public. Under the new system, the report consisted of two parts. The first part was a brief statement by the President to Congress, emphasizing his legislative proposals. The second part was the report of the Council to the President, which contained an economic review of the past year with a long-range look ahead. Nourse tried to keep the review part of the report strictly factual, with no hint of the Council's position on policy questions. Leon Keyserling, on the other hand, thought it should include explicit policy recommendations, and when he became chairman upon Nourse's resignation, this procedure was followed.

Arthur F. Burns in his turn made the entire annual report consist only of the President's message to Congress. Burns felt that a public and ardent defense of the Administration lessened the Council's objectivity.[51] The report thus became the President's statement, in effect an economic version of the State of the Union message. It embraced the whole range of the Administration proposals and defended them on economic grounds. The Council has since supplied a working draft for the President's annual economic report as well as its own semiannual "Economic Review."

Although its reports seem to be the Council's major activity, it also serves as a consultant on economic aspects of policy in general. Of course, the President is free to assign the

Council whatever projects he thinks might benefit from professional economic analysis. In addition, the Council uses its own initiative in submitting other memoranda on a wide range of other subjects. With the President's consent, the Council accepts work from other federal agencies. For example, it aids the Department of State in preparing United States position papers for meetings of the United Nations, the North Atlantic Treaty Organization, and the Organization for European Economic Cooperation. The Council does the same thing for other agencies with regard to major domestic policies. This has become a very important Council activity.

Congress intended that the Council should also act as a channel through which important economic groups could express their views on economic questions. To implement this purpose, the Council calls in representatives of various groups as it feels the need to consult with them or as they express a desire to consult with it. Informal staff contacts with these groups are maintained the year round to obtain reactions to Council reports and opinions concerning current or proposed policies.

Summarizing the role of the Council, Bertram Gross, who was at one time its executive secretary, said:

Theoretically a staff involved in its principal's decision-making may, as it were, occupy an anteroom to his office which provides the only means of access to him for business of a particular kind. Such a staff not only communicates *with* the principal, but *for*, and often *in lieu* of him. Conversely, a policy-advising staff can be sequestered in a cul-de-sac, having direct communications only with the principal, and never, in his behalf, with outsiders. Like most staffs, the Council stood between these two conceptual extremes. At the outset, however, its role as a thinking center was one which was more glamorized. Under the Employment Act, it was not to administer any legislative programs and it never has. Rather, a few people were to be relieved from program operation so that from the vantage of a central perspective, they might consider how all parts of the government's economic program fitted together.[52]

The Council has not been a primary research and statistical fact-gathering agency; instead, it has used the services of existing government agencies. It has worked with the Budget Bureau in improving operations of federal statistical agencies, but it has been primarily a co-ordinator and interpreter of data, rather than a collector. The Council issues no directives to anyone. "It is not charged with seeing that any particular job gets done. It has no function of administrative coordination." [53] But the Council itself has frequently recognized that its power to request information from operating agencies and its power to report are in themselves important co-ordinating devices. The mere fact that the Council can ask questions, collect data, and call conferences will point out conflicts as well as omissions in the programs of operating agencies. This is particularly evident in the discussions leading up to the preparation of the annual report to the President. Through daily informal contacts with other executive agencies, the members and staff of the Council learn about ideas and plans while they are still in a development phase, and thus the Council is able to "anticipate interagency disagreements and either suggest compromises or be prepared to take sides." [54]

Thus the Council has operated as a staff agency for the whole executive branch, gathering information from other staff agencies as well as from line agencies, participating in discussions, and influencing plans in the course of development. It has not depended solely or even principally upon contacts with the President himself. Virtually every policy recommendation it has made has grown out of interagency discussion. More than anything else, it is the Council's active role in formulating current policy which has distinguished it as a planning instrument from the earlier National Resources Planning Board.

A Council on Metropolitan Areas

The foregoing brief analysis of the record of the National Resources Planning Board, the Office of War Mobilization, and the Council of Economic Advisers has been made in order that the lessons of their experience may be applied to the creation of a staff agency on metropolitan areas. That experience makes it clear that such an agency ought to be created by statute, as was the Council of Economic Advisers, and that the statute ought to do four things: set forth a statement of policy in general terms, require an annual report from the President on metropolitan areas, provide for a Council on Metropolitan Areas, and create an appropriate committee of Congress. The congressional declaration of policy ought to recognize that the growth of metropolitan complexes and the shift of population into urban centers has created a national problem which demands co-operation among all levels of government, and that the federal government should provide leadership within the federal system in the development of sound policies which will aid states, cities, and other local governmental agencies in solving this problem. The declaration of policy may be elaborate or sparse, but the essential thing is that it recognize the responsibility of the federal government in the area and spell it out in detail. Certainly it should include recognition that the federal government has more than a passive role. The advantages to be gained from congressional profession of responsibility for action on the problem would seem, on the basis of the Council of Economic Advisers' experience, to outweigh the generally sound theory "that the President should not have the internal affairs of his Executive Office frozen by statute." [55]

Experience shows that a staff agency engaged primarily in research and long-range planning operates better as a board than as a single individual. Although the Office of War Mobilization was headed by a single director, it was concerned primarily with day-to-day policy co-ordination. The Council on Metropolitan Areas, like NRPB and the Council of Economic Advisers, should be concerned with data collection and analysis. This type of function puts a premium on representation of different points of view and the development of a consensus on which sound policy can be built.

Thus a multimember body has obvious advantages over an agency with a single director.

The statute ought to provide therefore for a multiple (three to five) member Council, to be named by the President. The members should hold office at the President's pleasure with no fixed term, but like other presidential appointees they would presumably be replaceable when a new administration took office. Members of the Council should give their full time to the Council's work, again following the pattern of the Council of Economic Advisers. The Council should have a small full-time professional staff under the immediate direction of the chairman. Staff members in the upper levels, however, ought not to be subject to the merit system, and the Council ought to have a free hand to choose a staff in which it has confidence. This system would recognize the importance of close working relations between all the presidential staff agencies as part of the same administration. It would reject the idea that a staff agency dealing with professional matters should operate without regard to the political policies and over-all goals of the President.

Moreover, the lessons of the past make it amply clear that good working relations with Congress are a necessity, not only as between members of the Council and its staff and individual members and committees of Congress, but also in terms of a direct congressional connection between the Council's work and the business of Congress. A Committee on Metropolitan Areas, perhaps copied after the Joint Committee on the Economic Report, should therefore be established by Congress. It would receive the report on metropolitan areas submitted by the President, and hold hearings on it and on other legislation of interest to metropolitan areas. Its chief value would be in providing a contact in Congress with a group knowledgeable on metropolitan matters. Not only would the Council's annual reports be of educational value to the general public, but, unlike the National Resources Planning Board's reports, they would also have entree into the lawmaking process in Congress.

The statute creating the Council on Metropolitan Areas should provide that it should have such duties as the President might assign to it. One would assume, of course, that he would use the Council to prepare his annual report to Congress. This would require the Council to undertake continuing research on the nature and effect of federal programs as they have an impact on metropolitan areas. Some of this information is already available in other federal agencies, but the Council would have the task of bringing it together and of filling in the gaps wherever they exist. The Council also ought to tackle the whole question of statistics dealing with metropolitan areas.

Like the Council of Economic Advisers, the Council on Metropolitan Areas should have no direct responsibility for co-ordinating federal programs, but it should have the power to ask questions, collect data, and make recommendations to the President. The President should be able by executive order to give the Council wide discretion in initiating business. In addition, the President would probably instruct the Council, from time to time, to undertake particular studies and to pass judgment on various projects submitted to him by other agencies.

Experience shows too that the Council must establish rapport with the President and the executive departments and be accepted by them as a part of the presidential team. In practice, this means that the Council cannot remain aloof from the ordinary flow of business in the Executive Office, but must be an integral part of it. If there is a particular White House aide in the same field of activity, the Council must also "get along" with him. And should a Coordinator for National Capital Affairs be appointed, as the Bible Committee recommended, the Council would obviously work closely with him.

Like the Council of Economic Advisers, again, the Council on Metropolitan Areas should circulate its reports to other agencies in the Executive Office of the President, take part in staff discussions, and participate in the day-to-day work of developing policy. It should form committees of representatives from other federal agencies to work with it upon matters concerning metropolitan areas. This continuing pick-and-shovel work would enable the Council to perform a valuable educational service in making federal officials appreciate the scope of metropolitan problems and anticipate the impact of federal programs.

Though the idea of using field co-ordinators, similar to the Federal Congested Area Coordinators during World War II, who served as pipe lines for reports to Washington on the effects of federal war programs in their sections of the country, is attractive, Congress' suspicion of regional offices of this type, as indicated by its abolition of the field offices of the Budget Bureau, would make it unwise for the Council to establish permanent field offices. This hostility might be avoided by using regional desks at headquarters to help the Council keep abreast of developments in various parts of the country. Officers holding these desk posts could spend some time in the field in the region to which they were assigned.

Since an important part of the Council's work ought to be to keep in touch with research being done by private as well as state and local agencies and professional groups, a flexible system of advisory committees might be set up to aid in this task. At the beginning a single advisory committee selected by the Council on the basis of individual merit rather than as representative of professional groups might be most effective. Then, as need arose, *ad hoc* functional advisory groups might be created. It would be well to leave the choice of the members of these advisory committees in the hands of the Council rather than make them representative of state or local agencies.

As a staff agency charged with putting the federal government's house in order, the Council should not attempt to provide advice, personnel, or funds to states and local government agencies. Though the National Resources Planning Board did some effective work through its grants to states for planning, Congress viewed these activities with suspicion.

Like any presidential staff agency, a Council on Metropolitan Areas will work successfully only if the President believes in it and includes its findings in his thinking and planning. But if no staff agency is useful apart from the man whom it was created to serve, no President can operate today without the information his staff provides him. This is particularly true of metropolitan problems, where so little of the federal impact is understood or appreciated.

A great many other proposals for providing attention to metropolitan problems have been made, but of them all, a Council on Metropolitan Areas is the best solution. If the Council is not soon established, however, the task may be entrusted to other hands which could turn out to be much less satisfactory. Indeed, the number of proposals in this field has multiplied geometrically in recent years, and if the proper solution is long delayed, a less desirable one will no doubt be substituted. It is the purpose of the following chapter to examine these other proposed solutions.

5

A DEPARTMENT OF URBAN
AFFAIRS: PRO AND CON

THE idea of an executive agency devoted exclusively to urban affairs is not a new one. A variety of possibilities have been suggested in recent years, ranging from an interagency committee all the way to a Department of Urban Affairs at the Cabinet level. Some of the proposals have been for a temporary organization, some for a permanent one; none of them have agreed on what form the organization should take.

The simplest suggestion advanced has been for an interagency committee, to be made up of representatives from the several government agencies whose programs bear upon urban and metropolitan areas. This proposal has been discussed informally but has never been activated. Endless variations have been suggested as to what agencies should be included and as to what its exact terms of reference should be. The proposal ran into the problem encountered so frequently in dealing with federal programs, that no one knows precisely which agencies and what programs actually do have an impact on metropolitan government. In addition, the proposal ran afoul of the inbuilt weaknesses of all interagency committees. With no permanent secretariat, no provision for regular meetings, no delegation of precise authority, an inter-agency committee is at best a feeble administrative device for dealing with a problem as explosive as that of metro-politan areas today.

A Cabinet committee has also been suggested as a device to focus attention on the problem. In 1956, for example, President Eisenhower asked seven members of the Cabinet to serve as a Committee on Small Business, and in 1958 he requested five members to constitute a Council on Youth Fitness. He might do the same for metropolitan areas. If he used such a committee, however, a full-time secretariat should be provided, for Cabinet members are fully occupied in their own departments. The President might wish instead to bring in an individual for a short while to study the problem and report to him, as he did recently when he appointed Edward P. Curtis to study aviation facilities planning (1957), and Clarence B. Randall to study international trade (1958).

Another means of focusing public attention on the problem would be to make use of a special presidential commission to study it. Thus, in 1954 the President appointed a five-man advisory committee for a National Highway Program, headed by General Lucius Clay, on whose report the Highway Act of 1956 came to be based; and in 1956 he directed a thirty-four-member Committee on Education beyond the High School to examine problems in that area, and on the basis of its findings to develop proposals for action. Congress provided funds for that Committee's work, a series of studies and con-ferences was launched, and a final set of recommendations was drawn up. In other areas, President Eisenhower has appointed a Committee on Government Contracts, an Ad-visory Commission on Presidential Office Space, a Committee on Government Employment Policy, and a Science Advisory Committee. Such committees of prominent citizens, properly staffed and financed, can do an excellent job of analysis and recommendation.

None of these temporary and short-range devices, however, should be regarded as a good alternative to the creation of a Council on Metropolitan Areas. They are useful in educating the public and the President, but they cannot supply the President with the continuing staff assistance the metropolitan problem demands. Though any of these devices can be very helpful to the President in preparing legislation, what is needed for metropolitan areas is not the passage of a single act, but an agency which will provide the President with a continuous flow of information upon which he can base policy.

Even though the newly created Advisory Commission on Intergovernmental Relations [1] is to be permanent, it is not a satisfactory answer for metropolitan areas either. Growing out of the work of the Subcommittee on Intergovernmental Relations of the House Committee on Government Operations, the Commission is visualized as a body which will "bring together Federal, State and local officials on a continuing basis for discussion of the problems which concern all levels of government." [2]

The bipartisan Commission will consist of 26 members: 3 from the executive branch of the federal government, 3 senators, 3 representatives, 4 governors, 3 state legislators, 4 mayors, 3 county officials, and 3 private citizens. It is clear from its sponsors' statements that the Commission will be mainly concerned with allocation of functions among levels of government and with federal grant-in-aid programs. As a means of gathering information the Commission has some attraction, but it will have so broad a membership base and be so indirectly involved in metropolitan problems that it will have limited usefulness, so far as the nation's great urban communities are concerned. The establishment of a commission of this nature, indeed, may lead people to conclude that an agency which will devote its primary attention to metropolitan area problems has been established, when in fact it has not.

Proposals for a Department

The most widely supported idea for an executive agency in the area of urban and metropolitan problems is to create a Cabinet department devoted exclusively to them. The idea dates at least from 1912, when Philip Kates suggested the creation of a national Department of Municipalities.[3] The Kates proposal would have created a research and service department which as its first task would conduct "a comprehensive and authoritative study of the municipal problem in its basic principle . . . an industrial survey of national scope, with . . . attendant investigations into causes of congestion of population, and the remedies by improved communication and transportation and other means; into sanitary conditions . . . into housing, disposal of municipal waste . . . industrial working conditions . . . the working of other municipal systems than ours, and of other theories and methods of legislation [applicable to the American problem]."[4] The information thus collected, fully and quickly transmitted to the proper local officials, Kates thought, would give municipalities all the information which was "essential to the proper solution of [their] problems."[5] Kates' idea interested Woodrow Wilson "very much indeed," and he hoped "to have an opportunity to discuss it very seriously . . . with those interested."[6]

The opportunity evidently did not materialize, however, and the proposal was lost in the pursuit of the New Freedom and in the preparation of the United States for World War I which immediately followed it. It was revived in 1919 in a slightly altered form by Harlean James, who thought that a Department of Civic Economy in the national government, "rightly conceived and vigorously carried out," would be invaluable in helping cities and towns to meet the challenge of the postwar period.[7] Miss James conceived of her Department of Civic Economy as performing primarily an educational service. "Such a department," she wrote, "should conduct research studies and make experiments on a scale possible only for the federal government" and should make its findings available to "the sleepy crossroads corner in the remote county" as well as to "the noisy traffic-ridden city." [8]

Miss James' idea did not bear fruit either, and for another decade or so no new proposals toward this end seem to have been made. In 1934, however, Charles E. Merriam, then with the National Resources Board, remarked that it was important that "the voice of our cities be heard in the capital, [and] it is equally important that the United States Government have some responsible administrative representation in the cities. . . . there is no urban United States representative corresponding to the county agent in the rural districts." [9] Although Merriam went on to profess that he did not know "just what form this new development may take or whether a number of Federal agencies may not jointly share Federal responsibility," he was certain that "the whole question of the relation of Federal Administration . . . to city government . . . looms up larger every day." By 1942, Merriam had become convinced that a separate administrative unit in Washington was necessary "in view of the proportion of our people who dwell in cities and the importance generally of cities in our political and economic system," and he recommended that there be "set up in the national government a bureau or department of urbanism." [10]

Since the end of the war, the idea has been advanced quite frequently. Just recently, Nathaniel S. Keith, a former federal housing official, proposed the creation of a Department of Community Development. Commenting on his idea, Keith declared that "the realities call for the establishment of a federal department as a focus for the necessary federal attention and assistance" to community development. "The establishment of a federal Department of Community Development would give needed stature to the federal interest in this field and would provide Cabinet-level policy co-ordination for all federal activities with an impact on community developmental problems." The following operating functions, Keith thought,

ought to be consolidated in the new department: research in housing and community development problems; assistance to regional, metropolitan, and urban planning; assistance to housing; assistance to urban renewal; assistance to the planning and financing of local public works; assistance to highway development and metropolitan area transportation. "The administrative consolidation of these functions in a single federal department," he concluded, "would provide the necessary fulcrum for consistent application of these programs in the field." [11]

In one form or another, the idea of a department has won a number of outspoken proponents. Representative J. Arthur Younger gave impetus to the idea in an article about it in a Sunday supplement.[12] Since then, it has become a popular subject for newspaper editorials across the country,[13] even in some of the small newspapers, and it has been incorporated into the last three annual policy recommendations of the American Municipal Association.[14] A number of other organizations have accepted the idea, including the National Association of Housing and Redevelopment Officials, the National Housing Conference, and the American Society of Planning Officials, and the hard-pressed mayors and local officials of a good many of the nation's largest cities have pledged their efforts to its establishment.[15]

The idea has also caught the attention of a number of members of Congress, and several of them have introduced bills into Congress to create such a department. Three such bills were introduced in the Eighty-fourth Congress, one by Representative J. Arthur Younger (R) of the Ninth District (San Mateo County) of California,[16] one by Representative Irwin D. Davidson (R) of the Twentieth District (New York City) of New York,[17] and one by nine senators, some of them from the nation's most urban areas: Herbert Lehman (D) of New York (New York City), Hubert Humphrey (D) of Minnesota (Minneapolis), Paul Douglas (D) of Illinois (Chicago), Wayne Morse (D) and Richard Neuberger (D) of Oregon

(Eugene and Portland), Warren Magnuson (D) of Washington (Seattle), Thomas C. Hennings (D) of Missouri (St. Louis), Pat McNamara (D) of Michigan (Detroit), and James E. Murray (D) of Montana.[18] Each of the three bills was referred to the Committee on Government Operations of the appropriate chamber. Only the Younger bill received a hearing, however, and no further action was taken before the end of that session. No action at all was taken on the other two bills, so that all of them died at the end of the Eighty-fourth Congress.

Virtually the same bills were submitted to the Eighty-fifth Congress. In the House, Representative Younger reintroduced his bill,[19] and Representative Martha W. Griffiths (D) of the Seventeenth District (Detroit) of Michigan offered another.[20] The Senate version was offered by some of the same senators, but this time under the leadership of Senator Joseph Clark (D) of Pennsylvania, a former mayor of Philadelphia. Senators Jacob Javits (R) of New York, Russell Long (D) of Louisiana, and Clifford Case (R) of New Jersey joined Senators Humphrey, Morse, Neuberger, Magnuson, and Murray in sponsoring the bill.[21] All three bills were referred to committee, but no hearings were held, and, as before, all of them died at the end of the session.

In the Eighty-sixth Congress, four bills were introduced in the House, one by Representative Albert Rains,[22] an influential member from Alabama, another by Representative Hugh Addonizio of New Jersey,[23] and the same bills as before by Representatives Griffiths and Younger. In the upper house, however, Senator Clark and the other senators had shifted their support to the metropolitan study commission idea and did not submit again the departmental bill of the preceding Congress. Senator Kenneth B. Keating of New York introduced a companion bill to Representative Younger's.[24]

The proposal for a department warrants analysis and discussion if for no other reason than the fact that it has won so much endorsement. One must recognize, of course, that proposals to create new executive departments are made frequently, and some of them have received a great deal of support, both in Congress and outside, without being accepted. In the past decade, proposals for departments of Civil Defense, Transportation, Water Resources, Public Works, and Science and Technology have all been advanced without success. A Department of Urban Affairs, however, suggests an easy solution to a complex problem, which in many ways is broader in scope and more immediate in its need for action than any of the other problems. Moreover, a discussion of such a concrete proposal can do much to clarify the proper way to deal administratively with a problem of this magnitude. Since proposals for an executive department will doubtless continue to be offered in the future as the solution to the problem, it is time that the merits of the idea be thought through.

Organization and Powers of the Department

All the bills so far presented to Congress have had certain similar features. All call for the creation of a new executive department, variously entitled the Department of Urban Affairs, the Department of Housing and Urban Affairs, and the Department of Urbiculture. All propose the same type of administrative organization, at least in broad terms. A Secretary, an Undersecretary, and a varying number of assistant secretaries heading major departmental divisions are provided for in each bill. Likewise, all the bills set forth the same general goal for the Department, though, as one might expect, they differ considerably in their exact wording. The Younger bills have the most limited scope. As H. R. 1019 (Eighty-fifth Congress) put it, "Many of the most pressing problems facing the people of the United States grow out of the lack of knowledge and understanding of proper techniques in utilization of urban land, [thus] there is a corresponding national interest in the development of the science of urbiculture." Therefore,

Recognizing the invaluable contribution made by the Department of Agriculture in promoting increasingly efficient use of farmlands, the Congress enacts this Act in order to provide a corresponding executive department to develop methods of dealing with pressing social, economic, and civic problems growing out of inadequate knowledge of the principles of using and developing urban lands, and to make these methods available to the people of the United States through suitable educational programs.[25]

Representative Griffiths' bills note "that the pressing needs of cities and metropolitan areas are such that Federal action should be taken to assist in meeting these needs through education, research, technical services, and such other programs as the Congress may later prescribe." Moreover,

The Congress finds also that a number of important Federal programs . . . have a vital impact on local communities and metropolitan areas; and that there is need for a central place in the Federal Administrative structure to assess the overall results of these programs, to help coordinate these activities, and to represent the needs of urban areas at the national level.[26]

The Senate bill (S. 2159) for the creation of a Department of Housing and Urban Affairs was very similar. It declared

(1) that a large majority of the American people now live in urban and metropolitan areas, and that almost all population growth in the last two decades has occurred in these areas; and

(2) that the number of Federal programs which have a vital impact on urban and metropolitan areas are numerous and varied; and

(3) that the general welfare and security of the Nation and the living standards of its people require that the Federal Government . . . [assist] . . . the States and local governments in meeting the problems caused by the continuing growth and concentration of population; and

(4) that for these reasons there should be a Federal department . . . to deal with those urban and metropolitan problems in which the Federal Government has a direct or cooperating interest.[27]

Three of the bills would have abolished and transferred the functions of certain existing agencies to the new department: Representatives Griffiths' and Younger's, those of "the constituent agencies of the Housing and Home Finance Agency," [28] and S. 2159, those of the Housing and Home Finance Agency and the Federal Civil Defense Administration. All three bills also contained a section which would have permitted the President to "exercise his authority under the Reorganization Act of 1949 with a view to further consolidating within the Department such functions and agencies of the Government as will further the purposes" of the Act creating the department. [29] The Rains and Addonizio bills would leave the transfer of functions, including housing, entirely to the President.

The Younger bill also provided that the Secretary should "establish research and educational programs to accomplish the purposes set forth" in the Act, and the Senate bill instructed the Secretary of the Department to "conduct a continuing study of problems peculiar to urban and metropolitan areas, including problems of coordinating Federal-State programs in such areas," to "provide technical assistance to State and local governmental bodies in developing solutions to such problems," and to "make such recommendations to the Congress, as a result of the studies to be undertaken . . . and after consultation with appropriate representatives of State and local governments, as he shall determine to be appropriate." [30]

As a result of the passage of any one of the bills, or of a mixture of them, another executive department, directed generally at urban and metropolitan problems, and combining research, service, and educational functions on the one hand with co-ordination and program operation functions on the other, would be added to the structure of the federal government. Initially, at least, no new functions would be added, but those which are now scattered throughout the federal government would be centralized in a single administrative unit.

Arguments for a Department

Supporters of the new department build their case on a number of grounds. Perhaps the most frequently offered justification is the fact that in a nation which is becoming increasingly urban, special recognition of urban affairs at the Cabinet level is a necessity. Senator Clark, in a statement explaining the purpose of S. 2159 to the Eighty-fifth Congress, remarked that "metropolitan growth is posing one of the greatest challenges of the second half of the 20th century. We cannot meet this challenge with government machinery designed for the 19th century." [31] As a matter of necessity, the federal government must "adapt its administrative organization" to enable it to meet more effectively the problems of today's urban and metropolitan areas.[32] Just as a Department of Agriculture was created as a farmers' agency in recognition of the primary importance of agriculture in 1889, and a frankly pro-labor Department of Labor was established when increased industrialization made it seem important to "foster, promote, and develop the welfare of the wage earners of the United States," [33] so is the development of a Department of Urban Affairs important and necessary today. Representative Younger, testifying before the Subcommittee on Executive and Legislative Reorganization of the House Committee on Government Operations in 1955 in behalf of his first bill, remarked that "very much the same argument that was advanced for the establishment of the Department of Agriculture" could be advanced for a Department of Urbiculture.

In 1862, when the [Office] of Agriculture was established, approximately 80 percent of our population lived on farms or in rural areas, and only 20 percent in urban territory. Now, in 1955, that situation has entirely changed. . . . In 1862 the problems which came to the Federal Government for solution arose from the rural areas because 80 percent of the population lived in rural areas. With 85 percent of the population concentrated in the urban areas, naturally the problems which come to the Federal Government for solution arise from those areas. . . . I think that . . . we should concentrate . . . Federal concern over the problems that originate in the city areas into a department that [has] a head with a Cabinet status. In simple terms, that is what this bill was designed to do.[34]

Representative William L. Dawson of Illinois, the chairman of the Subcommittee, remarked upon hearing his colleague's testimony: "Here in the Congress I have noticed that the farmers are well represented. They have the Department of Agriculture as well as the legislative committee set up here. They are taken care of and, as you say, the people are no longer on the farms. I think the Congress and our Government should revamp itself to meet the situation because Government is for the people." [35]

Representation of Urban Interests

Creation of a department and the designation of a Cabinet representative for urban affairs, the argument continues, would provide stronger leadership for and better representation of urban interests in national policy making. At present, there is no focal point for urban affairs in the executive branch of the federal government. A great many agency and bureau heads represent one aspect or another of the urban and metropolitan problem, but their efforts are often contradictory and are in no sense all-inclusive. The result is that national policy in this important field can be formed only on the basis of incomplete or inaccurate data about cities and their problems and needs. "It does seem to me," Representative Dawson noted, "that it is indicated that the problems of cities be given a departmental status, and it so seems to me from my experience as a Congressman here in Washington, and observing the various departments make their needs known to the Congress." [36] Maintaining that farmers have the Department of Agriculture to point out their needs to Congress and to protect their interests and promote their welfare, he argued, "The problems of the cities are not voiced here as such. Because of the great impact of those problems upon not only the cities but upon the country as a whole, I think that there is a crying need to the extent that the country should begin to think about a department to handle this." [37]

This reasoning would seem to be supported by studies in the field of public administration. Arthur Macmahon and John Millett, for example, declare that the "head of a department . . . has an individual consultative relationship to the President, to the Administration as a whole, and to Congress," a relationship of such importance that the Secretary of a department becomes "the Administration's natural consultant" in regard to the problems in his area.[38] To date, there has been no such consultant available specifically for urban affairs. Schuyler Wallace finds that since the President's Cabinet frequently serves not merely as "an administrative but also an advisory agency on broad questions of public policy . . . representation [thereon is] highly desirable." [39] Both by being available as a consultant on urban affairs to other officials in the federal government and by contributing the urban point of view to the determination of national policy, a Secretary of Urban Affairs would fill a need which has already been met in all other important policy areas. In a nation so predominantly urban, proponents of a department insist, to deny representation to urban affairs is no longer tenable.

Size of Urban Programs Warrants Departmental Status

Aside from the need to have urban interests represented in national policy making, those who advocate a department point out that by now the federal government has many programs which affect urban areas and that together they are important enough in the total picture of the federal government's activities to warrant elevation to departmental status. The federal government's housing programs alone, to say nothing of its civil defense program and others with distinctly urban aspects, certainly have become important enough and involve large enough expenditures of personnel and money to be raised to departmental status. They should, proponents of a department argue, be recognized as permanent interests of the government by being given regular Cabinet status—by being, in short, combined into a separate and distinct executive department. Thus Walter B. Mills, Jr., President of the National Association of Housing and Redevelopment Officials, in a letter to Representative Dawson in connection with H. R. 1864, declared that his organization was "strongly of the opinion that the Federal Government's activities in the field of housing, slum clearance, and urban redevelopment of urban centers have reached proportions warranting the creation of a Department . . . having full Cabinet status."[40] In the same vein, William C. Wheaton of the National Housing Conference maintained before the Dawson Subcommittee that the "relative size of the Housing and Home Finance Agency as compared with other executive departments" entitled it to departmental status. "If we look at the expenditures, we find that the gross expenditures of the Housing and Home Finance Agency exceed that of five other Cabinet departments . . . [it] has more employees than one department."[41] Certainly, Dr. Wheaton argued, the HHFA ought to be converted to departmental rank, especially when its total financial commitments are compared with those of the other civilian departments. Those commitments, Dr. Wheaton thought, "probably exceeded all of the other departments saving only the Treasury . . . and the Department of Health, Education and Welfare."[42]

Nor did Dr. Wheaton or other proponents of a department have to look far for support of their contention. The first Hoover Commission used the same type of argument to support its proposal for the creation of a Department of Social Security and Education. Having recommended the creation of a United Medical Administration to take care of the federal government's health programs, the Commission went on to say, "There remain, however, certain most important bureaus [and] agencies relating to education which must be organized into a workable department." And as the reasons for that conclusion, it noted: "The size of these agencies . . . is . . . indicated by the fact that they embrace about 20,000 employees. The administration expenditures [of the several agencies combined] would be roughly $50,000,000. The grants-in-aid to be distributed would approximate $800,000,000." [43] When operations of separate agencies reach such proportions, the Commission seemed to say, they naturally should be combined into one department. More recently, a proposal has been advanced to centralize the federal government's science activities in a Department of Science and to transfer to the new department the functions of the Atomic Energy Commission, the National Science Foundation, the Bureau of Standards, and the Patent Office, among others. The proponents of this measure, like those of a Department of Urban Affairs, justify the action on the ground that in terms of money and manpower involved the time has come to recognize the importance of the government's scientific interests.

For departmentalization, they assert, is the only really efficient way of handling related program operations of such magnitude in the federal government. Scattering of functions among a number of different units means that it is not possible anywhere to get a view of the problem to be solved as a whole. Senator Clark built much of his case on the advantages that a Department of Urban Affairs would bring in co-ordinating existing programs concerned with urban affairs and in simplifying the governmental structure by reducing the number of independent agencies reporting directly to the President.[44] The American Municipal Association in its 1956 policy statement likewise stressed the "greater . . . efficiency" which would result from centralizing the various activities affecting cities in one "unified administrative organization at the federal level." [45] No study which has been made of the executive branch fails to emphasize the evils attending the great proliferation of independent executive agencies that has occurred in recent years and the advantages to be gained by a reduction in their number and a co-ordination of their efforts. Indeed, the first finding of the Hoover Commission was precisely along this line: "Federal programs . . . must be grouped by related function and divided among a small number of principal assistants who are the heads of departments. . . . Until dispersed units are pulled together, and authority is placed in department heads as chief assistants to the President, there will be conflict, waste, and indecisiveness in administration." [46] To bring even the housing activities together under one department, if not also those relating to civil defense and possibly others, would thus seem to be in direct accord with the principles of efficient government administration.

Facilitation of Research

The creation of a department would have the added advantage, the argument proceeds, of making it possible more easily and quickly to conduct the great amount of research that needs to be done before actual solution of urban problems is possible. Research needs to be undertaken, for example, on the problems posed for urban mass transportation facilities by the rapid expansion of metropolitan areas in the past quarter century and on the problems growing out of "the lack of knowledge and understanding of proper techniques in utilization of urban land." [47] Other questions, such as "parking, traffic . . . central business district, port development . . . [and] metropolitan governmental problems . . . including problems of annexation and metropolitan urban services distribution" [48] offer equally great possibilities for study. All such problems could be much more effectively studied if brought together under an agency which would have the facilities to attract the services of the nation's outstanding experts on urban problems. Such a program would have the double advantage of avoiding duplication and repetition and at the same time covering all the important questions now facing cities and metropolitan areas. Today such studies are made in bits and pieces, if made at all, and not only are they therefore uneconomical, but their results are not often widely publicized. A federal department not only would develop information but would have channels available both to distribute it and to assist city and county officials in applying it. The department might thus become, its proponents argue, an urban planning assistance agency for the nation.

Informational Center

A further justification offered for a Department of Urban Affairs is that it would provide a central point in the federal government where cities could come for help and information. The American Municipal Association originally based its support of a department largely on these grounds: "The Congress should authorize a new federal cabinet post for urban affairs. Unlike other segments of our political economy, such as industry, labor and agriculture, local governments have no place to turn to in their many dealings with the federal government." [49] Instead of one place, there are many. A mayor must often make six or eight visits to get a complete picture, and, to make it even worse, the information he gets at one point is likely to be contradicted at the next. The mayor of Seattle, Allan Pomeroy, expressed the feelings of many of his fellows when he pointed out that "above all, such a department would provide a central clearinghouse for all the specialized problems having to do with intergovernmental relations as they affect central cities and their metropolitan areas." [50] And Carl Feiss, former Urban Renewal Administrator, noted the great advantages of effecting through the creation of a single department "a simplification in the lines of communication between the Federal, State, [and] local agencies so that local public officials would have a real opportunity of finding the right person at the right time for the right purposes and the right programs in order to simplify and expedite the very complicated problems that the localities are facing . . . in this tremendous urbanization that is taking place." [51]

Practical Political Argument

Although not advanced so openly as the foregoing arguments on behalf of a Department of Urban Affairs, another argument has been as influential. This is the argument of practical politics. Gerrymandered as most state legislatures are in favor of rural areas, they have not listened with sympathetic ears to the pleas of urban citizens. In some cases, the dominant upstate (rural) areas are of one political persuasion, the downstate (urban) areas of the other, and this has further complicated the relation between the legislatures and the cities.[52] In disgust and desperation, therefore, city officials have increasingly turned toward Washington for help and guidance. In national politics, although the cards are still stacked against urban voters, at least they are not stacked so high. City officials and urban citizens are convinced that with their own department, and even more their own Secretary, who would serve as their advocate, at last they might begin to get the sympathy and assistance they have long asked for. As Representative Younger has put it, "Agencies and commissions are temporary and, what's more, they're also the stepchildren of government. The chairman of a commission . . . is many, many rungs down the ladder from the Secretary of a Department who has daily access to the President's ear. The only favorite sons in Washington are the heads of the executive departments."[53] It follows, therefore, that "only a full-time, full-ranked Secretary . . . can effectively serve the cities of this nation."[54]

Those who favor a new department declare, furthermore, that there is considerable evidence in other fields to demonstrate that the Secretary of a department does in fact serve as a special advocate for his "constituents." To some degree at least, every Secretary of Agriculture, Labor, or Commerce takes care of the interests of his special clientele and tries to present a good record of performance for the party's sake—and for his own—at the next election. He builds such a record by aggressive leadership in programs in the area of his responsibility. Urban matters, however, have not been carried to the political level by such an advocate. The Administrator of the Housing and Home Finance Administration simply is not the political figure that a member—any member—of the traditional Cabinet is. Urban officials see the advantages to be gained in exploiting the political possibilities of a Cabinet post, and though the other justifications they offer are offered seriously and honestly, the political aspects of the situation have obviously been considered.

Arguments against a Department

However appealing the case for a Department of Urban Affairs may be, the other side of the coin ought to be considered carefully before a decision is made. Indeed, those opposed to a department have the stronger case. They argue that such a department would be politically unwise, administratively unsound, and functionally unnecessary. The creation of a Department of Urban Affairs, or Urbiculture (a department by that too clever name seems unlikely in any event),[55] is unwise on the ground of semantics alone. Semantics can be over-emphasized, of course, but the words so far suggested for the department's title constitute a real handicap to its adoption. "Urban Affairs" is naturally contrasted with "rural affairs," and all the old stereotypes about "rural" and "urban" would be aroused by its establishment. "Urban" means cities, and cities are still pictured as sinful and unhealthy as opposed to the farm and the country, which are equated with clean living, hard work, and thrift. Cities are thought to be dominated by bosses and political machines, in contrast with the democratic, independent way of life on the farm. It is not enough to say that this is an incorrect, distorted picture, both of urban and of rural living, nor is it sufficient to point out that cities down through the ages have been centers of freedom, that even today they are more progressive than the rural areas, which are traditionally conservative. Whatever the truth of these characterizations, the important fact is that the rural and small-town population in the United States traditionally views cities with suspicion, and these are the groups that dominate legislative bodies in the states as well as in Congress.

Added to this is the fact that "urban" also will be contrasted with "suburban," and the suburbanite is even more anti big city than his country cousin. At least he is anti downtown big city. One of the principal reasons for the existence of metropolitan areas has been the movement of population to the suburbs made possible with the development of the automobile. To the suburbanite, "the city" means where he works in the daytime. It means crowds, noise, subways, and social groups he does not like. He feels differently about the suburbs. Politically, the suburbanite is becoming increasingly important. His numbers alone make him a political factor to be counted. In alliance with rural voters, he is a formidable power. Representatives from strictly rural areas may be declining in strength as population moves away from the farms, but the small towns and especially the suburban areas are steadily gaining in population, political power, and importance. All three would be against a Department of Urban Affairs. Why, they would argue, should the whole nation underwrite a segment of the population who are quite able to take care of themselves? Cities are rich; they do not need help from the federal government. An executive department devoted to their interests would simply be a means by which big cities would get increased federal aid, perhaps to their detriment.

Though opponents of a department might admit that urbanism is a national problem, they argue that ours is a federal system of government, with certain well-defined areas of power given to the federal government and others reserved to the states. Problems of local government, they assert, whether in large or in small urban centers, are primarily a concern of the states and the local communities themselves. The federal government has no responsibility for cities as such, and therefore there is no need for a department. These may not be sound arguments, but they have lots of emotional appeal. They have been used in state legislatures for years with great success. They are and will continue to be just as effective in Congress, where smart "city slickers" are feared almost as much as they are in state legislatures.

Political Difficulties

Not only would these emotional factors make the creation of a Department of Urban Affairs politically difficult, but they would subject the operation of the Department to continual friction with Congress. Every time the Department's budget was scrutinized by Congress, every time a hearing was held on its legislative proposals, the tension between them would be aggravated. Could the Secretary of Urban Affairs deal successfully with Congress under these circumstances?

The very speed with which the idea has been developed and pushed also works against its adoption. Not only does Congress not like innovation, it is not apt to act on so radical a proposal without having before it conclusive evidence that the cities have done all they can to help themselves solve their own problems. To date, such evidence is not forthcoming. Congress likes even less to alter the administrative structure of the federal government until it is sure of the soundness of the proposal. In the past, periods of thirty to forty years have elapsed between the creation of one new executive department and the next. Agencies, bureaus, and commissions are not a great affront to congressional sensibilities; but the creation of a department, affecting as it would the very core of the executive branch, is another matter altogether. Any proposal for a new department, however sound, traditionally has rough going in Congress. As one of the witnesses before the Dawson Subcommittee in connection with H. R. 1864 pointed out, "A major stumbling block for H. R. 1864 is that the creation of a department of urbiculture would elevate consideration of urban problems so high and so fast from present levels of consideration that the sudden jump would be unacceptable to some people." [56] Chiefly, it would be unacceptable to Congress, at least in its present state of mind and membership.

As a matter of practical politics, to propose a Department of Urban Affairs is futile at present because the idea has not built up the kind of political support which would make it possible. President Eisenhower and his top administrative officials have shown no interest in it whatsoever. On the contrary, there is some evidence that they would be strongly opposed to such a department. Nor for that matter has there been any grass-roots support for it, notwithstanding the formal resolutions of a number of national civic organizations. Even as Representative Dawson acknowledged in the 1955 hearings, "You appreciate that there must be a public interest and demand for this legislation. . . . There must be created within this country a desire to have established a department which is concerned with the problems of the urban dwellers. . . . Sentiment for the idea . . . is necessary in this form of government to make it become a law." [57] Until such sentiment is built up, to talk about its adoption is futile.

A Secretary of Urban Affairs, actively looking to the interests of cities in Washington, would, moreover, add greatly to the centralization of governmental power in federal hands. As Governor Nelson Rockefeller of New York, who called the proposal for a Department of Urban Affairs "appalling," went on to point out, there is need for co-ordination of federal programs involving urban and metropolitan areas, but to vest that power in a new department would be to create an "all-powerful coordinator . . . in Washington." "On reflection," Rockefeller concluded, "it is self-evident that a Federal department with as much power as this would require would be a Frankenstein." If such a department were ever established, "home rule would become a memory." [58]

Finally, the creation of such a department is politically unlikely because of recent actions regarding the Housing and Home Finance Agency and the Federal Civil Defense Administration, the functions of which were to be transferred to the

Department of Urban Affairs. During its debates on recent housing bills, Congress has given every indication that it contemplates the continued existence of HHFA as the administrative unit for housing programs. By executive order, the Federal Civil Defense Administration has recently been merged with the Office of Defense Mobilization, to form the Office of Civil and Defense Mobilization. The probability that the functions of either agency might be shifted to a new department in the near future is remote.

Administrative Conflicts

Not only are there strong political arguments against the creation of a Department of Urban Affairs, but there is a strong case against it on grounds of administrative soundness. Creation of a department has come to be regarded as a panacea for all administrative ills. Yet a study of the service departments over the years, and of the Department of Defense in particular, since its creation in 1947, produces considerable evidence that departmentalization is not a guaranteed cure for administrative difficulties. Establishment of a department, indeed, may only delay the cure or force it to take place in different surroundings. Back of the proposal is the idea that a simple organizational change will provide the answer for urban and metropolitan problems. This is a false belief. The mere creation of a new administrative unit is not the answer to a problem as complex as that presented by the phenomenon of metropolitanization. Creation of a department would beg the most important question of all, What is the federal government's proper role in urban areas? The answer is not merely to assign urban affairs to a single organizational unit. It is a matter of principle and philosophy, not of method. To create a method without first having established a philosophy to base it on is to put the proverbial cart before the horse. Coming as it does at this time, when the basic issues of intergovernmental relations in metropolitan areas are still unresolved, such a proposal is clearly premature.

Moreover, a Department of Urban Affairs as proposed would be based on a geographical concept rather than on a functional one. To admit it would be to introduce a maverick into the administrative corral. The work of such a department, if all the programs carried on by the federal government affecting cities were placed under its jurisdiction, would necessarily cut across the functions of a great many existing agencies and departments. Indeed, once the Pandora's box is opened, how is it to be closed? What programs do not have an urban interest, save those pertaining strictly to agriculture? If housing and related activities and civil defense are the first to be included, how can arguments for the inclusion of a host of others be denied? Thus, in the hearings on the first Younger bill, the representative of the American Municipal Association declared that in his opinion the new department "should include such items as highways and urban transit, airports and airport administration, public health matters . . . water and air pollution, and juvenile delinquency" in addition to housing and urban development and renewal and civil defense.[59] What would be the effect at least on the departments of Commerce, Interior, and Health, Education and Welfare of the creation of a Department of Urban Affairs? It would certainly conflict with their organization and ongoing programs, to say nothing of the complexities it would introduce into the programs of many independent regulatory agencies. To insert an executive department based on a geographical pattern into a system primarily organized functionally would make for more, rather than less, confusion in the administrative structure.

It is argued that the new department would simply parallel the existing Department of Agriculture and serve city dwellers in the same way that Agriculture serves the farmers. But even if it be admitted that Agriculture is principally concerned with farmers, yet its organizational base is strictly functional. A comparable situation would be created if the new department were made simply the Department of Housing. This title, however, would not give it cognizance over the broad area of urban problems which its sponsors desire. What would be done with activities like airports, highways, and water pollution? Is it suggested that these functions too be divided along geographic lines and that urban highways be placed in the new department but rural highways left where they are now? Would highway matters be divided between two departments? Would the same duplication be repeated for water and air pollution, airport construction and maintenance, water supply, hospital construction, and all the manifold other urban programs of the federal government? Indeed, with what department and agency of the federal establishment would a department conceived upon geographic lines not conflict? To ask the question is to supply the answer. To create such a department would be to create an organizational misfit.

Moreover, it cannot be conclusively demonstrated that merely because certain activities of the federal government reach a particular magnitude they should automatically be brought together under a single executive department. The Veterans Administration would seem to be a case in point. In terms of the number of employees, size of budget, and amounts of money distributed, it would long ago seem to have deserved elevation to departmental status. Yet it has functioned with benefit to the group it serves through the years without Cabinet status. What advantages would have accrued from converting it into an executive department? Proponents of a Department of Urban Affairs claim that one advantage would be better representation in the administrative structure. The heads of HHFA and OCDM now sit with the President's Cabinet when matters pertaining to them are discussed. What would be gained by giving them secretarial status?

But it is argued that instead of occasional participation in the Cabinet, the Urban Affairs Secretary would be a full-time member. This argument is based on the assumption that the Cabinet is in fact a policy-forming body. Actually the President makes policy, and the Cabinet may or may not be consulted. Confusing the British system, with its theory of Cabinet responsibility, and the American system, where it is sometimes said the Cabinet members are the natural enemies of the President, is responsible for this misapprehension. Under the American system access to only one man, the President, is important, because he bears the chief burden for policy making. Entree at the White House is much more important than Cabinet status. Harry Hopkins, during World War II, was a good example of a man who did not have Cabinet status but who was much more powerful than any Cabinet officer because of his entree to the President. Indeed, entree to the King was what gave Cabinet officers in England their position of power in the first place. One of the principal prerogatives of an English Secretary of State was "the privilege of the closet," which meant the right of entree to the King and the right of consulting with him alone.

Close ties with congressional committees and well-organized pressure groups also account for the success of an administrative agency. Certainly the Veterans Administration owes much of its prolonged success to these factors. A seat in the Cabinet for the Veterans Administrator would not have been nearly so important in making it possible for him to carry out his agency's program. On the same basis, it cannot be maintained that departmental status and Cabinet representation alone would produce the effective "representation" of urban interests that proponents of the idea claim it would. Good entree at the White House, good working relations with Congress, and effective group pressure produce better results in many cases than a seat in the Cabinet.

Better Means Available

Finally, the opponents of a Department of Urban Affairs argue that it is unnecessary now. Attention to metropolitan problems, they say, is not guaranteed merely by the creation of an executive department. It can be secured as well under the existing arrangement of agencies, once they all recognize "that our metropolitan communities provide the environment within which the greatest number of people live and the largest part of the nation's business is carried out." [60] What is needed more than an organizational reshuffling is a policy within the entire executive branch to guide all federal agencies in their urban and metropolitan activities. If such a policy existed, "then the . . . Council of Economic Advisers would be devoting a large share of its attention to the economic problems of urban communities within the framework of the national economy. The . . . Bureau of Public Roads would have a finely articulated program for relating the construction of the interstate highway system to the needs and requirements of the group of cities within each of the regions of the United States. The agencies concerned with water resources would be at least as much concerned with the river basins within our metropolitan communities as they are with the problems of irrigation in the West." [61]

Establishment of a department would not necessarily be of any assistance in achieving co-ordination. Co-ordination in the executive branch results from common understanding and a will to co-operate among the personnel concerned; these can be achieved among diverse agencies as well as in a single department. Such simple devices as the exchange of personnel between one agency and another and the institution of periodic consultation between program officers would go far toward bringing about co-ordination. Indeed, a department as big as the proposed Department of Urban Affairs would have its own co-ordination problems which would have to be settled in some way. One important objection to adopting the proposal is based on past experience within the federal government. Over the years, it is notorious that the housing and civil defense officials have vociferously disagreed with each other. Would bringing them together eliminate their differences? How would they be reconciled? Which interest would dominate? A solution which would ignore long-standing conflicts of personnel and philosophy is not a solution at all.

Nor can it be demonstrated that the research and educational programs which are so urgently needed with regard to metropolitan problems can be carried out best by a single department. How much research of a general nature is worth while? In regard to mass transportation, for example, must not a solution be fitted to the needs of each individual metropolitan area? Indeed, opponents of a department argue, is there a need for the federal government to conduct such research at all? Today there is a host of agencies, public and private, carrying on research on these problems. Commenting on Representative Younger's first bill to establish a department, the editors of *The American City* said:

> In the opinion of *The American City* the need for an over-all . . . Department . . . is much less than was the case four decades ago.* This is owing, in part . . . to the spread of the council-manager form of municipal government and the establishment of local planning and zoning boards . . . to the excellent aids to municipal efficiency rendered by such national organizations as the "1313" group with headquarters in Chicago and such citizen associations as the National Municipal League and the Governmental Research Association and . . . to the effective work of the various foundations, educational institutions, state leagues of municipalities, and other agencies working for municipal improvements and civic advance. In other words, much . . . research and guidance . . . is now available for municipalities from sources other than the federal government; and municipal efficiency can thus be achieved with much less reliance on Uncle Sam than seemed to be essential four decades ago.[62]

Others are willing to admit that research on metropolitan area problems is needed, but argue that this is a staff function and would best be handled by a staff agency. They say that there should be an agency in the federal government concerned with urban and metropolitan areas and their problems, but that it should be a staff agency whose concern it would be to develop the facts about metropolitan area problems, which the President and his department and agency chiefs

---

* When *The American City* carried Philip Kates' article.

would take into account in framing policy. It is worth noting that the American Municipal Association, which advocated a line Department of Urban Affairs at its 1956 congress, had cooled off considerably toward the proposal by 1957. The declaration of policy adopted by the 1957 congress recommended instead creation of a staff agency, a Council of Urban Advisors, to study metropolitan problems and recommend solutions on the one hand, and to suggest a policy for the coordination of all federal programs affecting urban areas on the other. Sober second thought seems to have led AMA to the conclusion that although there is truth in the argument that research on urban problems is necessary, this does not require the creation of a new executive department.

Finally, say the opponents of the department, the greatest danger of all lies in the possibility that the creation of a Department of Urban Affairs would be accepted by government officials and others as settling the whole problem, when in reality it would provide only an organizational detail. Certainly city officials, the lobbyists they employ, and their organizations might welcome an executive department to use as a waste basket into which they could dump all the metropolitan problems referred to them and thus discharge their responsibilities.

A Department Rejected

One cannot but conclude that the opponents of a department have the better case. Formulation of a philosophy and evolution of a firm policy based thereon should precede designation of the agency to carry it out. Who executes policy is much less important than what the policy is. What is needed is not merely moving chessmen around on the board, but adopting rules for the game. Given the need for focusing the attention of the federal government on metropolitan area problems, creation of a Department of Urban Affairs or its equivalent is not the way to accomplish the objective. The proposal does not make political sense, it is not in accord with the administrative concepts on which the rest of the executive branch is based, and functionally it would add to the difficulties of effective administration.

Perhaps the most that can be said for a Department of Urban Affairs is that discussion of the idea keeps the need for action with regard to urban problems before the public. But such a department is not feasible at the present time. It is not beyond the realm of possibility, however, that, as federal activities in metropolitan areas continue to grow, as inevitably they will, an executive department may one day be established. If it is, past experience would indicate that it will result from a gradual evolutionary process over a period of years, as was the case with the Department of Agriculture and the Department of Health, Education and Welfare. In the meantime, there is much greater need for a presidential staff agency than for a new line department.

6

THE CASE FOR
FEDERAL ACTION

Much more important to the solution of metropolitan area problems in the long run than the decision whether a Department of Urban Affairs is to be established or not is a sound answer to the larger question of federal versus state responsibility in the matter. Any consideration of that question must take into account the American federal system. President Eisenhower himself posed the question in his 1957 Williamsburg speech, asking how, in coming to the assistance of state and local governments, the federal government could be confined to its proper role. Ever since President Eisenhower took office, some municipal officials have felt that there has been "a deliberate and determined effort on the part of the Administration to shed itself of every existing federal program it can conceive of as even remotely being a proper responsibility of the States." [1] To many, the continued expansion of federal activities in response to the crises of the past two decades has raised fears about "the continued vitality of our federal system." Indeed, it seems possible to some that if this trend continues the states will be reduced "to mere administrative provinces." [2] It is no secret that President Eisenhower shares these views, as evidenced by his Williamsburg speech, his wholehearted endorsement of the recommendations of the Joint Federal-State Action

Committee, and his recent veto messages. This is the climate in which metropolitan area problems are being considered today in the nation's capital, and even after 1960 it would be unrealistic to expect an immediate resolution of the issues raised in this debate.

Few would argue with the basic premise that the primary responsibility for solving the problems of metropolitan areas lies with local and state governments. Under our constitutional system, no other assignment is possible. On the other hand, few will disagree with the assertion that the very size and nature of the problem, if nothing else, make it a national issue, demanding national action.

Nature of the Metropolitan Problem

Before the federal government's role can be delineated, there must be some clear thinking about the implications of metropolitan life in the United States today and the nature of the problem this new way of life has created. More and more of the nation's population is living in urban areas. This fact has been repeated until it has become almost trite. The metropolitan problem in one sense is a compound of urban problems. But it is more than that. Luther Gulick has recently described it as the discontent of millions of human beings, dissatisfied with life in the great cities.

People are not satisfied with their homes and housing, with their trip to and from work, and with the aggravations, costs and delays of traffic and parking. They are distraught by the lack of schools and recreational facilities for their children and themselves, and they are concerned by social pressures, neighborhood conditions, youthful delinquency and crime. People find shopping difficult and more regimented, and the ever more needed services hard to get and expensive. They struggle with water shortages, with bad drainage and sewer conditions, with dirt and noise which they don't like. They find the city centers "old style," inconvenient, dismal and repulsive, and the old buses, streetcars, trains and other methods of mass movement uncomfortable and slow. . . . And when people move to the suburbs and take work in a new suburban factory, store or other enterprise, they find that many of the evils they sought to escape move in right after them, with mounting taxes to plague them there too.[3]

To be sure, it is easy to picture current conditions against what people would want if economic resources were not scarce. But economic resources are scarce—as they have always been—and people who depend on material things for the satisfactions of life will always be unhappy. Nevertheless, this widespread social dissatisfaction is one aspect of the metropolitan problem.

In part, the metropolitan problem is a psychological problem. The ties that bind the metropolitan community are not those that bound the typical rural community of the last century. Though there may be and often is a certain degree of neighborhood consciousness, and even of loyalty to an individual city in the metropolitan complex, there is no loyalty to the metropolitan area as a whole. In a real sense, when one speaks about metropolitan areas, the line of Gertrude Stein, "There is no there there," applies. Ever since the days of ancient Greece, man's first loyalties have been to his city, and this tradition still prevails in our own culture. Thus the achievement of a solution to the problems of metropolitan areas is handicapped by the fact that the metropolitan area is not even a symbol which attracts men. There still is no awareness of the larger community in the minds of residents of metropolitan areas.

The metropolitan problem is also one of urban economics. The past decade has witnessed unprecedented demands for housing, schools, highways, streets, hospitals, parks, modern commercial and industrial facilities, and all the other amenities that go with community life in the second half of the twentieth century. These demands will continue and in all probability will even become greater. The tremendous increases in productivity in the American economy and the steady uptrend of the American standard of living will undoubtedly result in a steadily increasing need for community services. These new pressures come at a time when governments in metropolitan centers have still not solved the problems created by today's population. Millions of American city dwellers live in substandard housing. Schools are overcrowded. Traffic congestion is rampant. There is a large backlog of need for modern water and sewage treatment facilities. The strain on municipal finances is currently aggravated by tight money and skyrocketing interest rates. In the face of all this, there is hardly a city in the nation that has the economic resources to solve its present problems, let alone those just over the horizon.

But more than anything else, the metropolitan problem is a political problem, and its solution must be through political means. The system of local government in use in the United States today dates from the eighteenth century, from a time when the problems of government were chiefly those of a rural population. The times have changed, but the system still prevails, aided and abetted in its survival by powerful vested interests, determined to prevent accommodation to the present. As the years have gone by, the states have sought to meet problems arising in urban areas without reorganizing local governments. Cities, counties, and towns have been joined by myriad single-purpose special governmental districts, which are allowed not only to overlap one another in a crazy-quilt pattern, but to cross and recross city, county, and town lines with reckless abandon.

Between 1952 and 1957, 519 new special district governments were created in metropolitan areas alone. As of January 1958, there were more than 15,000 local governmental units of one sort or another in the then 174 metropolitan areas in the United States, an average of 86 per area. Nine metropolitan areas had 250 or more local governments each, including the New York–Northeastern New Jersey area with more than 1,400 local units and the Chicago area with more than 900. Everywhere, metropolitan areas are characterized by divided governments and diffused political power.

Moreover, the character of the thing called a "metropolitan area" has changed since it was first defined by the Bureau of the Census in 1910.[4] Then it was regarded as a city having a population of at least 200,000 plus such densely populated places as lay within 10 miles of the boundaries of the central city. In 1910, no two metropolitan areas in the United States touched. Usually they were separated by miles of agricultural country or even wasteland. But today one metropolitan area grows into another until they form great metropolitan regions. By now, there are twenty-two such clusters in the United States. Where once each metropolitan area was a separate economic unit, today whole regions, composed of groups of metropolitan areas, are growing up. As a result, the time-honored formula that each metropolitan area is a separate unit and thus that its political needs can be met by annexing the suburbs no longer makes sense in many parts of the country. Certainly, annexation is no solution for a metropolitan cluster that runs from Springfield, Massachusetts, to Washington, D. C., and on to Norfolk, Virginia, a distance of 600 miles, with a width ranging from 10 to 60 miles. In fact, what form of governmental structure at the local level could possibly meet the governmental needs of so vast a social and economic aggregation? To assert that the problems of these areas can best be solved by local governments is ridiculous.

The metropolitan problem is made particularly difficult, in short, because a metropolitan area is not a legal entity as such, and thus has no recognized status in the governmental apparatus. Cities, towns, and counties do have separate legal status, but they deal only with affairs within their physical boundaries. Although there may be hundreds of municipal corporations within a single metropolitan area, the whole area does not exist as a government unit. Though the metropolis is the dominant pattern of American life, it is a pattern without legal recognition.

Inability of States to Meet the Problem

Every state, of course, has the power to bring at least some order out of this jurisdictional chaos and thus to facilitate an attack on problems in its own metropolitan areas. Nor is there any way by which states can escape their responsibility for their failure to act. By and large, state legislators and state executive officers are more oriented toward the rural voter and thus more representative of rural interests and concerned about rural problems than they are of urban voters and about urban interests. Thus they either fail to see the need for action in the first place, or tend to give urban problems short shrift when they are finally brought to their attention. In part, the states have been slow to act on the metropolitan problem for the same reason pressure groups and Congress have not acted: because the problem is not a monolithic one. Probably, very often, state legislatures have been faced with a wide divergence of metropolitan opinions about what should be done. Until representatives in the legislatures from these areas themselves can come to terms on the approaches to be taken, it is futile to expect the rest of the state legislature to act for them. In part, the states have ignored their metropolitan problems because they have felt unable to accomplish a solution within the limitations of their financial resources. To be sure, in the immediate postwar years the states had a financial surplus, but increased activity in many areas since then has in many cases exhausted their resources. Moreover, the tax advantage has lain increasingly with the federal government. To obtain new sources of revenue, it has pushed into the fields heretofore occupied by the states and their subdivisions. This has meant for the states a contracting area of potential taxation within which to meet the demands of an expanding number of services. In 1940, state and local governments received 60.6 per cent of the tax dollar collected in the United States, and the federal government 39.4 per cent. In 1956, just sixteen years later, the federal government received 72.3 per cent of the tax dollar and the states and local governments only 27.7 per cent.[5] This is a startling reversal, and it raises considerable doubt whether the states, even if they have the will to tackle metropolitan problems, can find a way to solve them alone.

Interstate Metropolitan Areas

The most important reason why the states cannot act, however, is that many metropolitan areas are not within the jurisdiction of any single state. According to the 1950 Census, 23 standard metropolitan areas extended across state boundary lines, and another 28 bordered very closely on a state line. Inevitably many of these will expand across state lines. Figure 2 shows five typical interstate metropolitan areas. Even in 1950, the population of the 23 areas which then crossed state lines amounted to almost 33 million, and of that number, more than one-fifth lived in a different state from the one in which the core city of the area was situated. The six largest accounted for over one-sixth of the total population of the United States, and the areas bordering on a state line accounted for almost another 10 million people. Thus a total of some 43 million people lived in such areas, or more than one out of every four people in the entire nation. The proportion is even higher today. Speculating upon the implications of these facts, Daniel R. Grant concluded that "with the bulk of our population increase presently taking place in the suburban fringes of metropolitan areas, there may well be more people living in interstate metropolitan areas than in intrastate cities of all sizes within the next generation or so." [6] Thus the interstate area is rapidly becoming the pattern for urban living.

Yet innumerable difficulties confront state action in providing adequate arrangements for interstate areas, particularly if they would involve the creation of an interstate agency with general governmental powers. Some of the difficulties are constitutional—many state constitutions would have to be amended to permit such action; others are legal—an extensive revision of state statutes would be necessary to make it possible; and

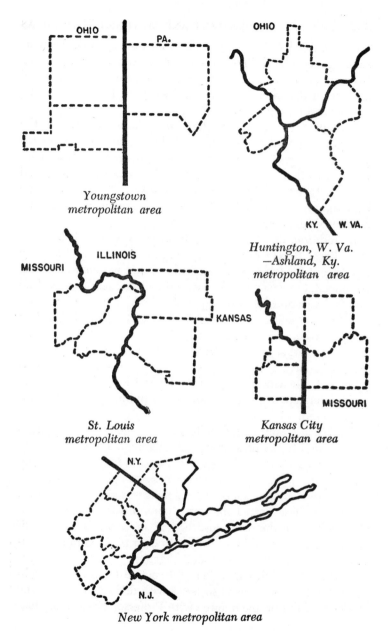

Youngstown
metropolitan area

Huntington, W. Va.
—Ashland, Ky.
metropolitan area

St. Louis
metropolitan area

Kansas City
metropolitan area

New York metropolitan area

Fig. 2. Some interstate metropolitan areas

some are fiscal. It is all very well to set up a specialized inter-state agency like the Port of New York Authority, which can live well on toll charges, but to create a general governmental agency on the interstate level and to grant it general taxing powers involves grave difficulties.

Perhaps even more important than these obstacles is the strength of popular emotional attachment to the present organization of government. People have always identified themselves with their city and their state. These are the traditional symbols to which their loyalties are given. A new interstate governing body for a whole metropolitan area would evoke no emotional response.

In addition, the American political party system is built on state lines. Rarely does a party organization cross the state line except for loose alliances made during national elections. An interstate agency would have no real political base and no political constituency. Consequently, the idea has little appeal to practical politicians. Nor does it attract political theorists, many of whom have doubts about interstate governing bodies, which are not subject to direct popular control. The only devices that have been developed for popular control, theorists point out, lie within state lines, and the question of how to make interstate agencies responsive to public opinion remains unanswered.

Finally, not only vested political but vested economic interests are tied to the present system. Differences in state regulations, tax systems, and license provisions in interstate areas all operate to the benefit of some business groups and to the disadvantage of others. Those who benefit would oppose change. Added to these vested interest groups are the thousands of officeholders in the many jurisdictions in interstate metropolitan areas. They would see a threat to their position in the creation of an interstate governmental agency.

In the light of this situation, state action to solve the problems of interstate areas is so beset with difficulties that many students of the problem agree with Professor Grant that "federal intervention is inevitable in one of two forms . . . [either] federal assumption of primary responsibility for those interstate metropolitan functions for which no adequate local authority exists . . . [or] federal stimulation, perhaps even coercion, of states and local governments toward creating new interstate instruments of integrated local government for the whole area." [7] Either way, it appears that some sort of federal action with regard to interstate metropolitan areas is required if their problems are to be solved.

International Metropolitan Communities

A number of important metropolitan communities lie athwart international boundaries, and this is another reason why states cannot handle the problem alone. The Detroit-Windsor and Buffalo areas on the Canadian border and the El Paso area on the Mexican border are already well-developed metropolitan areas, as figure 3 shows. The entire Rio Grande Valley, the San Diego area, and the Great Lakes–St. Lawrence region give promise of rapid urban development, which will result in an increase in metropolitan problems. Already sewage disposal, water supply, smoke abatement, water levels for navigation, and restrictions on truck transportation have become problems demanding attention and solution.

Take for example the Mexican boundary. Outside of Douglas, New Mexico, the ground slopes toward Mexico, and sewage flowed across the border. At Mexicali, raw sewage dumped into a river on the Mexican side of the border flowed into the business section of Calexico on the United States side. Prolonged negotiations between the two governments finally led to the erection of two sewage treatment plants, one at Douglas, the other at Mexicali, the costs of which were shared by the two national governments. The rapid settlement of the lower Rio Grande Valley, however, indicates that the day is not far off when a solution to the problem of water pollution in the entire river basin must be found. Then the erection of adequate sewage systems and treatment plants will have to be undertaken as a unit, since most of the communities in the valley use the river for water supply as well as sewage disposal.

There are other problems as well. El Paso, the only metropolitan area in the upper Rio Grande Valley, has difficulties because of the shifting course of the river. Urban development

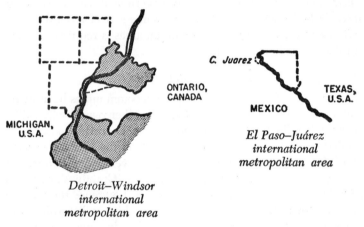

ONTARIO,
CANADA

MICHIGAN,
U.S.A.

*Detroit–Windsor
international
metropolitan area*

C. Juarez

MEXICO

TEXAS,
U.S.A.

*El Paso–Juárez
international
metropolitan area*

Fig. 3. The Detroit and El Paso international metropolitan areas

has been held up there for long periods of time while the Mexican and United States governments tried to decide who owned the new land along the river. More troublesome to the economic development of the region are restrictions on free movement of trucks across the border. California and Arizona permit reciprocal licensing of trucks, but Texas does not. Even the location of customs facilities has an impact on the border communities. These are only a few of the problems which plague these communities. None of them can be solved within the context of local government alone. Since they involve relations between sovereign powers, their solution properly lies within the federal government's jurisdiction.

The United States–Canadian border presents even more immediate and complex problems. For example, water pollution is forbidden in boundary areas. Away back in 1912, when the

International Joint Commission first began operations, it made an investigation of pollution, and ever since that time it has had jurisdiction to take the steps necessary to remove it. Yet forty years and more have passed, and still pollution of the boundary waters is taking place to an extent which is injurious to health and property, principally by reason of domestic sewage and industrial waste.[8] It is evident from its own reports that despite continued efforts to prevent pollution, the International Joint Commission has not been successful in solving this problem, particularly in heavily populated metropolitan regions. Today the most serious pollution problems are in the waters of Lake Huron and Lake Erie and in the upper St. Clair and lower Detroit rivers. To remove pollution there will probably require the expenditure of hundreds of millions of dollars on the Canadian side and somewhat less on the American side. The situation has been made immeasurably complex not only because this is a metropolitan problem and an international problem, but also because of the way the two federal systems operate. The Dominion government has taken the position that the construction of sewage treatment plants is a provincial matter, and the Province of Ontario, though it is willing to guarantee municipal bonds and build sewage trunk lines, maintains that the local governments should bear the cost of building the plants themselves. For its part, the United States government has been willing to do no more than the minimum allowed under the Federal Water Pollution Control Act, and none of the border states involved have shown any interest in the problem at all. As a result, the whole matter has been left in the lap of a hundred or more local communities on both sides of the border, despite the fact that it fairly cries for a unified approach. All the while the situation grows steadily worse.

In 1949, the International Joint Commission began a study of air pollution problems upon the receipt of numerous complaints in the Windsor-Detroit metropolitan area, which lies on both sides of the Detroit River for a distance of 30 miles and goes inland for about 15 miles. It included about 3,000,000 people on the Michigan side and 160,000 on the Canadian side. The region contained the third largest concentration of industry in North America. Scientific studies indicated the presence of a very high concentration of dust and chemicals in the air over the region. The dust fall in the Windsor region was nearly double that found in Pittsburgh. During the navigation season, the Detroit River carried one of the largest vessel traffic loads in the world. There were more than 30,000 vessels passing each year at Detroit, many of which were old-type lake vessels burning coal. They were responsible for a great deal of air pollution. In 1950, it was reported that 77.5 per cent of the vessels were smoking excessively and that they smoked over 50 per cent of the time.[9] The International Joint Commission did undertake an educational campaign among shipping companies and was able to reduce pollution temporarily. Nevertheless, air pollution continues to be a major problem in communities on the Canadian border. Its solution is obviously beyond the reach of local governments acting alone.

The International Joint Commission was also given jurisdiction over cases involving the use, obstruction, and diversion of boundary waters. The treaty prescribes an order of precedence for the use of boundary waters, as follows: domestic and sanitary purposes, navigation, power, and irrigation; and it provides that no individual or corporation may erect a dam on a boundary stream without the permission of the Commission. Thus in the very exercise of its treaty-making power, the federal government is already involved in metropolitan area problems. Commission investigations included the advisability of a waterway through Lake Champlain to connect with the Hudson River, which would involve water rights not only of the city of Montreal at one end and of New York City at the other, but also of some half dozen American and Canadian cities in between.

In recent years, matters having to do with electric power allocation and development, which have many repercussions in metropolitan areas, have been referred to the Commission. An important case now pending concerns the request of the Canadian government that electric power from Grand Coulee Dam be furnished the city of Vancouver at the same rate as that given to the city of Seattle. This would place Vancouver in a much better competitive position vis-à-vis the American Pacific Northwest cities. The Canadians have also announced that they are seriously considering a proposal to reverse the flow of the Columbia River in Canada, an action which would greatly reduce the amount of water in the Grand Coulee and Bonneville dams. To support their right to make this diversion, the Canadians cite a twenty-year-old decision of the United States Attorney General which was originally applied to the Mexican border, concerning the right of upstream nations to do what they want with the water. The Canadians in effect said that, unless the whole border area were treated as a single unit for electric power purposes, they would retain water in streams flowing across the border for their own use.

From their very nature, it is obvious that problems such as these that affect metropolitan areas on our national boundaries cannot be handled either by the communities themselves or fully by the states. And the mechanisms created by the federal government so long ago to settle disputes in boundary areas are limited in scope, and operate as adjuncts to its conduct of foreign affairs. Since then, border communities have grown greatly, and they promise to develop even more in the years ahead. Detroit, Buffalo, Seattle-Vancouver have all become great industrial areas, and the completion of the St. Lawrence Seaway will surely stimulate further development. Indeed, considerable development is already well under way. Neither the State Department nor the International Commissions were intended to deal with the complex problems that these great metropolitan areas present. Though it goes without saying that on all matters of foreign relations the federal government properly occupies the center of the stage, and that any solution to the problems of government in metropolitan areas along our national borders must take place within that context, it cannot be emphasized too strongly that Washington has not yet faced up to the facts of the situation. Until the federal government does so and decides what its policy will be with regard to them, neither the local communities nor the states involved can be expected to solve their problems.

Contacts across the border generally are not close at the local level, with certain notable exceptions, as for example in the Buffalo area. When problems arise, protests come to the State Department, frequently through congressmen. Sometimes our neighbors originate the complaint through their Foreign Office. Some problems can be settled by the International Boundary Commission, established by treaty between the United States and Mexico in 1884, and the International Joint Commission, created by treaty between Canada and the United States in 1909. But neither the State Department nor the International Commissions are equipped to deal with problems of metropolitan government. There are no municipal or metropolitan government specialists *per se* in the State Department or on the staffs of the Commissions.

Foreign service officers are selected for their knowledge of diplomatic history, not for their knowledge of local government. One Desk Officer interviewed by the authors began the conference with the remark: "Good heavens, I hope you are not going to ask me how a city council is elected, because I really haven't the faintest idea." State Department personnel do a conscientious job in negotiating with their opposite numbers in foreign offices across the border, but they know so little about the problems of government in metropolitan areas that they overlook many important factors. To make it even worse, the State Department operates on a rotation principle. Officers are moved frequently. Thus not only do most officers come to their jobs ignorant of metropolitan area problems, but just when they may have developed some familiarity with the problems in a particular area—in border communities, for example— they are transferred to new duties, and their experience amounts to naught. Finally, the problems of border communities are lost in the routine business of geographic area desks. There is no special device by which to isolate them and bring them up for action and solution.

The two International Commissions are no better. Hailed when they were created as examples of successful international co-operation and as means of negotiating particular problems, they were not conceived of as having broad assignments which would include the solution of metropolitan area problems. Their primary concerns are with technical engineering problems and with points of international law, and, as a result, they are staffed by engineers and lawyers. Moreover, they function as quasi-judicial bodies and were intended to be remote from the main stream of governmental activity, insulated from the process of everyday policy formulation.

In summary, there is no effective machinery in the federal government for recognizing and solving problems that arise in international metropolitan communities. Each time a problem arises it must be approached in a very cumbersome way, either through special legislation or through the quasi-judicial processes of an international commission. Yet the number and complexity of the problems of ordinary living in these communities increase daily.

Need for Federal Action

If the primary responsibility for solving the metropolitan area problem rests with the states and their local subdivisions, it is nevertheless true that by now the solution of the problem, not only for interstate and international metropolitan areas but for those within single states as well, has become too important to be put entirely on the shoulders of only one of the partners in the federal system. This new pattern of settlement is a national phenomenon and as such necessarily involves the other partner, the federal government, in its accommodation. Not that the entire problem of adjustment should simply be transferred to Washington; it cannot and should not be. But neither can the federal government be indifferent to the fate of nearly two-thirds of the nation's population, which will shortly be living in those areas. After all, as Mayor Richard J. Daley of Chicago pointed out recently, metropolitan area problems concern the federal government "because they concern people. The Federal Government is concerned with people," and the bulk of those people "are in cities all over America." [10] The effective government of so much of the country's population and the solution of the problems which face them are necessarily matters of prime importance to Washington. Indifference to the problem as a whole, or the extension of mere sympathy and encouragement to the states in their efforts to solve it, or even a continuation of the existing hit-and-miss program will no longer do. It has been obvious for some time not only that the "people and the governments of the metropolitan areas cannot solve their problems with the governmental and private devices now available," [11] but also that the states, acting by themselves, can supply only part of the deficiency. The rest must be made up in Washington, if it is to be made up at all.

The lack of state action and the force of mere numbers are not the only reasons for federal action in the solution of the metropolitan area problem. The role metropolitan areas play in the national economy is enough in itself to make their fullest possible development a vital concern of the federal government. Indeed, "the problems of our metropolitan communities are so directly tied to growth in population, to growth in industry and commerce, to income, employment and unemployment, and to the movement of persons and goods . . . that the problems of any one metropolitan community cannot possibly be handled in isolation and apart from the whole national system of cities and regions." [12] Both transportation and communication networks are centralized in the nation's metropolitan areas. In them is centered our industrial prowess. In them live the bulk of all our skilled artisans, as well as of our executive personnel. It does not exaggerate too much to say that on their welfare depends not only the welfare of the entire nation, but its security in the world of today.

Economic and Social Importance

Unfortunately, exact statistics are not available to demonstrate precisely the full economic stake which the nation has in its metropolitan areas. It is indicative of the general lack of recognition given to the problems of metropolitan areas that as yet no adequate statistical basis has been developed for urban research. However, enough of the relative position of the standard metropolitan areas in the national economy can be gleaned from the *County and City Data Book* of the Bureau of the Census to demonstrate that those areas account for over 75 per cent of the national total in manufactures, in wholesale and retail sales, and in receipts in the service trades, as well as for the bulk of all non-farm real estate in the country. In addition, a "crude effort" made in 1953 to derive a percentage of the national income originating in these areas set it "in a range of 65 to 70%." [13] A government which is pledged by law to assume responsibility for full employment and national prosperity necessarily has a major interest in the areas which produce such a great majority of the nation's wealth.

Moreover, it is chiefly in the nation's metropolitan areas that the cultural, educational, and scientific centers of American life are found. The rest of the nation has long looked to the cities for cultural leadership through newspapers and radio, theaters and libraries, universities and museums. Hospitals and research groups are predominantly located in cities. In an era of increasing recognition of the importance of science and education to successful long-term competition for world leadership, the federal government's interest in maintaining the health of such centers is obvious. Although no tradition of direct governmental responsibility for the arts and sciences has developed in the United States, the dependence on them of both the nation's security and its future growth implies active governmental concern about their continued strength. To the degree that their strength is derived from their location in metropolitan areas, the federal government cannot avoid assuming some degree of responsibility for the development of those areas.

More than anything else, however, federal action with regard to government in metropolitan areas is demanded by the kind of problems those areas face today. Far from being matters of local or even state-wide concern, the most vital metropolitan area problems are at the same time problems of utmost concern to our national defense, to the conservation of natural resources, and to the maintenance of national health and welfare. They are problems of national dimensions, affecting the lives of all Americans, no matter where they live. So closely knit is our economic and industrial system today that what strikes at the metropolitan nerve centers of the nation is felt throughout the country. As shown above, it was demand for aid in solving these problems on the part of individual cities that first brought the federal government into the picture. The fact that many of them have become aggravated with the passage of time makes an integrated federal program imperative. Even if the theory of federalism would seem to allot the responsibility for some of the problems to the states, because of their very nature the federal government cannot avoid responsibility for aiding in their solution.

Defense Considerations

In case of the involvement of the United States in another major conflict, metropolitan mass transit, without substantial assistance, could not absorb the added burden that would be placed upon it by wartime industrial demands, handicapped as it would be by gasoline rationing and restriction of automobile production. Probably no problem is more readily apparent in most metropolitan areas than the inability of older transit systems to handle present-day traffic, to say nothing of future transportation requirements. Central cities in many metropolitan areas are ghost towns from 5 P.M. to 7 A.M. Workers flock to the suburbs after work—"the dormitory suburbs," they have been called—only to flock back again the next morning. Mass transit facilities must be able to accommodate the flood twice a day, yet are expected to remain idle and unused the rest of the time.

In recent years the trend toward private automobiles has further weakened the economic position of mass transit facilities, both by offering strenuous competition to them on the one hand and by clogging streets with surface traffic on the other, thereby making efficient service impossible. Clogged streets result in dropping downtown property values, and decreasing property values are quickly followed by economic readjustments which profoundly affect employment, sales, and production in downtown areas, which again react negatively upon mass transit facilities. A vicious circle of major proportions is thus well established in most metropolitan areas, yet no local body is competent to tackle the problem and to assure that the area as a whole will continue to be provided with a decent, effective, and economic mass transportation system. Today, metropolitan mass transit facilities have reached so low an ebb that it is doubtful in many cases whether they could be counted on in any future defense preparations this country might be forced to make. Yet, as President Eisenhower himself has said, "America is in an era when defensive and productive strength require the absolute best that we can have." [14]

The mass transit problem is only one part of the nation's transportation problem, and it cannot be solved by itself. As Senator Keating has recently pointed out, the federal government, in its regulation of railroads, cannot overlook its responsibility to the commuter.[15] Though some parts of the problem are susceptible to state and local action, in many metropolitan communities no solution can be found without the active participation of the federal government. Annoying as this whole situation is to everyday peacetime living, it is a matter of vital concern in considering the nation's defense.

The highway problem is equally serious, and here again, defense considerations alone make federal responsibility a necessity. The House Committee on Public Roads, commenting in 1956 on the expanded National System of Interstate Highways, noted that it "contains only 1.2 per cent of total United States road mileage, [but] when completed . . . it may be expected to carry twenty per cent of the nation's total traffic load." [16] The defense importance of that system is obvious. But defense is not the only consideration. As President Eisenhower told the Governors' Conference in 1954, in a message to the meeting held at Bolton's Landing, New York, the country urgently needs better and safer highways both to keep pace with its over-all economic development and to reduce the appalling toll of death and injury from traffic accidents. In 1952 President Eisenhower recognized the need for "a grand plan for a properly articulated highway system that solves the problems of speedy, safe, transcontinental travel . . . intercity transportation . . . access highways . . . and farm to farm movement . . . metropolitan area congestion . . . bottlenecks and parking." [17] Since then the new highway program has been launched, but solution of the highway problems both of central cities and of their metropolitan fringes is requisite to the development of an adequate national highway program.

In many areas today, the demand for outdoor recreation resources and facilities far outstrips supply. Yet metropolitan communities, where the bulk of the American people live, are not generally able to develop adequate plans to meet their recreational needs. Because so many metropolitan areas are already interstate and international, and others are becoming so, to meet the demand for recreational facilities in time and on a large enough scale requires federal action. Moreover, because of the federal government's extensive commitments in highway construction in urban areas and in a variety of urban renewal and redevelopment projects, it must be a part of the team when plans for future land use to provide for recreational facilities are being formulated. In addition, as the Arden House Conference on Metropolitan Problems noted, the current concern with juvenile delinquency gives "added urgency" to the whole recreation problem.[18] As one way to combat juvenile delinquency, which again has become a problem of national dimensions, the Conference suggested federal co-operation in meeting the recreational needs of school-age boys who otherwise would be confined to city streets all summer.[19] Indeed, the creation of the National Outdoor Recreation Resources Review Commission by the Eighty-fifth Congress indicates a recognition of the need for federal action in this field.[20]

Public Health Requirements

As noted above, almost every metropolitan area suffers to some degree from the lack of a sufficient supply of water. The rivers which supply many of the nation's most important metropolitan areas are interstate or international. For example, as figure 4 shows, the Columbia and the Connecticut river basins are sources of water not for a single state but for entire regions, including a number of states. The Delaware, the Ohio, the St. Lawrence, and, of course, the Mississippi are further illustrations of the point. Every survey made in recent years of national water resources agrees that their most efficient development lies in comprehensive planning of an entire river system for many purposes.[21] Such planning is very complex; it must include more than the local governments concerned, more than the states involved. For "it is the people that a Nation's water resources policy must be designed to serve." "A well-rounded national water resources policy . . . must be a broad reflection of the lives of the people on their farms, in their villages and cities, in their regions, and in the Nation as a whole." [22] Such a policy can be evolved only by the initiative and under the leadership of the federal government.

Water pollution is closely related to the problem of water supply. "Pollution can be just as effective in reducing a water resource for use as drought. Pollution control, therefore, is now recognized as a key to the national problem of water conservation." [23] The expansion of population and industry in the nation's metropolitan areas has been one of the prime causes

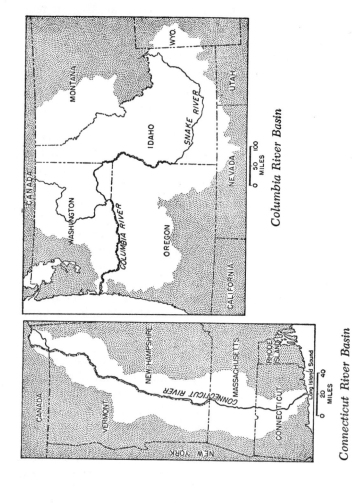

Columbia River Basin

Connecticut River Basin

Fig. 4. Interstate river basins

fer the tremendous increase in the amount of sewage and industrial waste dumped into the nation's waters in the past thirty years. Sewers and sewage disposal plants were largely designed for and confined to the central cities when they were originally constructed. As population expanded into the suburban fringes of those cities after 1920, vast problems of waste collection and sewage disposal arose as the result of the lower suburban density of population and of the unequal distribution of taxable property among the suburbs, as well as of the inadequate co-ordination which results from the maze of overlapping governmental jurisdictions characteristic of metropolitan areas. Even today, sewage and waste disposal plants are provided independently by municipalities and industries on a small-scale and uneconomic basis. As a result, the raw sewage equivalent dumped into American streams and rivers has increased by almost 50 per cent since 1920, and industrial wastes have increased by over 100 per cent in the same period.[24] On the basis of such evidence, the Kestnbaum Commission concluded that stream pollution is "one of the Nation's most serious public health problems." [25]

The House Committee on Public Works figured in 1955 that municipal pollution abatement needs for the next ten years, if met, would cost $5.33 billion, and that another $5.5 billion would be required for the construction of adequate new sewer systems in the same period.[26] The fact that many of the rivers and streams involved are navigable streams already under federal jurisdiction, and the number of instances in which the waste from cities and industries in one state pollutes the waters of another state, led the Kestnbaum Commission to recommend "increased participation of the National Government in coping with this hazard to domestic and industrial water users." [27] On the ground of the national health and welfare alone, the federal government's responsibility for action with regard to this problem in metropolitan areas is manifest.

Slum clearance and urban renewal, as has already been pointed out, is another metropolitan area problem of obvious importance to the federal government if national health is to be maintained and if cities are to remain the vital industrial workshops of the nation. At the core of every metropolitan area in the nation today are one or more old central cities, the hearts of which have been blighted more or less seriously by unsightly and unhealthy slums. It has been the desire of most city dwellers to have the modern equivalent of forty acres and a mule— a house of their own in the suburbs and a car to carry them back and forth to work—that has produced the metropolitan explosion. As thousands of people in downtown residential areas have realized their dreams and left the core cities to live in the suburbs, many old downtown residential areas have deteriorated to the point where they have become cancers gnawing at the vitals of the whole area's prosperity. Virtually every American community has felt the scourge of the slums. "Slums have spread so far, their costs have become so great, that they have become a problem of national dimensions and concern." [28]

By now, urban blight and slums constitute one of the greatest peacetime economic problems that confront America. For cities must be renewed; they deteriorate more rapidly than they can be constructed, added to, or repaired. Yet the "real and total costs of urban renewal are almost beyond cities' and citizens' comprehension." They will total almost "two trillion dollars by 1970," concludes one expert in the field. Even though the "responsibilities and requirements involved are predominantly those of private enterprise . . . necessary Federal participation expenditures alone will rival those for national security." [29] Slums have become more than an economic problem. They constitute a serious social problem as well, involving important considerations of human welfare. The Congress of the United States itself recognized these considerations in its "Declaration of National Housing Policy," prefacing the Housing Act of 1949, which states that "the general welfare and security of the Nation and the health and living standards of its people require . . . the elimination of substandard and other inadequate housing through the clearance of slums and blighted areas, and the realization as soon as possible of the goal of a decent home and a suitable living environment for every American family, thus contributing to the development and redevelopment of communities and to the advancement of the growth, wealth, and security of the Nation." [30] That good housing and a sound living environment for American families are most important aspects of human welfare,[31] and as such are areas of activity which cannot be ignored by the federal government, is no longer debatable. Many of the problems which the federal government is now attacking in the field of public health are but parts of the larger problem of slums. To solve them requires solution of the basic problem as well.

Although air pollution—"Garbage in the Sky" [32]—is a relatively new metropolitan problem, it has already assumed alarming proportions. In his special message to Congress on national health problems, January 31, 1955, President Eisenhower noted that "as a result of industrial growth and urban development, the atmosphere over some population centers may be approaching the limit of its ability to absorb air pollutants with safety to health." [33] Indeed, air pollution is now seen as a possible source of lung cancer, asthma, and other diseases. But, as the President observed, air pollution is primarily a problem of metropolitan areas. The effects of polluted air are not confined to the air over the metropolitan area from which it originates, nor indeed to the boundaries of any area or state. Polluted air moves wherever the winds carry it, with the result that air pollution is fast becoming a menace to the nation's health, and to the safety and comfort of people in many areas and in widely separated parts of the country. Nor are its effects interstate alone; they are even international. The problem is made all the more serious because of experiments with atomic explosions. In this connection, Dr. Alan T. Waterman, Director of the National Science Foundation, noted that "the problems of radio-active air pollution resulting from operations directly controlled by the Federal Government lie peculiarly within the province of the Federal Government. . . . therefore . . . the Federal Government should undertake responsibility for the control and prevention of such hazards." [34] Both because of the growing danger of air pollution to national health in general and because of the federal government's part in creating the menace in the first place, the necessity of federal action to aid in solving the air pollution problem is beyond question.

Civil Defense

The 1950 Census showed that 40 per cent of the population of the United States and over half of all persons employed in manufacturing live in just forty metropolitan areas, and since then, the proportion has increased. It is obvious that in this thermonuclear age a single explosion can effectively destroy an entire metropolitan center, and prospective weapons promise the possibility of even more widespread destruction. Present legislation in the United States still leaves responsibility for solving the problem of civil defense divided between the states and the federal government. But there is increasing evidence that the possibilities of national catastrophe are so great that a larger and more active federal role is mandatory. [35] A recent study by the House Military Operations Subcommittee predicts that a thermonuclear attack on the 150 largest cities in the United States could wipe out 70 per cent of the nation's industry and kill about 90 per cent of the population. In the face of such a threat, the Subcommittee concluded that "to save over 90 per cent of the population and restore the pre-attack American standard of living in less than ten years should be sufficient incentive to give civil defense its rightful place in the defense system." Only by the federal government's assumption of primary responsibility in this field can that place be assured.

Co-operative Federalism

The list of metropolitan area problems could be expanded much further, [36] and in each case need for the assumption of federal responsibility could be demonstrated. The need is not for the federal government to take over the entire metropolitan area problem, lock, stock, and barrel. Democracy must of necessity resist the temptation to concentrate all powers of the state in one organ. The need is rather for the federal government to recognize and accept its share of responsibility on the one hand, and on the other hand to devise a coherent and comprehensive policy, within the framework of the federal system, to guide it in its actions. To date, Washington has done neither, nor does it appear that action in either direction will soon be forthcoming. Indeed, no consensus has yet been reached about what the federal government's role should be. Thus it has not been possible to devise any kind of policy. As Robert Daland noted recently, "It is almost a shock to realize that while we can turn to revealing analyses of [federal] agricultural policy, labor policy, tax policy or resources policy, we have no exposition of urbanism policy." [37] Such a policy must be developed, however, if the federal government is to assist effectively in the solution of the metropolitan problem.

The philosophy of the Eisenhower Administration as expressed by the President himself innumerable times is that the federal government's power must always be "counterbalanced," "checked," "hedged about," and "restrained" in order to prevent it from poaching on the states' preserves. To President Eisenhower, the main functions of domestic government lie within those preserves. Thus, although both President Eisenhower and the Kestnbaum Commission recognized the existence of the metropolitan area problem, the solution they suggested lies within the framework of this philosophy; namely, that the states should and could take the major responsibility for solving it. Indeed, the report of the Kestnbaum Commission emphasizes the role of the states, and Mr. Kestnbaum himself has said that "many of the most fundamental recommendations contained in the [Commission's] report are directed to the states and to local governments and their implementation is dependent very largely on State action." [38] Both the Commission's report and its *Advisory Committee Report on Local Government* contain a whole list of exhortations to the states to solve the metropolitan area problem:

It is clearly the responsibility of the States to assume leadership in solving the problems of metropolitan government.

Representation in the state legislatures should be on a fair and equitable basis.

State constitutions should not include undue limitations on the right of legislatures to levy and distribute revenue.

State legislation should make available to local governments the widest possible range of revenue sources.

The States should redistribute to local governments a substantial portion of the revenues they collect.

State governments should recognize the pressing metropolitan problems not only in their central cities but also in the emerging communities in the unincorporated fringe areas and in the suburban cities.[39]

And there are others still. All serve to emphasize the Commission's conviction that the problem of government in metropolitan areas, like most other domestic problems, must be solved primarily by the states.

All these recommendations were made in 1955, but in the years since, the states have done virtually nothing to put any of them into effect. Mr. Kestnbaum himself admits discouragement on this score.[40] Indeed, all that he can really say is that "certain aspects of the Report are receiving . . . attention by groups within the States," and that "there are many evidences of a growing acceptance of the Commission's proposal that States engage in a process of self-scrutiny."[41] Despite the manifest failure of the states to act, Mr. Kestnbaum still feels convinced that it is their responsibility. If they do not act, there is nothing to be done about metropolitan areas. Mr. Kestnbaum does believe, however, that some day, in some metropolitan area, things will become so critical that the state will finally act. Then the dam will be broken, and the wheels will begin to grind. But is this the kind of policy the nation can afford?

The basic difficulty is that the Administration seems committed to the old-fashioned notion that federalism is an "either-or" proposition, that it consists of two separate spheres, and that the states carry the main burden for action on the domestic front. Even a cursory examination of Supreme Court decisions over the past half century, however, demonstrates that such a notion was long ago outmoded. Congress in many instances, as has been indicated above, has also made it clear that it does not hold to this view. And however much the Kestnbaum report seems to say otherwise, a careful examination of it reveals that it too worked from a different premise. For the Commission rejected the "either-or" theory as extreme, saying that "the National Government and the States should not be regarded as competitors for authority but as two levels of government cooperating with or complementing each other in meeting the growing demands in both." [42]

To be sure, the strengthening of state government is an important objective. State governments should be more representative; state fiscal systems should be reformed in numerous ways to permit metropolitan areas to obtain their fair share of the state's financial resources; and states should revise their constitutions and their statutes to permit more effective handling of metropolitan areas. But such things are long-term goals. They cannot be attained in just a few years. In the meantime, metropolitan problems mount almost in geometrical progression. The metropolis and all the problems it brings with it demand attention now. The problems are too grave and the risk too great to wait any longer. The urgent need today is for action, growing out of bold and creative thinking across the broad front of metropolitan area problems. The sheer force of population growth will force some sort of solution. It is up to Washington to assure the nation that the solution finally adopted will be the wisest and best for the long-term welfare and security of the nation as a whole.

Such a course of action should be one of co-operative federalism, a principle which has long been accepted as a wise basis for action in the United States. Agriculture is one of the fields where the principle in operation has yielded bountiful results. But although it has been applied piecemeal in the solution of many urban problems, it has been used with a bad conscience and with numerous apologies. As a result, the metropolitan problem has not been approached as a whole, nor have the responsibilities of the federal government been frankly recognized. Given a true understanding of the nature of modern American federalism, the national government can provide leadership, research, and incentives which will go a long way toward solving the problems of government in metropolitan areas. In the words of Senator Vance Hartke of Indiana, "The Federal Government . . . can provide the incentive to pool information, talent, energy, and resources to focus attention on metropolitan problems and suggested solutions. It can help anticipate and plan. It can help gain public support and understanding. . . . [what is needed is] a strategy for urban development. To be meaningful the strategy should have national leadership." [43]

Woodrow Wilson long ago saw the flexibility of our federal system as one of its greatest advantages. Today the need is greater than ever to take advantage of that flexibility. The federal government must take the initiative in meeting the challenge of the metropolis. As the Rockefeller Brothers Fund report stated, "The metropolitan sprawl does not stop at city, county, or even state boundaries. It is generally intergovernmental, often interstate, sometimes international. Imagination and experimentation will be needed to develop the political structures necessary for the . . . governmental services" required to solve its problems.[44] The federal government must give metropolitan areas, with their huge populations, their dynamic economies, their world influence and social importance, a greater share of its attention than they so far have been accorded.

7

RECOMMENDATIONS

As the federal government moves to act on the metropolitan area problem, it begins with a severe handicap. It lacks knowledge, first of all, of the extent and complexity of the problem the nation faces. Not only is there no basis of fact regarding the total impact of its many activities in metropolitan areas on which to build, but its statistical procedures are not designed to produce the raw data for metropolitan areas as such, from which the basic facts can be derived. Even in its collection of urban data, there are a number of obvious gaps. The definition of a standard metropolitan area used by the Bureau of the Census still needs to be revised. Even the new definition of a "Standard Metropolitan Statistical Area" is built on a county basis. But counties which impinge on metropolitan areas often have a vast hinterland of sparsely settled rural territory which is far from being metropolitan in any sense of the term. San Bernardino County in southern California is a good example. Whereas the western end of the county is in fact part of the Los Angeles urban complex, the eastern part runs two hundred miles back into the desert. Yet all of it, by the Bureau of the Census definition, is part of the Los Angeles metropolitan area.

Moreover, knowledge is lacking about what happens when a federal program is put into effect in a metropolitan area so far as the total resources and social structure of the community are concerned, and even less is known about the total effect of a series of federal programs on a single metropolitan area. This was pointed out emphatically in the Kestnbaum report. Part of the trouble results from not knowing exactly how much federal money is spent in individual metropolitan areas. These data are available in the files of the operating agencies, but have never been put together in terms of metropolitan areas. As a preliminary step, exact data should be gathered on federal expenditures in major metropolitan areas over the past decade. Subsequently, a study should be made of the total impact of federal programs on government in metropolitan areas.

Because exact data are lacking, as this study has repeatedly emphasized, all recommendations for action to solve metropolitan problems must be predicated on a great deal of assumption. Nor is it possible, for the same reason, to spell out in great detail what should be done. A more solid basis of factual knowledge than is now available would be required for such a project. The recommendations which follow are therefore based, of necessity, on the facts which are most clearly evident.

There is reason to believe that federal programs are piling up on each other faster than metropolitan areas can digest them. Each is planned separately, and there is no correlation among them. Programs are launched in isolation, without reference to their impact on the areas to which they are directed. As a consequence, federal programs are badly co-ordinated so far as metropolitan areas are concerned, both among themselves and in terms of state and local programs in the same areas. Federal programs having a bearing on metropolitan problems should be re-examined in order to assure better coordination and to provide the maximum flexibility and a minimum of standardization as to detail and procedure.

Moreover, the federal government in its grant-in-aid programs should encourage the creation of larger units of government to fit present social and economic realities in metropolitan areas. In particular, it ought not to require the continued existence of outmoded local governmental units by limiting its grants to cities when action over a larger area is needed. The example set in the housing program, to provide assistance for broad over-all metropolitan planning, should be followed in other areas. The federal government should assist in the preparation of plans by providing technical aid, information, and financial assistance, and it should require all federal and federal grant-in-aid programs, including highways and recreation, as well as housing and urban renewal, to be related to comprehensive metropolitan plans.

Federal programs for the most part are concerned with unrelated physical things—buildings, highways, airports—but there is a magnificent unconcern about the people who are displaced by these activities. The elimination of slums, for example, is going on at such breakneck speed that many more people are left homeless than ever before, crowding is getting worse, and delinquency is increasing. To be sure, one cannot make omelets without breaking eggs, but the life of a community is as important as its physical development, and both should be taken into account. Moreover, it should be recognized that massive urban relocation breaks up long-established community patterns. Replacing slum dwellings with new and sterile housing projects which offer no encouragement to rebuilding community life will have serious repercussions on metropolitan living. The relocation of these displaced people and the solution of all the social problems their movement entails should be the joint responsibility of the federal government and the local communities.

In interstate metropolitan areas, the federal government should recognize its special responsibilities by offering incentives to the states involved to co-operate with one another and with the federal government in attacking particular problems on an area-wide basis. The states should be encouraged to make broader use of all sorts of co-operative arrangements, including interstate compacts, in attacking metropolitan area problems. Congress could do much to encourage the use of compacts by simplifying its own legislative procedures for dealing with them and by the passage of general permissive legislation. The federal government should give the nation a good example by speedily implementing the recommendations of the Bible Committee for the Washington metropolitan area. It should also grant the District of Columbia greater freedom to solve its own problems, and by a policy of self-restraint should refrain from constant interference with local policy formation in the District.

With regard to international metropolitan areas, the federal government should recognize that such areas have many of the same governmental problems that domestic metropolitan areas have, and it ought to facilitate the creation of local planning agencies or other appropriate devices for each of these areas. Moreover, since many problems of these areas will still have to be handled through ordinary diplomatic channels, the federal government should make certain that the International Commissions and the Department of State have personnel on their staffs who are familiar with metropolitan government and its problems.

Under the American system of government, unless the President provides leadership, no great amount of progress can be made in solving any problem. None of the recent presidents have been concerned with government in metropolitan areas; their neglect has affected both the legislative and the executive branches, and has been felt from top to bottom of the administrative pyramid and far beyond into the tentacles of the operating agencies. Presidential interest in metropolitan areas must be aroused before effective action can be expected. Lacking presidential leadership, Congress has been slow to appreciate the magnitude of the problem. Consequently, it has not given a high priority to considering ways in which the federal government could aid in solving it. Structural changes, such as those suggested below, can provide for better integration of federal programs, but mere structural change cannot make its maximum contribution until both the President and Congress have been made fully conscious of their responsibilities for action.

Urban needs have not received anything like the recognition

that has been given to agriculture and the needs of rural areas because in many federal agencies there is a conspicuous lack of people with training and experience in the governmental problems of metropolitan areas. One of the reasons American agriculture has made the great strides it has in less than a century is that the federal government has recognized its importance by recruiting thousands of agricultural specialists. To date, not even the beginnings of anything comparable have been developed for metropolitan needs, although almost two-thirds of the population of the United States now live in metropolitan areas. The federal government does not lack skilled engineers to build urban highways or airports to serve urban areas, but it does lack personnel who are skilled in the general problems of urban government. Special urban units should be established and those already in existence should be strengthened in the federal agencies whose programs particularly concern metropolitan areas.

One of the structural changes which are needed is the establishment of a staff agency to furnish the President with continuous staff assistance on metropolitan problems. The importance of this kind of assistance has been emphasized in a preceding chapter. Stated briefly, a Council on Metropolitan Areas should be established by statute in the Executive Office of the President. The Council should consist of three to five full-time members, one of whom should be designated as chairman and be assigned broad administrative authority over the work of the Council. In addition to such day-to-day duties as the President might assign it, the Council should organize a program of continuing research on the impact of federal programs on metropolitan areas. Though the Council should have no authority to co-ordinate federal programs, it should have power to collect data, ask questions, and make recommendations to the President. It should keep abreast of developments in the field through the device of regional desks rather than by means of permanently established field offices. An advisory group representing private research bodies as well as state and local governmental units and interested professional groups should be appointed to consult with the Council in the performance of its duties.

The federal government's program for metropolitan areas should be firmly anchored in the structure of Congress as well as in the White House. This can best be accomplished by requiring the President to submit an annual report to Congress on metropolitan problems, just as he does on the economic state of the nation, and by creating an appropriate Committee on Metropolitan Problems to which the President's report could be referred for study and action. These devices have been used successfully with regard to economic matters, and they could be used with equal success here. The creation of such a committee, however, should not deter the present House Subcommittee on Intergovernmental Relations (the Fountain Subcommittee) from continuing its studies of intergovernmental problems in general, with special attention to the important problem of federal-state relations.

In addition to these general recommendations, there are actions which the federal government can take in relation to specific programs which would make its work in urban areas much more effective.

Highways

1. The federal highway program should be made an integral part of metropolitan land use planning. Federal aid to highways should be closely geared to the other federal aid programs in metropolitan areas—housing and slum clearance, the development of recreational areas, airport construction, civil defense, and so on. Plans should be co-ordinated nationally and also at the local level.

2. Since the federal highway program deals with only one part of the whole transportation problem in the United States, it should be developed in conjunction with long-range planning in regard to the other factors of the transportation picture.

Particularly in metropolitan areas it should be tied closely with the means of mass transportation.

3. The Bureau of Public Roads should recognize the special needs of urban and metropolitan areas through the creation of appropriate units to deal with them in its administrative structure. This would involve the recruiting of personnel familiar with the broad problems of government in metropolitan areas as well as with technical and engineering problems.

4. The federal government ought to be concerned about the relocation of people who are moved from sites taken for federal programs. This would involve careful prior arrangements with communities in the metropolitan area concerned to assure that adequate housing is available for those who are evicted and that relocation can be achieved with a minimum of human distress.

Water Resources

5. Present federal water resource development programs should be re-examined in terms of present and potential metropolitan needs for domestic and industrial use, and for recreation. Flood control, irrigation, and navigation have too long held the attention of Congress to the exclusion of urban water needs.

6. The federal government must recognize the implications of the suburban explosion on water needs. New suburbs compete for water with older central cities which have long-established claims to available water sources in the area. Simple grants-in-aid to individual suburban communities will do little to solve their problem. The establishment of metropolitan water districts should be encouraged by the federal government; at the same time, federal programs should be examined to make certain that they do not inadvertently work against the establishment of water supply systems for entire metropolitan areas.

7. The federal government should take steps to act on the findings of recent national water surveys, particularly with re-

gard to relating federal water programs to one another. At present, administrative responsibility is scattered through a number of federal agencies, with the result that there is often competition between federal water use programs. The whole problem of lack of communication and co-ordination, both between one federal agency and another, and between federal agencies and state and local water units, needs to be appreciated and solved.

Water Pollution

8. Federal pollution control programs should put greater emphasis on the needs of rapidly growing suburbs in metropolitan areas where sewage disposal problems are most acute. Since 1956, with the passage of the Federal Water Pollution Control Act, there has been a co-operative federal-state-local water pollution control program. The needs of metropolitan areas, however, and especially the needs of suburbs therein, have not been adequately taken into account. What is needed in many cases is not isolated sewage treatment plants, but the development of sewage trunk lines and feeder systems serving the entire metropolitan area.

9. Under the present law, communities within metropolitan areas cannot pool federal grants for the construction either of joint treatment facilities or of sewage trunk lines. The effect of the present policy is to encourage the use of inadequate and outmoded political forms and thus to fragmentize a function that would be best handled by a larger unit. Federal legislation should be amended to permit local co-operation in the handling of this problem on a metropolitan basis.

10. Water pollution control demands federal action. The recommendation of the Joint Federal-State Action Committee that this function be returned to the states should be rejected by Congress. Instead, the federal grant-in-aid program for water pollution control activities should be strengthened and expanded.

Air Pollution

11. Research on the cause and prevention of air pollution is a pressing need today. The public health aspects of air pollution alone make this a national problem demanding immediate attention. The present Air Pollution Control Act should be extended to permit uninterrupted progress.

12. The federal government ought to initiate a nation-wide study of the means by which all levels of government can cooperate to control air pollution, since no state, acting alone, can solve the problem.

13. The federal government should offer incentives to metropolitan areas to approach the problem of air pollution on an area-wide basis.

14. In regard to its own atomic energy programs, the federal government should recognize and act on its responsibility for controlling nuclear fallout over major population centers.

Airports

15. The "jet age" requires a federal planning program of broad scope which will take into account the airport needs of metropolitan areas. Only the federal government can undertake such a planning role. The planning function, indeed, is the most important one the federal government can perform.

16. Far from withdrawing federal aid to airports, the federal government should increase its appropriations for this purpose.

17. Formulas for the distribution of federal-aid airport funds should be established in such a way as to encourage planning, construction, and operation of airports on a metropolitan basis. The present formula is wholly inadequate to accomplish this objective.

18. The problem of noise will become increasingly severe. A proper master plan for airports would take this fact into account.

19. The relation of military airports to civilian airports in

metropolitan areas continues to be critical and should be considered in long-range planning.

20. Since the greatest increase in air traffic in metropolitan areas in the future will probably be in the number of general (privately owned) aircraft, the relation of commercial and military traffic to private aircraft use must be given attention in planning federal programs.

Military Installations and Defense Industries

21. The federal government should recognize that military installations and defense industries have a major impact on governmental problems in metropolitan areas.

22. Where metropolitan planning machinery exists, location of military installations and defense industries should be required to conform to local land use plans. In areas where military installations are projected, and metropolitan planning agencies do not exist, the federal government should take the initiative in bringing together city planners and local representatives to consult upon appropriate locations.

23. The program to aid federally impacted defense areas should be reoriented to give greater weight to the effect of federal activities in metropolitan areas.

Civil Defense

24. The federal government should convert its recognition of joint responsibility with the states for civil defense into a concrete program of action which acknowledges the paramount importance of metropolitan areas to the nation's security.

25. Not only should the federal government's aid programs be increased in amount, but the distribution formula should be heavily weighted to encourage the formation of metropolitan civil defense arrangements.

26. The federal government should decide the extent to which national civil defense requirements will impinge on fu-

ture metropolitan development, and should develop a policy to guide metropolitan areas in the future.

Housing and Urban Renewal

27. Present housing legislation needs to be simplified and clarified. Statute has been piled upon statute, amendment upon amendment, until it takes skilled legal advice to determine what is permissible and what is not, and how it can be done. The whole system of federal housing legislation needs to be revised and simplified.

28. Cumbersome procedural requirements should be abolished. Federal housing agencies should continue to re-examine their administrative procedures to ensure that they operate to facilitate the effective use of statutory provisions rather than to create unnecessary delays and road blocks.

29. All federal programs dealing with land use, including housing, highways, slum clearance, and urban renewal programs, ought to be integrated so that the needs of the whole metropolitan area with regard to land use planning are taken into consideration.

30. A balanced program is needed which will provide adequate multifamily rental units for middle-income groups and for senior citizens in the central city, as well as single-family homes in the suburbs.

31. Low-income public housing should give greater consideration to the social needs of the people who live in it. Public housing units should be more attractively designed. They should look less institutional, less like jails or hospitals. More important, they should be designed in recognition of the sociological factors that make for successful community living. They should provide play space for children, meeting places for adults, and recreational programs for senior citizens, out of which a real community can be developed.

32. The federal government ought to continue to aid official metropolitan planning groups in developing comprehensive

plans. Indeed, as more planning agencies are created, federal funds should be increased so that grants-in-aid may continue to be made available on an equitable basis for sharing the cost of preparing area-wide plans.

33. The federal government should continue to provide a substantial grant-in-aid program for urban renewal and for housing. Without federal leadership and financial support, no sizable impact can be made on modernizing the urban pattern of living.

34. Far from withdrawing from the field in favor of the states, the federal government must increase its participation in housing and renewal programs if the needs of the nation are to be met.

Allocation of Resources

It is obvious that many of these recommendations entail the expenditure of money; in some cases, of large amounts of money. Critics of any federal program these days are prone to point first to proposed costs and to raise the hue and cry of inflation and the national debt. To be sure, economy is always necessary, in government as in private industry. True economy, however, involves planning ahead and spending now in order to save later. Government's main job on all levels is the allocation of scarce resources. This certainly includes allocations for the future as well as for the present. Federal expenditures made now to secure better metropolitan living in the future can prevent situations from arising which would be infinitely more expensive to solve a decade from now, if, indeed, they could then be solved at all.

On the other hand, many of the recommendations made in this report would result in better co-ordination of programs and in the elimination of overlapping and duplication, as well as in other savings, and thus, by the more efficient use of resources, would serve to reduce the present as well as the future costs of those programs now operating in metropolitan areas. And if, as is hoped, the states react to federal stimulation by finding ways of increasing their own contributions to the solution of metropolitan problems, the necessity of larger federal expenditures will be proportionately reduced.

The point is that economy is relative to the objective. The objective of the nation with regard to metropolitan areas in the years ahead should be to enable governments in those areas to offer their citizens the highest possible standards of service, convenience, efficiency, and beauty. If the costs are large, so is the object for which money is spent.

Co-operative Action

No action by the federal government alone, however, will suffice. The federal government should assure itself that cities and states themselves have done as much as they can before they turn to Washington for aid, and there is much that state and local governments can do to assist in attacking metropolitan area problems. The states for their part can through legislation make it possible for interstate metropolitan areas to organize to meet their governmental needs more effectively. Where the state must be the intermediary in federal grant-in-aid programs affecting metropolitan areas, it should assure city and other governmental units in those areas adequate representation in the planning and administration of the programs. Finally, local governments in metropolitan areas need to push ahead much more vigorously to establish area-wide planning agencies in order to fit themselves to take the most effective advantage of federal programs.

Since no governmental action on any level can be long sustained in legislative bodies without organized popular support, metropolitan areas should seek to develop forceful representative groups to plead their case in the state house and in Washington. Metropolitan communities need to develop a civic consciousness, on an area-wide basis, which can be felt by Congress and the President. Such a consciousness is necessary if federal programs are to operate with the greatest degree of effectiveness at the local level.

The primary need today is for frank recognition of the federal government's responsibilities toward metropolitan areas, within the framework of co-operative federalism, and for development of a basic federal policy in accordance with that recognition. Taking cognizance of the fact that government in metropolitan areas is a national problem and that it involves interstate and international situations which neither the local communities nor the states can handle alone, the federal government should acknowledge that it is a proper subject for federal action. Recognition that the federal government has a proper role to play in the government of metropolitan areas involves more than the present piecemeal approach. It requires an understanding that this is a single problem with many facets and that its solution should be approached with a unified program. A policy based on that acknowledgment will make it possible to bring the full resources of the federal government to bear, in co-operation with states and local governments, in attacking metropolitan problems. Thus the techniques of co-operative federalism, which have been so successful in meeting other problems, can be applied to metropolitan areas.

Such a policy will involve joint federal-state-local planning and action, but only the federal government can supply leadership on a national basis. The greatest need in the cities today is not water or sewers, or wider streets, or more schools, or housing, important as they are. What is needed most is drive, organization, and leadership. There is no shortage of cement and steel and bricks. But there is a shortage of clear thinking, of effective political leadership, and of appropriate governmental institutions, plans, and policies. The federal government has a clear responsibility to act to alleviate that shortage.

BIBLIOGRAPHICAL NOTE

IT is virtually impossible any longer to compile a bibliography in the field of metropolitan areas, at least to compile a bibliography of any long-term use. For one thing, so much material is pouring out in ever-increasing quantities from an ever-growing number of sources that before the ink would be dry on one such bibliography, it would be time to begin another. Moreover, much of the material is of ephemeral interest and soon becomes outdated. A more basic reason why no attempt is made here to provide a bibliography, however, is the fact that earnest efforts have already been made to compile a comprehensive bibliography in the field, and brief supplementary bibliographies continue to appear intermittently. Thus there is no need for such an undertaking here.

The masterful volume *Metropolitan Communities, A Bibliography*, published in 1956 by the Government Affairs Foundation, and its companion volume *Metropolitan Surveys, A Digest*, published in 1959, are basic to every work in the field and should be exhaustively consulted by anyone beginning work on government in metropolitan areas. The bibliography begun with *Metropolitan Communities* has been continued by the Conference on Metropolitan Area Problems in the columns of the bimonthly *Metropolitan Area Problems News and Digest*, which can be obtained by addressing the Institute of Public Administration, 684 Park Avenue, New York 21, New

York. There, developments in metropolitan areas are reported, and studies, books, and articles on all types of metropolitan area problems are adequately described. Although the *National Civic Review* (formerly *National Municipal Review*) does not attempt a bibliography of metropolitan area items, it does describe developments in metropolitan areas and report them to its readers every month. The cumulative issues of *Public Affairs Information Service* also provide a valuable index to the literature on the subject, under the headings "Metropolitan Areas" and "Metropolitan Government." These three, and of course the *Municipal Year Book,* are the chief regular sources of information on metropolitan area publications and developments.

The *Readers' Guide to Periodical Literature* occasionally lists an article under a metropolitan area heading. The same applies to the *Index to Legal Periodicals*. Both may on occasion prove helpful for the popular-type article or for more specialized legal analyses.

The metropolitan area problem is part and parcel of the larger problem of intergovernmental relations; consequently, bibliographies of publications in that area are also useful. One of the best and most recent bibliographies is the one prepared by the Legislative Reference Service of the Library of Congress for the Subcommittee on Intergovernmental Relations of the House Committee on Government Operations, entitled *Intergovernmental Relations in the United States: A Selected Bibliography,* published as a committee print in 1956. This was based largely on a similarly entitled bibliography prepared by the Legislative Reference Service for the Commission on Intergovernmental Relations (the Kestnbaum Commission) in 1955.

Though most of the material listed in the bibliographies cited above consists of articles and reports, an increasing number of books pertaining to the field is also being published. Among the worth-while books which appeared in the field within the last few months of 1958 and the first few months of 1959, for example, are:

Urban Sprawl and Health, by the National Health Council (New York).

The Exploding Metropolis, by the Editors of *Fortune* (Garden City: Doubleday and Company).

Suburbia: Its People and Their Politics, by Robert C. Wood (Boston: Houghton Mifflin Company).

Cities in the Motor Age, by Wilfred Owen (New York: The Viking Press, Inc.).

In addition, a number of metropolitan dailies throughout the country have produced important series of informative articles on the special problems induced by metropolitan growth. Particularly notable are those in the *Washington Star,* the Bergen (New Jersey) *Evening Record,* the Dallas (Texas) *Morning News,* the Dayton (Ohio) *Daily News,* and the New Orleans (Louisiana) *Item.* The *New York Times* and the *New York Herald Tribune* have both published a number of impressive studies.

Since many of the problems of government in metropolitan areas are functional in nature—water, sewage disposal, airport construction, and so on—the trade and professional journals in these functional fields frequently contain pertinent articles. Most of these are listed in the *Public Affairs Information Service,* but some are not. The proceedings of annual and occasional special conferences and symposia in governmental and allied fields are also useful sources of information. Virtually every league of municipalities holds an annual meeting; an increasing number of industrially sponsored conferences are held, such as the one in the fall of 1957 by the Connecticut General Life Insurance Company; and university-sponsored meetings are becoming more common. The official and unofficial reports of all these contain much that is useful to the researcher in the field.

The growing international interest in the metropolitan problem is evidenced by the contract entered into by the United Nations in October 1958 with the International Union of Social Authorities for a three-year survey of the kinds of services central governments extend to municipalities. The report, which is expected in 1961, should be of great interest to American students.

In the last analysis, much valuable material is still hard to locate and acquire. Some studies are made for private use only, others are only for limited circulation, and still others are not published at all. The field is still so young that virtually anyone working in it will have to rely heavily on interviews, as did the authors of this book. The people concerned with thinking about and solving metropolitan problems have, many of them, not had an opportunity to write about them; thus the best bibliography available would still be incomplete.

In the narrower area of the subject of this monograph, it is even more difficult to compile a good bibliography. All the foregoing comments apply, but in addition a comment must be made on the tremendous resources of the federal government itself. Every issue of the *Congressional Record,* many a report of a Senate or House committee, many a press release or fact sheet issued by an administrative agency bears on the subject of the federal government and metropolitan areas. The difficulty is that for bibliographical purposes there is no co-ordination or centralization of all this mass of material, no index available, no way to get a thorough purview—except by patiently wading and plodding through the pile itself. Even then, however, much of the material will turn out to be tangential and will be found to go very quickly out of date.

The principal sources of information on the federal government at the time of writing are, however, cited in the notes to this study, which themselves constitute something of a bibliography.

NOTES

1

FEDERAL PROGRAMS IN METROPOLITAN AREAS

1. Fredrika Bremer, *The Homes of the New World: Impressions of America* (New York, 1854), vol. I, p. 47.

2. See Warren S. Tryon, ed., *A Mirror for Americans* (Chicago, 1952), esp. vols. II, III.

3. Ernie Pyle, *Home Country* (New York, 1947), p. 3.

4. Henry van Dyke, *The Spirit of America* (New York, 1910), p. 122.

5. Harry Kantor, *Governing Our Metropolitan Communities* (Univ. of Florida, Public Administration Clearing Service, Civic Information Series, no. 9; Gainesville, 1958), p. 1.

6. See Editors of *Fortune*, *The Exploding Metropolis* (Garden City, 1958).

7. An urban place was defined in 1790 as a place of 2,500 population or more.

8. Census reports throughout the nineteenth century reported population by cities, and those in 1880 and 1890 paid particular attention to the social statistics of cities.

9. Except in New England, a standard metropolitan area was defined by the Bureau of the Census in 1949 as a county or group of contiguous counties which contained at least one city of 50,000 inhabitants or more. In addition, contiguous counties were included in the area if they were essentially metropolitan in character. In 1959 redefined as standard metropolitan statistical districts.

10. Donald J. Bogue, *Population Growth in Standard Metropolitan Areas 1900–1950* (Washington: Housing and Home Finance Agency, Div. of Housing Research, 1953), p. 9.

11. See Carl Bridenbaugh, *Cities in the Wilderness* (New York, 1938), esp. chaps. iii, iv, for a discussion of urban development in the Colonial period; see the same author's *Cities in Revolt* (New York, 1955) for a discussion of urban development up to 1776; see

also Richard C. Wade, "Urban Life in Western America: 1790–1830," *American Historical Review*, 64:14–20 (Oct. 1958).

12. See A. M. Schlesinger, *The Rise of the City, 1878–1898* (New York, 1933), for a thorough discussion of the rise of cities as a result of the Industrial Revolution.

13. Robert E. Merriam (Assistant Director, U. S. Bureau of the Budget), address before Annual Conference, Maryland Municipal League, Ocean City, Md., June 14, 1957.

14. The definition of "metropolitan area" used by the Budget Bureau in this connection is that of the New York Regional Plan Association. It includes more territory than the definition used by the Bureau of the Census.

15. 47 Stat. 725.

16. 48 Stat. 128.

17. 48 Stat. 1246.

18. 50 Stat. 20.

19. 58 Stat. 284.

20. Joint Com. on Housing, U. S. Congress, *The High Cost of Housing*, 80th Cong., 1st Sess., Jan. 12, 1948.

21. This plan was made in pursuance of the provision of the Reorganization Act of 1945, 59 Stat. 813.

22. See Quintin Johnstone, "The Federal Urban Renewal Program," *University of Chicago Law Review*, 25:300–354 (Winter 1958).

23. Housing and Home Finance Agency, press release, June 17, 1957.

24. 68 Stat. 590, esp. sec. 701.

25. Housing and Home Finance Agency, *Urban Planning Assistance Program, Fact Sheet*, June 30, 1959.

26. President Eisenhower's veto message, *New York Times*, July 8, 1959, p. 18.

27. See Senator Clark's article, "The Hope for Housing," *The Progressive*, Apr. 1959, reproduced in *Congressional Record*, 105:A2910–12 (Apr. 10, 1959).

28. Com. on Banking and Currency, U. S. House of Representatives, *Investigation of Housing, 1955*, 84th Cong., 1st Sess., pt. 3, p. 18.

29. Ibid., pt. 2 (Los Angeles), pt. 4 (Cleveland), and pt. 6 (Birmingham, Ala.).

30. Senate Rep. No. 1448, 84th Cong., 2d Sess., p. 6.

31. William H. Whyte, Jr., "Are Cities Un-American?" *Fortune*, Sept. 1957, reprinted in *The Exploding Metropolis*, by the Editors of *Fortune* (Garden City, 1958), p. 25.

32. Ibid., p. 44; for a case study in public housing, see also Martin Meyerson and Edward C. Banfield, *Politics, Planning and the Public Interest* (Glencoe, Ill., 1955).

33. *Report of the Urban Renewal Study Board to Mayor Thomas D'Alesandro, Jr.* (Baltimore, 1956), p. 14.

34. Com. on Government Operations, Subcom. on Intergovernmental Relations, U. S. House of Representatives, 6th Ann. Rep., *Replies from State and Local Governments* . . . , 85th Cong., 1st Sess., June 17, 1957, p. 14.

35. Com. on Banking and Currency, U. S. Senate, *Hearings on the Housing Act of 1958*, 85th Cong., 2d Sess., p. 293.

36. Ibid., p. 141.

37. See reports of city administrator of New York on relocation for the period 1955–58.

38. Com. on Banking and Currency, U. S. Senate, loc. cit.

39. See the study of the Boston West End project being made under the auspices of the National Institute for Mental Health, Bethesda, Md.

40. For an interesting discussion of the federal government's activity in the water resources field, see the statement of Brigadier General John L. Person before the House Com. on Public Works, May 12, 1959, reprinted in *Congressional Record*, 105:A4940–41 (June 9, 1959).

41. James Fesler, "National Water Resources Administration," *Law and Contemporary Problems*, 22:444 (Summer 1957).

42. Tennessee Valley Authority, *Annual Report for 1957*, pp. 10–20.

43. Presidential Advisory Committee on Water Resources Policy, *Water Resources Policy* (1955), p. 2.

44. Commission on Organization of the Executive Branch of the Government (First Hoover Commission), *Reorganization of the Department of the Interior* (1949); Commission on Organization of the Executive Branch of the Government (Second Hoover Commission), Task Force on Water Resources and Power, *Report on Water Resources and Power* (1955).

45. President's Water Resources Policy Commission, *Report* (1950).

46. Temple University, *Survey of Federal Reorganization* (1953).

47. Missouri Basin Survey Commission, *Missouri Land and Water* (1953).

48. Presidential Advisory Committee on Water Resources Policy, op. cit.

49. First Hoover Commission, *Reorganization of the Department of the Interior*, p. 37.

50. President's Water Resources Policy Commission, op. cit., vol. I, p. 10.

51. Second Hoover Commission, *Report on Water Resources and Power*, vol. III, p. 1235.

52. Ibid., pp. 1235, 1245.

53. Remarks of Senator Mike Mansfield before the Senate, Jan. 27, 1959, *Congressional Record*, 105:1045–47 (Jan. 27, 1959).

54. See Robert and Leona Rienow, "The Day the Tap Runs Dry," *Harper's Magazine*, Oct. 1958.

55. President's Water Resources Policy Commission, op. cit., vol. I, p. 177. These figures represent gross withdrawals at the source; net consumptive use is very much less.

56. Ibid., p. 181.

57. Ibid., p. 184.

58. Senate Rep. No. 462, 80th Cong., 1st Sess., p. 2.

59. 62 Stat. 1155.

60. Second Hoover Commission, op. cit., vol. III, p. 1231.

61. Com. on Public Works, Subcom. on Rivers and Harbors, U. S. House of Representatives, *Hearings on S. 890 and H. R. 9540*, 84th Cong., 1st and 2d Sess., July 20, 1955–Mar. 15, 1956, p. 138.

62. *Congressional Record*, 105:A2334 (Mar. 18, 1959).

63. Com. on Public Works, Subcom. on Rivers and Harbors, op. cit., p. 136.

64. Ibid., p. 152.

65. See chap. 4 below.

66. American Society of Planning Officials, *The Airport Dilemma* (Chicago, 1938).

67. President Eisenhower's memorandum accompanying his veto message on Airport Act of 1958, *New York Times*, Sept. 3, 1958.

68. American Society of Planning Officials, op. cit.

69. Dwight H. Green, "Comments Concerning the National Airport Program," *Temple Law Quarterly*, 60:20 (July 1946).

70. 60 Stat. 170, sec. 9 (a), (b).

71. Civil Aeronautics Administration, *The Federal-Aid Airport Program* (Oct. 1, 1955), p. 5.

72. 69 Stat. 441.

73. U. S. Department of Commerce, press release, Apr. 2, 1957.

74. *Congressional Record*, 105:4644 (Mar. 25, 1959).

75. Ibid., p. 4643.

76. William B. Hartsfield (Mayor, Atlanta, Ga.), *Aviation Prob-*

lems for Cities (Washington: American Municipal Association, May 1957).

77. Idem, *Statement before the Air Coordinating Committee,* June 6, 1957 (American Municipal Association press release).

78. American Municipal Association, *The National Municipal Policy,* 33d Annual American Municipal Congress, Nov. 28, 1956, sec. XV–4.

79. See Richard E. Mooney, "Shortage in Jet Runways," *New York Times,* Oct. 12, 1958.

80. Com. on the Armed Services, U. S. House of Representatives, *Report to Accompany H. R. 13015 . . . ,* 85th Cong., 2d Sess., June 24, 1958, pp. 34–38.

81. Ibid.

82. *Washington Star,* Aug. 15, 1958.

83. The authors found that in Fayetteville, N. C., the city police force had to be doubled as a result of the administrative order permitting servicemen to leave near-by Fort Bragg in civilian clothes.

84. Survey made by the authors, summer 1957.

85. 54 Stat. 974, as amended; continued in effect until 1955. See also Robert H. Connery, *The Navy and the Industrial Mobilization in World War II* (Princeton, 1950).

86. Richardson Wood, "The Shambles around the War Plant," *Harper's Magazine,* Aug. 1951, pp. 48–53; "Mobile, Alabama: A Portrait of a Southern City after the War Boom," *Fortune,* Mar. 1946, pp. 106–17; American Society of Planning Officials, *Impact of Defense Industries on Communities, A Selected Bibliography* (Chicago, 1951).

87. Arthur W. Bromage and John A. Perkins, "Willow Run Produces Bombers and Integration Problems," *American Political Science Review,* 36:689–96 (Aug. 1942). Drawn upon freely.

88. Quoted ibid., p. 693.

89. Ibid.

90. Bureau of the Census, *Population Census* (Washington, 1950), vol. I, p. xxxiii.

91. Com. on Government Operations, U. S. House of Representatives, *Hearings on Civil Defense,* 85th Cong., 2d Sess., Apr.–May 1958, p. 397.

92. 64 Stat. 1245.

93. Com. on Government Operations, Subcom. on Military Operations, U. S. House of Representatives, *Hearings on Civil Defense for National Survival,* 84th Cong., 2d Sess.

94. Idem, 8th Rep., *Status of Civil Defense Legislation,* 85th Cong., 1st Sess., p. 2.

95. Idem, *Hearings on New Civil Defense Legislation,* 85th Cong., 1st Sess., pp. 44, 311.

96. Reorganization Plan No. 1, 1958.

97. Com. on Government Operations, U. S. House of Representatives, *Hearings on Civil Defense,* 85th Cong., 2d Sess., p. 368.

98. Ibid., p. 361.

99. Ibid., p. 381.

100. Ibid., p. 395.

101. Wilfred Owen, *The New Highways: A Challenge to the Metropolitan Region* (Connecticut General Life Insurance Co., Background Paper, Sept. 1957), pp. 5, 23.

102. 70 Stat. 374.

103. U. S. Bureau of Public Roads, *The Administration of Federal Aid for Highways* (Jan. 1957).

104. 58 Stat. 838.

105. 68 Stat. 70.

106. See the remarks of Representative Walter S. Baring of Nevada, *Congressional Record,* 105:A1832–33 (Mar. 5, 1959); see also Polly Praeger, "Extinction by Thruway: The Fight to Save a Town," *Harper's Magazine,* Dec. 1958.

107. Based on an interview with Donald W. Loutzenheiser (Chief, Urban Highways Branch, Bureau of Public Roads), Aug. 1956.

108. Ibid.

109. Com. on Public Works, U. S. Senate, *Hearings on Federal Aid Highway Act of 1958,* 85th Cong., 2d Sess., p. 613.

110. *Congressional Record,* 105:2571 (Feb. 24, 1959).

111. Ibid., pp. 2799–800 (Mar. 2, 1959).

112. "No More Traffic Jams?" *U. S. News and World Report,* July 20, 1956, p. 77.

113. *Congressional Record,* 105:A2849 (Apr. 8, 1959).

114. Owen, op. cit., p. 17.

115. H. G. Bartz, "The Perils of Air Pollution," *World Health,* Mar.–Apr. 1958, p. 7.

116. 69 Stat. 322.

117. *Congressional Record,* 104:A8181–82 (Sept. 11, 1958).

118. *Congressional Record,* 105:5 (Jan. 23, 1959).

119. Senator Joseph Clark, cited ibid.; see also Senate Rep. No. 182, 86th Cong., 1st Sess.

120. *Congressional Record,* 104:A8181–82 (Sept. 11, 1958).

121. *Congressional Record,* 105:A3464 (Apr. 28, 1959).

122. Even in "Special Analysis G" of the *Budget of the United States Government* for fiscal 1959, where federal aid to state and

local governments is detailed, the data are given in terms of function, agency, and program, and it is impossible to determine expenditures in metropolitan areas.

2

REPRESENTATION OF METROPOLITAN INTERESTS IN WASHINGTON

1. Quoted in American Municipal Association, *Proceedings, 1931–1935* (Chicago, 1936), p. 67.

2. Charles S. Ascher, "Federating the Leagues of Cities," *Survey,* Dec. 15, 1932, p. 685.

3. E. E. McAdams (then President, American Municipal Association), in *Addresses Delivered at the 18th Annual Conference of the American Municipal Association* (Chicago, 1941), p. 4.

4. See the statement in *The National Municipal Policy* adopted by the 33d Annual American Municipal Congress, Nov. 28, 1956, p. 2.

5. *National Legislative Bulletin,* Jan. 16, 1958, p. 2.

6. Clifford Brenner (press secretary to Mayor Dilworth), letter to Richard H. Leach, June 27, 1957.

7. William N. Cassella, Jr., and Victor Jones, eds., "Metropolitan Government," *National Municipal Review,* 47:177 (Apr. 1958).

8. New York, Chicago, Philadelphia, Los Angeles, Detroit, Baltimore, Cleveland, St. Louis, Washington, Boston, San Francisco, Pittsburgh, Milwaukee, Houston, Buffalo, New Orleans, Minneapolis, Cincinnati, Seattle, and Kansas City (Mo.).

9. United States Conference of Mayors, *1957 Annual Conference Program,* p. 12.

10. *City Problems of 1933. Annual Proceedings of the United States Conference of Mayors* (Chicago, 1933), p. 3.

11. Ibid., p. 10.

12. Ibid., p. 4.

13. United States Conference of Mayors, *1957 Annual Conference Program,* p. 2.

14. Com. on Banking and Currency, Subcom. on Housing, U. S. House of Representatives, *Hearings,* 85th Cong., 1st Sess., Mar. 4–15, 1957, p. 613.

15. Memorandum from Harry R. Betters, Executive Director,

United States Conference of Mayors, to member cities, Sept. 27, 1957.

16. For the full policy statement, see "Where We Stand," an insert in *The County Officer*, vol. 23, Jan. 1958. The quotation is from p. 3.

17. Ibid.

18. Ibid.

19. *Program, Urban County Congress of the National Association of County Officials*, Mar. 15–18, 1959, p. 2.

20. *National Municipal Review*, 45:287 (June 1956).

21. *American Planning and Civic Annual*, 1955, p. v.

22. *Looking Ahead*, Feb. 1957, pp. 1–3.

23. Harold D. Smith, in *Addresses Delivered at the 18th Annual Conference of the American Municipal Association* (Chicago, 1941), p. 97.

24. *Time*, Dec. 2, 1935, p. 10.

25. *City Problems of 1933. Annual Proceedings of the United States Conference of Mayors* (Chicago, 1933), p. 3.

26. Arthur W. Bromage, *Introduction to Municipal Government and Administration* (New York, 1950), p. 185.

27. "City Hall Hires Its Own Lobby," *Business Week*, June 1, 1957, p. 129.

28. Com. on Government Operations, Subcom. on Intergovernmental Relations, U. S. House of Representatives, *Federal-State-Local Relations*, 85th Cong., 2d Sess., pt. 2, p. 597.

29. Com. on Banking and Currency, Subcom. on Housing, U. S. House of Representatives, *Investigation of Housing, 1955*, 84th Cong., 1st Sess., pt. 2, p. 1.

3

CONGRESS AND METROPOLITAN AREAS

1. That Congress is busy is unquestionable. During the 85th Congress (1957–58), over 20,600 bills, resolutions, and joint resolutions were submitted for its consideration.

2. "Here's Your Report, Mr. President," *This Week*, July 5, 1959, pp. 4–5.

3. John F. Kennedy, "The Shame of the States," *New York Times Magazine*, May 18, 1958, p. 12.

4. Gordon E. Baker, *Rural versus Urban Political Power* (New York, 1955), p. 41.

5. Ernest S. Griffith, *Congress: Its Contemporary Role* (New York, 1956), p. 159.

6. Senator Joseph Clark, quoted in *Congressional Record,* 104:8002 (May 19, 1958).

7. Baker, op. cit., p. 48.

8. H. R. 11844, introduced Apr. 2, 1958, by Representative Brooks Hays of Arkansas; hearing held by Family Farm Subcom. of House Com. on Agriculture, July 8, 1958.

9. H. R. 5565, introduced Mar. 14, 1957, by Representative Harold Ostertag of New York.

10. See Wesley McCune, *The Farm Bloc* (New York, 1943), esp. chaps. ix, xi.

11. Kenneth Crawford, *The Pressure Boys* (New York, 1939), p. 6.

12. Stuart Chase, *Democracy under Pressure* (New York, 1945), p. 99.

13. Representative Harold Ostertag, *In the Nation's Capital* (mimeographed release no. 33, Nov. 21, 1956).

14. Senate Rep. No. 1448, 84th Cong., 2d Sess., p. 22.

15. Com. on Banking and Currency, Subcom. on Housing, U. S. House of Representatives, *Investigation of Housing, 1956,* 84th Cong., 2d Sess., p. 59.

16. Ibid., p. 56.

17. *Congressional Record,* 99:7012 (June 22, 1953).

18. Com. on Banking and Currency, Subcom. on Housing, U. S. House of Representatives, *Hearings on Housing, 1957,* 85th Cong., 1st Sess., p. 102.

19. Ibid., p. 61.

20. House Rep. No. 2963, 84th Cong., 2d Sess., p. 35.

21. For an example of the political maneuvering in Congress affecting the District of Columbia, see Alfred Steinberg, "Let's Set Washington Free," *Reader's Digest,* July 1953, pp. 97–98.

22. Ibid.

23. The figures given in "Washington: A City in Trouble," *Changing Times,* Oct. 1958, p. 20.

24. See *Economic Development in the Washington Metropolitan Area* (staff study prepared for Joint Com. on Washington Metropolitan Problems, 85th Cong., 2d Sess.), p. 4.

25. *Congressional Record,* 103:14512 (Aug. 26, 1957).

26. National Resources Committee, *Our Cities: Their Role in the National Economy* (1937), p. 80.

27. *Economic Development in the Washington Metropolitan Area*, p. 5.

28. 43 Stat. 463.

29. National Capital Park and Planning Commission, *Washington Present and Future. A General Summary of the Comprehensive Plan for the National Capital and Its Environs* (1950), p. 1.

30. Ibid., p. 5.

31. Ibid., p. 7.

32. 66 Stat. 785.

33. See *Governmental Agencies Concerned with Land Use, Planning, or Conservation in the Washington Metropolitan Area* (staff study prepared for Joint Com. on Washington Metropolitan Problems, 85th Cong., 2d Sess.), pp. 2–5; see also "Washington: A City in Trouble," *Changing Times*, Oct. 1958, p. 20.

34. H. R. 2236, 83d Cong., 1st Sess.; passed by the House June 22, 1953; passed by the Senate July 23, 1953.

35. This expectation was voiced by Representative DeWitt Hyde of Maryland, *Washington Star*, Aug. 30, 1957.

36. *Congressional Record*, 103:14512 (Aug. 26, 1957).

37. *Washington Star*, Aug. 30, 1957.

38. Joint Com. on Washington Metropolitan Problems, U. S. Congress, *Washington Metropolitan Area Water Problems*, 85th Cong., 2d Sess., p. 3.

39. Senate Rep. No. 1230, 85th Cong., 2d Sess., p. 4.

40. *Economic Development in the Washington Metropolitan Area*, p. 34.

41. Senate Rep. No. 38, 86th Cong., 1st Sess.

42. *Washington Post and Times Herald*, Feb. 2, 1959, quoted in *Congressional Record*, 105:1417 (Feb. 2, 1959).

43. S. J. Res. 42; see also Senate Rep. No. 456, 86th Cong., 1st Sess.

44. Carroll Kirkpatrick, "What Happened to the Farm Bloc," *Harper's Magazine*, Nov. 1957, p. 57.

45. Ibid., pp. 56–57.

46. John M. Maclachlan and Joe S. Floyd, *This Changing South* (Gainesville, 1956), p. 29.

47. Ibid., p. 38.

48. Ibid., p. 39.

49. See Rupert B. Vance and N. J. Demerath, eds., *The Urban South* (Chapel Hill, 1954), esp. chap. ii.

50. Quoted in *Knoxville News-Sentinel* (Knoxville, Tenn.), Nov. 7, 1958, p. 2.

51. *Congressional Record*, 105:3797 (Mar. 16, 1959).

52. See House Rep. No. 2533, 85th Cong., 2d Sess.

53. Ibid., p. 40.

54. See House Rep. No. 575, 85th Cong., 1st Sess.; see also Com. on Government Operations, Subcom. on Intergovernmental Relations, *Federal-State-Local Relations*, 85th Cong., 2d Sess., pts. 1, 2.

55. House Rep. No. 575, p. 13.

56. Commission on Intergovernmental Relations, *A Report to the President* (1955), p. 53.

57. Ibid., p. 49.

58. Ibid., chaps vii, viii, xi, xii, xiv.

59. Ibid., p. 171.

60. 69 Stat. 441.

61. Commission on Intergovernmental Relations, op. cit., p. 47.

62. *State Government*, 24:286 (Nov. 1951).

63. See Richard H. Leach, "The Status of Interstate Compacts Today," *State Government*, 32:134 ff. (Spring 1959); see also Richard H. Leach and Redding S. Sugg, Jr., *The Administration of Interstate Compacts* (Baton Rouge, 1959).

64. S. 2667, H. R. 5975, 8978, 8987, 8990, 85th Cong., 1st Sess.

65. Interstate Commission on the Potomac River Basin, *News-Letter*, Oct. 1957, p. 4.

66. Com. on Rules, U. S. House of Representatives, hearings before a special subcommittee on the *Proposed Establishment of Committee on Administrative Procedure and Practice*, 84th Cong., 2d Sess., May 22–24, 1956.

67. H. Res. 231, submitted Apr. 11, 1957.

68. Public Law 380, 86th Cong., 1st Sess.

69. Representative Harold Ostertag, *In the Nation's Capital* (mimeographed release no. 299, Mar. 14, 1957).

70. H. R. 5565, 85th Cong., 1st Sess., sec. 4 (a).

71. Ibid.

72. H. R. 2416, 86th Cong., 1st Sess.

73. S. 1431, H. R. 7282, 7378, 7465, 86th Cong., 1st Sess.

4

PRESIDENTIAL LEADERSHIP

1. Herbert Hoover, *The Memoirs of Herbert Hoover* (New York, 1952), vol. II, p. 228.

2. See particularly his speech in New York City, Dec. 11, 1931,

in *The Public Papers and Addresses of Franklin D. Roosevelt* (New York, 1938), vol. I, p. 497.

3. 67 Stat. 145.

4. Commission on Intergovernmental Relations, *A Report to the President* (1955), p. 9.

5. Ibid., pp. 52–53.

6. Lane Dwinell, New Hampshire, chairman; Theodore R. Mc-Keldin, Maryland; Victor E. Anderson, Nebraska; Robert E. Smiley, Idaho; Price Daniel, Texas; James P. Coleman, Mississippi; Dennis J. Roberts, Rhode Island; George M. Leader, Pennsylvania; George Docking, Kansas; and William G. Stratton, Illinois.

7. White House press release, Aug. 9, 1957.

8. Joint Federal-State Action Committee, *Summary of Meeting,* mimeographed release, Chicago, Ill., Oct. 3–4, 1957.

9. Idem, Washington, D. C., Nov. 14–15, 1957.

10. A part of the resolution on "Intergovernmental Relations" adopted by the United States Conference of Mayors, Sept. 13, 1958.

11. President's Committee on Administrative Management, *Report* (Washington, 1937), p. 32.

12. Commission on Organization of the Executive Branch of the Government (First Hoover Commission), *Report on General Management of the Executive Branch* (Washington, 1949), p. 1.

13. Commission on Intergovernmental Relations, op. cit., p. 87.

14. This executive order is a secret document and not available to the public.

15. Howard Pyle, interviews with authors, Sept. 3, 1956, and Aug. 27, 1957.

16. Com. on Government Operations, Subcom. on Intergovernmental Relations, U. S. House of Representatives, *Federal-State-Local Relations*, 85th Cong., 2d Sess., pt. 2, p. 598.

17. Robert E. Merriam, address before Annual Conference, Maryland Municipal League, June 14, 1957.

18. 42 Stat. 20.

19. See Com. on the National Budget, U. S. Senate, *Hearings*, 66th Cong., 2d Sess., 1920.

20. Fritz Morstein Marx, "The Bureau of the Budget: Its Evolution and Present Role," *American Political Science Review*, 39:682 (Aug. 1945).

21. Ibid., p. 893 (Oct. 1945).

22. Com. on Appropriations, U. S. House of Representatives, *Hearings on the Budget for the Fiscal Year 1958*, 85th Cong., 1st Sess., Jan. 24, 1957.

23. President's Advisory Committee on Management, "Improvement of Management in the Federal Government," *Public Administration Review*, 13:41 (Winter 1953).

24. The language of Executive Order 8248, Sept. 8, 1939, making the Bureau of the Budget part of the Executive Office of the President.

25. See Charles E. Merriam, "The National Resources Planning Board," *American Political Science Review*, 38:1078–88 (Dec. 1944), for a full discussion of the Board.

26. Executive Order 6777, June 30, 1934.

27. John Millett, *The Process and Organization of Government Planning* (New York, 1949), p. 140.

28. Ibid., p. 163.

29. Charles E. Merriam, op. cit., p. 1080.

30. Com. on Appropriations, U. S. House of Representatives, *Hearings on the Independent Offices Appropriations Bill for Fiscal Year 1944*, 78th Cong., 1st Sess., Jan. 11, 1943, pp. 50–89.

31. *New York Times*, Mar. 12, 1943.

32. *Congressional Record*, 89:979 (Feb. 15, 1943).

33. Ibid., p. 1072.

34. Ibid., p. 1977 (Mar. 15, 1943).

35. *New York Times*, Mar. 13, 1943.

36. Charles E. Merriam, op. cit., p. 1086.

37. Executive Order 9347, May 27, 1943.

38. 60 Stat. 24, sec. 4.

39. Stephen K. Bailey, *Congress Makes a Law* (New York, 1950), p. 52.

40. Ibid., p. 169.

41. *Hearings on H. R. 2202*, p. 959, quoted by Bailey, ibid., p. 169.

42. Bailey, ibid., p. 222.

43. R. S. Milne, "The American Council of Economic Advisers," *Political Studies*, June 1955, p. 125.

44. For an opinion that they should not, see Joseph Harris, *The Advice and Consent of the Senate* (Berkeley, 1953), p. 391.

45. Edwin G. Nourse, *Proceedings of the American Philosophical Society*, 94:311–16 (Aug. 1950).

46. Idem, "Why I Had to Step Aside," *Colliers*, Feb. 18, 1950, p. 51.

47. Ibid., p. 53.

48. See discussion of this position in Milne, op. cit., p. 127.

49. Nourse, "Why I Had to Step Aside," p. 51.

50. Idem, letter to the editor, *Business Week*, Jan. 5, 1957.

51. Arthur F. Burns, "Reading the Nation's Economic Health," *Business Week*, Dec. 8, 1956.

52. Bertram M. Gross and John L. Lewis, "The President's Economic Staff during the Truman Administration," *American Political Science Review*, 48:118 (Mar. 1954).

53. Council of Economic Advisers, *Fifth Annual Report to the President* (1950), p. 30.

54. Gross and Lewis, op. cit., p. 122.

55. Harry Truman, "My View of the Presidency," *Look*, Mar. 11, 1958, p. 29.

5

A DEPARTMENT OF URBAN AFFAIRS:
PRO AND CON

1. Public Law 380, 86th Cong., 1st Sess.

2. *Congressional Record*, 105:9353 (June 9, 1959).

3. Philip Kates, "A National Department of Municipalities," *American City*, 6:405–7 (Jan. 1912).

4. Ibid., p. 405.

5. Ibid., p. 407.

6. Woodrow Wilson, letter to editor, *American City*, Aug. 22, 1912, quoted in *American City*, 69:19 (Oct. 1954).

7. Harlean James, "Service—The Keynote of a New Cabinet Department," *Review of Reviews*, Feb. 1919, p. 190.

8. Ibid., p. 188.

9. Charles E. Merriam, "Cities in a Changing World," in *City Problems of 1934. Annual Proceedings of the United States Conference of Mayors* (Chicago, 1935), pp. 73–74.

10. Idem in Guy Greer, ed., *The Problems of Cities and Towns. Report of the Conference on Urbanism, Harvard University, March 5–6, 1942* (Cambridge, 1942), p. 29.

11. Nathaniel S. Keith, "Blueprint for Community Development," unpublished manuscript, pp. 8–9.

12. J. Arthur Younger, "We Need a Department of Urbiculture," *This Week*, Aug. 5, 1957, p. 8.

13. See, for example, "Urban Secretary Remains a Possibility," editorial, *Durham Sun* (Durham, N. C.), Aug. 8, 1958.

14. See chap. 2 above.

15. Representative Younger was kind enough to allow the au-

thors to read the letters he received in response to his article; a score or more of mayors offered him their support and assistance in getting such a department created.

16. H. R. 1864.
17. H. R. 10295.
18. S. 3159.
19. H. R. 1019.
20. H. R. 3383.
21. S. 2159.
22. H. R. 2423.
23. H. R. 4481.
24. H. R. 781, 984, S. 2397.
25. H. R. 1019, 85th Cong., 1st Sess., sec. 2.
26. H. R. 3383, 85th Cong., 1st Sess., sec. 2.
27. S. 2159, 85th Cong., 1st Sess., sec. 1.
28. H. R. 3383, sec. 4 (b).
29. S. 2159, sec. 4 (c).
30. Ibid., sec. 5 (a), (b).
31. Press release from Senator Joseph Clark's office, May 26, 1957, p. 1.
32. S. 2159, sec. 1 (3).
33. The wording of the act establishing the Department of Labor, 37 Stat. 736.
34. Com. on Government Operations, U. S. House of Representatives, *Hearings on Creation of a Department of Urbiculture*, 84th Cong., 1st Sess., July 26, 1955, pp. 3–4.
35. Ibid., p. 19.
36. Ibid., p. 23.
37. Ibid.
38. Arthur Macmahon and John D. Millett, *Federal Administrators* (New York, 1939), p. 4.
39. Schuyler C. Wallace, *Federal Departmentalization* (New York, 1941), p. 67.
40. Com. on Government Operations, U. S. House of Representatives, op. cit., p. 51.
41. Ibid., p. 34.
42. Ibid., p. 35.
43. Commission on Organization of the Executive Branch of the Government (First Hoover Commission), *Report on Social Security* (Washington, 1946), p. 5.
44. Press release from Senator Joseph Clark's office, May 26, 1957.
45. American Municipal Association, *The National Municipal*

Policy, 33d Annual American Municipal Congress, Nov. 28, 1956, sec. IV–4.

46. Commission on Organization of the Executive Branch of the Government (First Hoover Commission), *General Management of the Executive Branch* (Washington, 1949), p. 3.

47. H. R. 1019, sec. 2.

48. Herbert W. Stevens (Director of Planning, City of Cincinnati), quoted in Com. on Government Operations, U. S. House of Representatives, *Sixth Report*, 85th Cong., 1st Sess. (House Rep. No. 575), p. 377.

49. American Municipal Association, op. cit.

50. Com. on Government Operations, U. S. House of Representatives, op. cit., p. 428.

51. Com. on Government Operations, U. S. House of Representatives, *Hearings on Creation of a Department of Urbiculture*, 84th Cong., 1st Sess., July 26, 1955, p. 42.

52. For a general discussion of rural-urban conflicts, see also the comments in Commission on Intergovernmental Relations, *A Report to the President* (1955), pp. 38 ff. For specific studies, see Murray C. Havens, *City Versus Farm?* (Bur. of Public Administration, Univ. of Alabama, 1957); John E. Juergensmeyer, *The Campaign for the Illinois Reapportionment Amendment* (Institute of Government and Public Affairs, Univ. of Illinois, 1957); Edward H. Hobbs, *Legislative Apportionment in Mississippi* (Bur. of Public Administration, Univ. of Mississippi, 1956), as well as numerous other publications on the subject by university bureaus of public administration.

53. J. Arthur Younger, "We Need a Department of Urbiculture," *This Week*, Aug. 5, 1957, p. 8.

54. Mayor Ben West of Nashville, "Our Voiceless Towns and Cities," address before National Municipal League, Sept. 12, 1956, p. 10.

55. See W. Brooke Graves, *The Coming Challenge in Federal-State Relations. A Report for the Chamber of Commerce of the United States* (Washington, 1957).

56. Com. on Government Operations, U. S. House of Representatives, op. cit., p. 49.

57. Ibid., pp. 45–46.

58. Nelson A. Rockefeller, in *New York Times*, Sept. 24, 1957.

59. Com. on Government Operations, U. S. House of Representatives, op. cit., p. 45.

60. Harvey S. Perloff, "Responsibilities of Local, State, and Federal Government" (paper prepared for Conference on the Chal-

lenge of Metropolitan Government, American University, Washington, June 21, 1958), p. 5.

61. Ibid.

62. *American City*, 69:19 (Oct. 1954).

6

THE CASE FOR FEDERAL ACTION

1. Hugh Mields, Jr., "1958 Federal Legislative Review," *Western City*, Sept. 1958, p. 29.

2. Commission on Intergovernmental Relations, *A Report to the President* (1955), pp. 1, 2.

3. Luther Gulick, "Problems of U. S. Economic Development," in *Problems of United States Economic Development* (New York, 1958), pp. 317–18.

4. See Charlton F. Chute, "Today's Urban Regions," *National Municipal Review*, 45:274–80, 334–39 (June, July 1956).

5. Figures furnished Governor Harold W. Handley of Indiana by U. S. Department of Commerce, Oct. 1957.

6. Daniel R. Grant, "The Government of Interstate Metropolitan Areas," *Western Political Quarterly*, 8:90 (Mar. 1955).

7. Ibid., p. 106.

8. See pertinent sections of the annual reports of the International Joint Commission, published each year in Washington.

9. Morris Katz, *The Greater Windsor–Detroit Air Pollution Investigation*, address before Dominion Marine Association (press release, International Joint Commission, Jan. 21, 1953).

10. Com. on Government Operations, Subcom. on Intergovernmental Relations, U. S. House of Representatives, *Federal-State-Local Relations*, 85th Cong., 1st Sess., pt. 2, p. 397.

11. Commission on Intergovernmental Relations, *An Advisory Committee Report on Local Government* (1955), p. 26.

12. Harvey S. Perloff, op. cit.

13. Henry Cohen, "Census Improvements Needed for Urban Research," *Urban Land*, 14:5 (Feb. 1955).

14. President Eisenhower before Governors' Conference, July 12, 1952, quoted in President's Advisory Committee on a National Highway Program, *A Ten-Year National Highway Program* (1955).

15. *Congressional Record*, 105:3169 (Mar. 9, 1959).

16. House Rep. No. 2022, 84th Cong., 2d Sess., p. 8.

17. President Eisenhower before Governors' Conference, July 12, 1952.

18. "Six States and Their Metropolitan Problems," *State Government*, 30:237 (Nov. 1957).

19. Ibid.

20. See House Rep. No. 1386, 85th Cong., 2d Sess., pp. 2–3.

21. See chap. 1 above.

22. President's Water Resources Policy Commission, *A Water Policy for the American People* (Washington, 1950), p. 2.

23. House Rep. No. 2190, 84th Cong., 2d Sess., p. 2.

24. Ibid., p. 3.

25. Commission on Intergovernmental Relations, *A Report to the President*, p. 247.

26. House Rep. No. 2190, p. 3.

27. Commission on Intergovernmental Relations, loc. cit.

28. Housing and Home Finance Agency, *Urban Renewal, What It Is . . .* (1955), p. 3.

29. Reginald R. Isaacs, "The Real Costs of Urban Renewal," in *Problems of United States Economic Development* (New York, 1958), p. 339.

30. 63 Stat. 413.

31. Richard L. Steiner (Commissioner, Urban Renewal Administration), address before 84th Annual Forum of National Conference on Social Welfare, Philadelphia, May 22, 1957.

32. Title of an article in *Fortune*, Apr. 1955, pp. 142 ff.

33. Com. on Public Works, U. S. Senate, *Water and Air Pollution Control*, 84th Cong., 1st Sess., Apr. 26, 1955, p. 216.

34. Ibid., p. 208.

35. See Leo A. Hoegh, "Survival Planning in Metropolitan Areas," *Metropolitan Area Problems News and Digest*, 1:3–4 (Feb.–Mar. 1958).

36. For a list of the problems of a typical metropolitan area, see Senate Rep. No. 1230, 85th Cong., 2d Sess., p. 5.

37. Robert T. Daland, "Political Science and the Study of Urbanism," *American Political Science Review*, 51:507 (June 1957).

38. Letter from Meyer Kestnbaum to Richard H. Leach, Sept. 11, 1958.

39. Commission on Intergovernmental Relations, *A Report to the President*, p. 52; idem, *An Advisory Committee Report on Local Government*, pp. 30–32.

40. Letter from Meyer Kestnbaum to Richard H. Leach, Sept. 11, 1958.

41. Ibid.

42. Commission on Intergovernmental Relations, *A Report to the President*, p. 2.

43. *Congressional Record*, 105:A358–59 (Jan. 21, 1959).

44. Rockefeller Brothers Fund, *The Challenge to America: Its Economic and Social Aspects* (Special Studies Project Report IV; New York, 1958), p. 48.

INDEX

Addonizio, Hugh J., 117, 170, 173

Administrative agencies' handling of federal programs, 99–100

Administrative conflicts involving proposed Department of Urban Affairs, 187–188

Advisory Commission on Intergovernmental Relations, 126, 128, 166

Agricultural pressure groups, 98

Agricultural specialists, 229

Agriculture: and co-operative federalism, 223; fundamental unity of, 94. See also Rural orientation

Agriculture, Department of. See Department of Agriculture

Air pollution, radioactive, 55, 219, 233

Air pollution control, 55–56; international problem, 205, 219; interstate problem, 56, 219; legislation, 55, 56; primarily metropolitan problem, 55, 219; and public health, 219; recommendations, 233; responsibility for, 56, 219

Airport planning, 32

Airports, civilian, federal aid for: Eisenhower and, 133; history, 30–33 passim; recommendations, 233–234; on regional basis, 32, 33, 120; vs. military airports, 34, 233

Allocation of resources, 236–237

American Association of State Highway Officials, 70

American Bar Association, Section on Municipal Law, 84

American City, The, quoted, 191

American federal system. See Federal system

American Municipal Association, 64–74, 91, 135; and Department of Urban Affairs, proposed, 70, 71, 169, 178, 180, 187, 192; and federal governmental unit for metropolitan areas, 73, 74, see also American Municipal Association and Department of Urban Affairs; and federal grants to metropolitan areas, 73; and federal programs affecting metropolitan areas, 34, 43, 67, 70; functional approach, 69, 72, 73; informational services to members, 68; membership basis, 65, 69, 73; and metropolitan area problems, 69–74, 78, 85; Metropolitan Areas Committee of, 69, 72; National Municipal Policy, 67, 68, 69–72 passim; spokesman for cities, 65–69, not for metropolitan areas, 69, 73, 74; and (study) Commission on Metropolitan Problems, proposed, 127; and United States Conference of Mayors, 75, 80

American Municipal News, 68

American Planning and Civic Association, 86

American Society of Planning Officials, 169

Anderson, Robert, 131

Annexation of suburbs, 198

Arden House Conference on Metropolitan Problems, 214

Army Corps of Engineers, 7, 21

Urban land use. *See* Land use, urban

Urban places in United States, 1790 and 1950, 2

Urban programs divided among congressional committees, 100

Urban renewal: cost, 218; and highway program, 51, 54, 98; and land use planning, 11, 54, 214, 235; recommendations, 235–236; and relocation of displaced people, 19, 52. *See also* Housing; Housing program; Interrelation of federal programs

Urban Renewal Administration, 99; expenditures in New York metropolitan area, 7

Urbanization, 2, 4; of farm population, 115; and politics, 116; in South, 116

Urbiculture, 171; Department of, proposed, 171, 174, 182

Van Dyke, Henry, quoted, 1

Veterans Administration, 188, 189; housing program, 7, 10, 11, 15, 16

Vinson, Fred M., 149, 151

Wallace, Schuyler, quoted, 176

War industry, *See* Defense industry

War Mobilization, Office of. *See* Office of War Mobilization

Washington (D.C.) metropolitan area: Congress and, 102–119; interstate, 101, 105; legislation on, 104, 107, 109; mass transportation in, 101, 104, 108, 109, 111, 114; water pollution problem, 104, 123

Water, municipal uses of, 25

Water pollution: effect on water supply, 215; international problem, 203, 204; Potomac River,

104, 123. *See also* Water pollution control

Water pollution control: expenditures for, 28; Eisenhower and, 132; federal responsibility for, 123, 217; federal-state relations in, 132; history, 27–29; Joint Federal-State Action Committee and, 29, 132, 232; legislation, 27–29 *passim;* and metropolitan areas, 28–29; and public health, 217; recommendations, 232. *See also* Water pollution

Water resources: international problem, 203, 206; and public health, 215; surveys of, 22. *See also* Water resources program

Water resources program: federal agencies engaged in, 21; federal responsibility in, 215; history, 20–21; and metropolitan areas, 21, 23, 24–26; recommendations, 231–232. *See also* Water resources

Water supply. *See* Water resources

Waterman, Alan T., quoted, 219

West, Ben, quoted, 90, 136

Wheaton, William C., quoted, 177

White House Conference on Metropolitan Development, proposed, 87

Whittington, William A., 151

Willow Run defense plant, 40–41

Wilson, Woodrow: and Department of Municipalities, proposed, 167; and federal system, 224

Wolman, Abel, report, 123–124

Wolverton, Charles A., 101

Younger, J. Arthur, 116, 169–171 *passim,* 173, 174, 181, 187, 191

Youngstown metropolitan area, map, 201